LIFE'S PICTURE HISTORY

OF WORLD WAR II

This book is composed of the finest work produced by photographers and painters during World War II. Much of it was published in LIFE under the general direction of wartime Managing Editor John Shaw Billings and of Daniel Longwell, who succeeded him as Managing Editor in June 1944, when Mr. Billings became Editorial Director of all TIME Inc. publications. Selection and assignment of LIFE's photographers was the task ably performed by Wilson Hicks. On behalf of the editors of LIFE, this history was compiled by an editorial task force including:

Editor.....................Arthur B. Tourtellot

Picture Editor................Francis Brennan

Title Maps ....Richard Edes Harrison

Text Editor..............Richard W. Johnston

Text .... Robert Sherrod
    assisted by D'Arcy Van Bokkelen, Allen Dibble

Full page text...............John Dos Passos

Editorial Assistants.....Margaret Andrus, Jane Bartels, Mary Baynes, Leona Carney, Albert J. Dunn, Hilda Edson, Edward A. Hamilton, Michael Harrington, Nancy Levering, Patricia Purviance, Lilian Rixey, Jane M. Smith, Eleanor Tatum.

LIFE'S PICTURE HISTORY OF WORLD WAR II

TIME INCORPORATED · NEW YORK · 1950

Preface: A Salute

IT is very silly to say, as some do, that wars never settle anything. They have settled a great many things, such as the independence of the United States of America. It is a deep and true instinct of mankind to honor those who have fought, and especially those who suffered wounds and death in battle. This book honors, first of all and universally, those who fought honorably in World War II, the first war which was actually a worldwide war.

As Americans we honor with greatest pride and gratitude the tremendous and decisive achievements of American arms; we honor our allies of many nations and every race; we honor, too, those millions of enemy combatants who, however wickedly misled, fought courageously and who found wounds and death and all the miseries of war no less bitter on their side than on ours. To all who fought and died, we say: God rest them and God forgive us all.

Wars do settle some things, but wars are more than military action. This book is strictly a book of military history. It is therefore not a complete history of the war. It does not deal with the vast complex of political and social forces which precede and follow wars and are indeed intertwined with every battle. In our view the United States and her allies displayed more skill and valor in the military war than in the political conduct of the war. But these great issues will remain with us for a generation and lie outside the province of this book. We believe that our victory in World War II was essential in order to keep open the possibility of decent civilization on this earth. But civilization has yet to be saved and recreated; in particular, the principles of political freedom have yet to be established as the law of mankind.

The military war—the actual fighting of World War II—came to a successful conclusion for us in September 1945 with the final destruction of our enemies' capacity to resist our will. It then took its place on the great scroll of history as a completed entity. It was the greatest feat of arms ever accomplished on this planet. This book devotes itself to the recording of that tremendous feat. In large sweep or in fine detail, it is a ghastly, grisly story, but also one of high inspiration, of vast self-sacrifice, of a will-to-die for freedom.

This military war was notably reported in words and pictures by a far-flung corps of brave, intelligent men and women. Never were the people at home kept better informed of the course of conflict and never, in return, did they give their support more loyally to the fighting front. Wounds or worse were often the lot of the front-line correspondents and photographers. Here again the editors of LIFE are proud to salute this gallant band of journalists in general and our own photographers and reporters in particular who contributed so generously to the historic coverage in the following pages.

This is not the place nor the time to call the whole roll of more than a hundred LIFE and TIME photographers, artists and correspondents who, under our credentials, helped make this record. But, with our memory of them still green, special tribute is surely in order to those of our staffs who died in line of duty: MELVILLE JACOBY, who reported the heartbreak of Bataan and escaped to Australia only to be mowed down by a rampaging P-40; WILLIAM CHICKERING, whose stirring narrative of the recapture of the Philippines was broken off in mid-sentence when a kamikaze plane struck him on the flag bridge of a U.S. warship in Lingayan Gulf; LUCIEN

LABAUDT, a LIFE artist who died in a military plane crash in India before he could put brush to canvas on his assignment.

Three of our men were severely wounded. Eugene Smith, a LIFE photographer, had his face smashed at Okinawa as he pressed his camera even beyond the front lines of the savage fighting there. Edward Laning was a victim of Nazi shrapnel in Italy. Jack Belden, a LIFE correspondent who seemed born to war, slogged his way out of Burma with Stilwell to take two rifle bullets in the leg as he crawled over a stone wall to get a closer look at the Salerno landing.

It would be an invidious task to try to parcel out appropriate praise for all the LIFE and TIME men and women who turned in distinguished performances on war assignments. But names and deeds come flooding back in any recollection of those days, enough to fill many pages. At risk of injustice to others no less good, we are impelled to set down brief notices of some remarkable journalistic achievements.

The side-line invasion of Finland by Russia in 1939 came into sharp, bleak focus for the first time with the photo-reporting of Carl Mydans. He went on to the Philippines where he and his wife were captured, interned at Santo Tomas and finally exchanged in time for him to cover MacArthur's return to the Philippines. William Vandivert supplied the photographs to accent all the horror of the Nazi air blitz on London in 1940, with narratives by Walter Graebner. Photographer David Scherman and Charles Murphy, writing the commentary, made something heroic out of the low-comedy Nazi sinking of the third-rate Egyptian steamer *ZamZam* in the South Atlantic.

From inside Russia, Margaret Bourke-White photographed the Nazi invasion in all its desolation in 1941, was torpedoed in 1942 on the way to the North African landings, survived to make Italy and the "forgotten war" there her own particular picture province. Robert Capa, blooded in the Spanish Civil War, recorded the American landing on Omaha beach on D-day by coming ashore with the first troop wave, the relief of Bastogne by going in with the American tanks and the first "drop" across the Rhine by parachuting down with the airborne men themselves.

Among our correspondents, Robert Sherrod, after Pearl Harbor, took the Pacific theater as his own, provided specifics of our dire plight there and made personal history by landing shoulder to shoulder with the Marines at Tarawa, Saipan and Iwo Jima. (He wrote much of this book.) John Hersey got his baptism under fire in the Pacific and went on to Sicily where he collected material from which to write his Pulitzer prize novel.

There were many others—Ralph Morse aboard the U.S.S. *Vincennes* as she sank off Savo Island—Aaron Bohrod painting the stinking jungles of the South Pacific —Dmitri Kessel three-quarters frozen in the Aleutians—John Phillips knocking around Yugoslavia with an unknown guerrilla leader named Tito—Eliot Elisofon amid all the mud and misery of North Africa—Frank Scherschel on the deadly dangerous Murmansk run—George Silk pinning down in color French blood and death as they unfolded on a gutted road in southern Italy—Tom Lea who landed at Peleliu, and Floyd Davis who was on a big Hamburg raid, painting war in all its garish, dazzling colors—and George Strock taking what was probably the most tragic picture of the war, three American soldiers on the Buna beach, dead.

The list could go on and on without exhausting the first-rate. The professional work of all these men provide the bone and sinew of this book. They made this record—they and thousands like them, the combat photographers and artists in and out of uniform. This book is in some measure a salute to their bravery, their skill and their patriotism.

HENRY R. LUCE, *Editor-in-chief*

JOHN SHAW BILLINGS, *Wartime Managing Editor*

Contents

I
The Conquest of Europe

Europe: 1939-40

THE first of September 1939 dawned dry and clear over the plains of northeastern Europe. The early morning air shook with the roar of motors as formations of the Luftwaffe headed into the streak of light in the east. Soon the armored columns of the Wehrmacht were slam-banging along eastward roads. The tanks splintered the blue and white painted wooden barriers of the customs posts as they crossed the Polish border. It will rain, said the commentators in the West. If it rains the armored columns will bog in the Polish mud. Day followed day of brilliant sunshine. If it would only rain, prayed the commentators in the West. No rain fell. Within 24 hours the Luftwaffe owned the Polish sky. Within 24 days Poland, in the words of Stalin's spokesmen in the Kremlin, had ceased to exist as a state. With the collapse of the buffer state of Poland the whole European order, patched together by the Peace of Versailles, fell to bits; and Western Europe, almost overnight, lost the leadership of mankind.

The war of 1914–18 had halted the development of a European order for the world. The peace only intensified cleavages between the nations. Woodrow Wilson had constructed a league to resolve differences by parliamentary discussion but he was not able to convince even his own electorate that the settlements at Versailles were worth supporting. Only gradually did we learn the bitter lesson that we were part of the European order and that its breakdown was threatening our republic too.

During the years between the wars we witnessed, in a weakened and discouraged Europe, conflict between classes take the place of conflict between nations. We saw a new type of political organization come into being in Russia, where the Communist party seized control of a working-class revolt and in the name of Karl Marx built this control into a fear-dominated military state. We saw Mussolini discover in Italy that it was as easy to build a structure of autocracy out of the terrors of those who dreaded Communism as out of the hopes of those who wanted it. From Germany we heard Hitler's shrill hysterical voice as he put the methods the Fascists and Communists had invented for molding and moving masses of men to work to gear the military aptitudes of the German people into one of the bloodiest tyrannies that ever afflicted mankind.

THE stale-minded statesmen of Western Europe were no more able to cope with the new political techniques than their generals were able to anticipate the inventions of lightning war. Step by step they allowed the foundations of European democracy to be undermined. The Rhineland, Austria, the Spanish Republic.... Late in September 1938, after a summer of alarms and threats, the French and British prime ministers flew home from Munich, having assured Hitler, who gave them a good tongue-lashing for their pains, that they would not fight for Czechoslovakia.

Munich convinced Stalin, who since Lenin's death had been massacring his way to dominance over the Communist apparatus in the Soviet Union, that he had better throw in his lot with the winner. By mid-August 1939 he had reached an agreement with Hitler which secured Germany's eastern flank and gave Hitler the opportunity he was waiting for to try out his new notions of warfare against the Poles. The agreement was no sooner made than it was carried out with energy on both sides. While the Wehrmacht cut the Polish forces to pieces from the front, Stalin's armies and his execution squads mopped up the Polish rear. Russian garrisons entered the small republics on the eastern shore of the Baltic and by November Stalin was ready to press an offensive against the Finns. It took the Russian army all winter to blast through the Finnish lines and even then the Finnish people remained unbroken. While Hitler's generals scornfully watched the Kremlin's plans failing in Finland they were designing a similar operation against Norway.

Britain and France had declared war on Germany on September 3, 1939 in protest against the attack on Poland. Londoners and Parisians woke up next morning relieved to discover that they hadn't been blown up in the night and started to tell each other that this was a phony war. The French army took cover in the Maginot line, planned from lessons learned in the defense of Verdun. It had never been extended to the sea. To fill the gap the British landed an expeditionary force in channel ports. The French started wearily to take up the science of warfare where they had left it on Nov. 11, 1918. Hitler addressed the Reichstag in October saying all he wanted was peace. Belgium and Holland let it be known that they would be very, very neutral. The western front settled down to garrison routine.

HITLER meanwhile was busy at work. By early spring his Scandinavian plans were ripe. On the morning of April 9 the good people of Copenhagen pedaling to work on their bicycles found a German column tramping toward the royal palace. The same day telephone exchanges and radio stations and government buildings in Norway were seized by Hitler's adherents under Quisling. German airborne forces deployed on the airfields and troops smuggled in with full equipment on merchant ships poured out of the holds and took over the principal ports. Exactly a month later, while the House of Commons was debating the failure of the Allied counterattack at Narvik, the Luftwaffe surprised Belgium and Holland, and German armored columns started probing across Ardennes Forest into France. The French general staff had thought that region was too hilly and wooded for tanks and defended it only with reservists. What ensued was a curious repetition of the Battle of the Marne, with the sides and the result reversed. While the Franco-British line pushed ahead into Belgium, the Wehrmacht crossed the Meuse at Sedan and tore through the hinge between the Maginot defenses and the field armies. The Allied forces in Flanders were immediately outflanked. The French fought bravely but their planes were obsolete, their tanks were scattered. Their aged generals shared with their industrialists and their Communist-infiltrated working class a religion of defeat. Class war antagonisms made resistance to an invader impossible. From the moment the armored columns broke through at Sedan it was a foregone conclusion that Paris would fall and that Hitler would soon have Europe's capital in his hands.

Holland surrendered May 14, 1940. By the time Belgium capitulated on May 28 the British forces, their communications with the French cut off, their airshield driven back to island bases, were leaving heavy equipment behind and trooping along roads clogged with refugees toward the column of smoke that showed where the last port of escape on the seacoast was burning: Dunkerque. —JOHN DOS PASSOS

The blitzkrieg is tested in Poland, then turned against the West

THE 11-inch shot fired by the ancient German battleship *Schleswig-Holstein* (*above*) at 4:45 a.m. Friday, Sept. 1, 1939, literally reverberated around the world for six years, 21 hours and 23 minutes, until an uneasy peace was declared aboard another battleship in Tokyo Bay. It set off a Polish ammunition dump near Danzig, the first of many hits the Germans scored. At the same moment Adolf Hitler's planes, 2,000 of them, were winging eastward to destroy the Polish air force on its airfields before it could rise in protest. (Under the dictators' code only a sucker declared war before he struck.) Within a day air supremacy, the *sine qua non* of modern war, had been achieved. Hitler's 45 divisions—six of them with about 300 tanks each—rumbled through the dry Polish marshes. They cut off 15 of Poland's 45 divisions and left them for torment by Stuka dive bombers. Poles fought bravely. Brigades of horse cavalry broke their swords and lances on German armor. Panzers, those unrelenting steel divisions were named. Luftwaffe (the German air corps) was another name that struck terror in civilian and military hearts alike. Together these Teutonic words added up to the paralyzing blitzkrieg (lightning war).

German pincers broke resistance into pockets around Kutno, Kraków and a few other prepared defenses. Within a week General Heinz Guderian's tanks were poised before Warsaw, 155 miles from the German border. Meanwhile air-and-armor eliminated the pockets, but not before one Polish group had struck out from Poznań against the main line approaching Warsaw. This battle lasted until Sept. 19. Two days earlier, while Poland was helpless in agony, Russian columns crossed her eastern frontier. Warsaw held out until Sept. 27. Poles died to the tune of 11 stirring notes of a Chopin *Polonaise*, repeated on the radio every 30 seconds. At the end of the month all was over. Poland was divided almost in halves between Hitler and Stalin. Against Hitler's losses of 11,000 killed and 30,000 wounded, the Poles had lost an army of two million men and their country. Hitler brought something new to warfare besides planes and tanks and velocity. He had not expected Britain and France to go to war over Poland; when they came in he determined to show them how merciless he could make it. Prisoners of war were shot. In the new concept cities and civilians died with the troops. All must bow and suffer before the blitzkrieg. And civilization would never be the same again.

STUKA DIVE BOMBERS RANGED POLAND'S UNDEFENDED SKIES, HAMMERED AT HER RAILWAYS AND BROKE UP HER UNWIELDY MOBILIZATION

GERMANY'S NEW SWORD WAS THE PANZER DIVISION OF 3,000 TANKS AND VEHICLES WHICH SLASHED SWIFTLY ACROSS POLAND'S FLAT PLAINS

AT OUTSKIRTS OF WARSAW AFTER ONE WEEK OF BLITZ GERMAN SOLDIERS HALTED THEIR MOTORIZED ADVANCE TO RECONNOITER THE CITY

IN WARSAW'S SUBURBS ON SEPT. 9, ADVANCE PANZER TROOPS WHEELED UP A HOWITZER TO BOMBARD THE STUBBORN HEART OF THE CITY

DOMED CHURCH OF ST. ALEXANDER ROSE ABOVE PREWAR WARSAW

NAZI BLITZ-SIEGE LEFT ST. ALEXANDER'S A LOW SHELL OF RUBBLE

ANTIQUE BUILDINGS GRACED WARSAW'S OLDEST MARKET QUARTER

THREE WEEKS' SHELLING TURNED "OLD MARKET" INTO NEW RUINS

HORDES OF PRISONERS were all that remained of Poland's army after three weeks of war. The Poles had tried to defend the whole winding length of their frontier. When Nazi armored attacks broke through to Warsaw, entire armies were cut off and grouped together in contracting pockets from which the Germans took some 700,000 captives. Escaping eastward, 200,000 more were gathered in by the invading Red Army.

EXULTANT GERMANS, the officers snug in command cars, moved in swift, gigantic encirclements of the fiercely resisting Poles. Stuka dive bombers and panzer divisions split Polish defenses ahead of them, but the German infantry was still an important part of the team—modern infantry, that rode as well as marched and carried tremendous new firepower in the form of automatic weapons, machine guns, mortars and antitank artillery.

HAVING POSED IN TRIUMPH IN POLAND, HITLER AND FOREIGN MINISTER JOACHIM VON RIBBENTROP RETURNED TO THEIR TRAIN—AND THE WEST

Attack in West

was not launched until seven months after the fall of Poland —seven months of the lulling "sitzkrieg," or "phony war." On May 10, 1940, as he sent his divisions plunging into Holland and Belgium, Hitler declared, "The fight beginning today decides the fate of the German nation for the next 1,000 years!" The superbly trained Nazi soldiers seemed invincible. When the Dutch flooded their canals the Germans simply bridged them or paddled across in rubber boats. In Belgium they attacked Albert Canal defenses from trains (*above*). Hitler's bombers knocked out all but 12 Dutch planes the second day of the invasion. At one bridge fifth columnists pulled the wires before the structure could be dynamited. Sections of Rotterdam and Utrecht were leveled by German bombers May 14, and the Dutch surrendered that day, with only 3,000 casualties in an army of 260,000. Belgium, clinging to neutrality, refused to integrate its defense with the Dutch or French. The Germans landed glider troops on the Belgian fortress Eben-Emael and blew up its guns. Terrorized Belgians clogged the roads into France as British and French troops came the other way to meet the Nazis. When King Leopold surrendered only 6,000 of his soldiers had died defending their country.

AT DAWN, MAY 10, THE FIRST BOMBS HIT AROUND AMSTERDAM'S AIRDROME

DROPPING EVERYWHERE, TOUGH PARATROOPS RIDDLED THE DUTCH DEFENSES

NAZI MOTOR CONVOY side-stepped a Dutch roadblock of dynamited trees. Holland was small; the Germans were fast. Although the Dutch opened the dikes and let in the sea, nothing availed to halt the Nazis.

DENIED A BRIDGE at the frontier by Dutch dynamite, Nazi engineers crossed the river in rubber boats. Paratroops seized intact the bridges leading to Rotterdam, held them open for the German ground forces.

TERROR BOMBING OF THE CENTER OF ROTTERDAM ON MAY 14 LEFT HOMELESS CITIZENS MILLING ABOUT THE EDGE OF A 500-ACRE HOLOCAUST

HORRIFIED BY ROTTERDAM, HOLLAND SURRENDERED. NAZIS HERDED THEIR DAZED PRISONERS INTO RUINS OF A DUTCH FORT THAT FAILED

AFTER ONLY FIVE DAYS OF WAR THE DUTCH GATHERED AROUND GERMAN SOUND TRUCKS FOR THE FIRST OF FIVE YEARS OF NAZI DECREES

FORT EBEN-EMAEL (*right*) was captured by German engineers (*center*) who again utilized rubber boats to span Albert Canal. They relieved glider troops who had spiked most of fort's guns.

BATTLE-SHOCKED BELGIANS, some weeping, were flushed from their underground forts as the Nazis streamed across the Canal, drove the Belgian army back toward the advancing French.

SMOKE PALL OF BURNING OIL SIGNALED THE FALL OF ANTWERP ON MAY 18

BLASTING A PATH FOR THE BLITZ, A GERMAN SELF-PROPELLED HOWITZER FIRED POINT-BLANK AT FRENCH-HELD RAILWAY STATION IN HANGEST

WOUNDED POILU IS BORNE OFF IN NAZI HANDS

Fall of France

seemed inconceivable, even after the Low Countries were overrun. It could happen to the Poles, the Dutch and the Belgians—but surely not to the French, whose army long had been labeled "the finest in the world." Nobody was more surprised at what happened than Germany's generals. Who could guess that the Allied commander, General Maurice Gamelin, would rush 35 French and British divisions into Belgium and leave a gap to the south unplugged? When Field Marshal Karl von Rundstedt's "Army Group A," spearheaded by seven armored divisions, hurtled through the "impassable" Ardennes Forest, just north of the Maginot line, he was opposed only by nine divisions—seven manned by elderly reserves. Gamelin was fired, General Maxime Weygand called in. But for the French army—defensive-minded, politics-ridden, half-inclined to fight—it was years too late. French planes were no match for the swifter Messerschmitts. Some French divisions had no antitank guns. Since Poland the Germans had perfected close air support. Without waiting for artillery, von Rundstedt sent in dive bombers to scourge French defenses ahead of his tanks. Against such tactics the position was desperate when the Germans drove south across the width of France. On June 10 Premier Paul Reynaud begged President Roosevelt to send "clouds of warplanes" (which America had not). That day the opportunistic Mussolini declared war. Four days later the Nazis entered Paris, and also penetrated and passed beyond the Maginot line. By June 17 Marshal Henri Pétain, 84, Reynaud's successor as premier, was ready to yield France to the Third Reich.

BURNING OF ROUEN on June 10 marked German crossing of the Seine River. This was only five days after the Nazis turned away from smoldering Dunkerque and started drive toward Paris. In two days of hard fighting the German armies striking south of the Somme breached the thin, hastily improvised "Weygand line." East of Paris the Nazis quickly reached the Marne, and the battle of France became a disorganized rout.

ONE OF FRANCE'S FORLORN TANKS WAS DIVE-BOMBED INTO A DITCH

NEAR VERDUN THE GERMANS MOCKED THE MAN WHOSE LINE FAILED

16

ANOTHER ARMISTICE was signed at Compiègne June 22. When Marshal Pétain sued for peace, Hitler relished the full irony of history by ordering the French to meet him in the old railway car where Germany surrendered in 1918. There they were told to disband France's army, immobilize her navy, yield half of France to Nazi troops. As Hitler and his staff strutted away from the car (*above*), the band struck up *Deutschland über alles*.

FRANCE HAD FALLEN AND ONE AND A HALF MILLION OF HER CAPTURED SONS WERE HERDED INTO THE CROWDED PRISON CAMPS OF THE REICH

THE NAZI EAGLE descended upon Paris June 14 when a plane landed in the Place de la Concorde, bringing Hitler's personal adjutant to arrange a triumphal entry. On June 10 the government had left for Tours and thousands of frightened Parisians stampeded after it. In 1870 the capital of France held out against Prussian siege guns for 132 days; in 1940 it was declared an open city and the Nazis paraded in without firing a shot.

PARIS SIGNS NOW POINTED THE WAY TO THE GERMAN OVERLORDS

GERMAN SOLDIER TOOK TOURIST'S SNAPSHOT OF THE MADELEINE

FRENCHMEN SEIZED AS HOSTAGES LOST THEIR LIVES BLINDFOLDED IN FRONT OF THE FIRING SQUADS AT THE VINCENNES SHOOTING RANGE

THE GERMAN GARRISON paraded under the Arc de Triomphe and down the Champs-Elysées while the grim work of occupation went on in places like Vincennes. Paris was headquarters for the harsh rule of occupied France and, as stunned Frenchmen recoiled from the shame of Vichy, it also became a center of northern resistance. Nazis answered with more firing squads and in two years shot more than 1,000 patriots in reprisal.

19

IN PARIS ONE CONQUERING CORPORAL VISITED THE TOMB OF ANOTHER. LIKE NAPOLEON, HITLER STILL FACED A BIG PROBLEM—ENGLAND

Dunkerque

TRAPPED ON A NARROW FRENCH BEACH, A QUARTER-MILLION BRITISH SOLDIERS STILL FOUGHT DEFIANTLY WHILE HOPING FOR A MIRACLE

WAR came slowly to Britain. Four divisions were across the Channel by October 1939, settling on the French-Belgian line. By March 1940 only six more had followed. Even the new First Lord of the Admiralty, Winston Churchill, so long a Cassandra among the amiable appeasers, placed his faith in the superiority of the defensive in warfare. His navy's clashes were all the action the British had in the first eight months of the war. A German submarine sank a British battleship in Scapa Flow itself; the battle cruiser *Scharnhorst* destroyed the armed merchant cruiser *Rawalpindi* off Iceland. Vengeance came late in 1939 when three British cruisers cornered the pocket-battleship *Graf Spee* in the estuary of South America's River Plate and drove her skipper to scuttling and suicide. But in April 1940 Britain still basked in false security and Prime Minister Neville Chamberlain surveyed the nation's "fighting strength" with pride: "Hitler missed the bus." As though in answer, Hitler overran Denmark in a day and swooped upon Norway. The British fleet retaliated with a crippling defeat of the German navy, and Allied troops successfully made three major counterlandings. The first week of May, however, the British were driven from Namsos and Narvik, and stopped before Trondheim, signaling the loss of Norway, and the fury of press and Parliament fell upon Chamberlain. Quoting Oliver Cromwell, one M.P. cried, ". . . Depart, I say; and let us

have done with you. In the name of God—go!" The government fell and the King asked Churchill to take over. It was Friday, May 10.

That day history violently shattered the fools' trance called the phony war. Only six days later the new Prime Minister had to face the dreadful possibility that Britain's main army overseas would be irrevocably lost. His troops, under French command, had been drawn deep into Belgium, and then blocked out as the Germans swept to the sea. No reserves were available to stop them, "one of the greatest surprises" of Winston Churchill's 65 years. On the 19th Churchill posed the problem: suppose it became necessary to evacuate the British forces? As the picture worsened the Admiralty and shipping ministry began rounding up all available bottoms: 36 transports, 30 ferry boats, a variety of coastal vessels. Forty Dutch *schuits*, which had fled to Britain, were manned by Royal Navy crews. Operation Dynamo began May 26. To protect Dunkerque, the last possible port from which evacuation could be made, Churchill ordered the small garrison at Calais to fight to the death. The canals at Gravelines were flooded and a gradual British withdrawal to the sea began. As the soldiers swarmed on the beaches and the Dunkerque piers the R.A.F. threw an umbrella overhead to fight off German attackers. The miracle of Dunkerque began, sustained only by the forlorn hope that perhaps 45,000 men might be evacuated before the rest were overcome by German armor.

21

THE Dunkerque perimeter narrowed to a thin strip of flaming beach—toward the end it was only 10 miles long. More than 300,000 British and French troops scrambled for the boats and ships of the rescue fleet as bombs burst on the sands and columns of smoke rose from the burning port. On May 26 only 4,247 men were lifted to safety. The next day 5,718 were rescued, then 18,527 more, and on May 29, 47,310, when the British navy—plowing through mine fields and incessant bombing and shelling, and losing 24 ships—drove close to the edge of the blazing shore. With hundreds of civilian craft and some French warships joining in, 53,823 men were rescued on May 30, and by June 4—the day Operation Dynamo was considered completed—336,427 men, including 123,095 French, had been snatched from death or capture.

SEAMEN OF BRITAIN STILL RULED THE NARROW SEAS

THE crisis of Dunkerque was enormously sharpened, during the first fearful days of the evacuation, by collateral disasters. The night of May 26, when the lift was only beginning, the remnants of the Calais garrison surrendered. The next midnight King Leopold delivered the Belgian armies to the Nazis. Confronted by this news, the naval commander at Dunkerque said bleakly, "Evacuation tomorrow night is problematical." Yet the evacuation *did* continue, the perimeter *did* hold—partly because of the courage and devotion of British and French sailors and civilian seafarers, and partly because of valiant flying by the R.A.F. The Royal Navy and the few French naval units brought off two thirds of those rescued; the hundreds of volunteer boatmen accounted for the rest. The R.A.F. shot down 159 German aircraft. As it was, an estimated 2,000 men were lost at sea, as well as 243 ships and boats and most of the British army's equipment, including 120,000 vehicles, 2,700 artillery pieces and 90,000 rifles. But this was small booty for General Guderian's Panzer corps, which on May 26 had been poised for the kill. Suddenly, and fantastically, Guderian was ordered to stop within medium artillery range of Dunkerque. Why? Field Marshal von Rundstedt insisted after the war that Hitler issued the order to save tanks for the push through France. But British historians claim von Rundstedt's diary shows it was his own idea. In any event, Hitler—confident that the British would sue for peace—shrugged away the miracle of Dunkerque and the German army turned toward Paris.

GUIDED BY THE VAST SMOKE PLUMES OF DUNKERQUE, WARSHIPS, TRAWLERS, BARGES AND EVEN MOTORBOATS PLIED THE CHANNEL FOR 10 DAYS

II
The Siege of Britain

Britain: 1940-41

NEVILLE CHAMBERLAIN's government collapsed under the first shock of the German punch through the Low Countries and Winston Churchill took his place with a coalition ministry which included Labor M.P.s. A man of enormous energy and imaginative courage, Churchill had a singlehearted love of his country's greatness that embraced everything British from the royal crown to the riveters in shipyards on the Clyde. It was not for nothing that he had been brought up in the shadow of the column in the park at Blenheim inscribed in cadenced and Augustan prose with the victories of his ancestor Marlborough. He was master of the language of England's great days—in his first speech as prime minister he said:

> I would say to the House, as I said to those who have joined this Government: I have nothing to offer but blood, toil, tears, and sweat. We have before us an ordeal of the most grievous kind. We have before us many, many long months of struggle and of suffering. You ask: What is our policy? I will say: It is to wage war, by sea, land and air, with all our might and with all the strength that God can give us: to wage war against a monstrous tyranny, never surpassed in the dark, lamentable catalogue of human crime. That is our policy. You ask: What is our aim? I can answer in one word: Victory. . . .

Like most Germans, Hitler admired the English, but felt that Germans could run the British Empire much better than Britons could. He was hoping to come in as a partner in the grand old imperial firm, a partner who would eventually take over the business. But now what he had most feared took place. Dunkerque, the defeat and the inner victory, awakened the English people. No foreigner visiting that congested heart of a moribund empire in the days of appeasement abroad and the dole at home could have predicted that a population which seemed so hopelessly stratified by antagonisms and inequalities between classes could so immediately find common purpose. In Churchill's voice, speaking the mighty language of their ancestors over the radio, all sorts and conditions of Britons discovered a pride and passion to defend their island. His words rang in the ears of the fishermen and yachtsmen and the merchant crews who manned the boats at Dunkerque; in the ears of the girls in the telephone exchanges who kept communications going through air raids, and of the rooftop watchers so soon to be called on to wear out all their strength in the long battle against the Luftwaffe:

> We shall go on to the end, we shall fight in France, we shall fight on the seas and oceans, we shall fight with growing confidence and growing strength in the air, we shall defend our Island, whatever the cost may be, we shall fight on the beaches, we shall fight on the landing grounds, we shall fight in the fields and in the streets; we shall fight in the hills; we shall never surrender. . . .

SOON the British people were translating his words into action, but the battle was not as they had imagined it. The invasion was by incendiary bombs and high explosives. The weapons with which they fought were fire engines and buckets and sandbags and stirrup pumps and longhandled shovels and jacks and crowbars to lift the girders of fallen buildings. The chivalry was in the young fighter pilots who met the enemy in the sky overhead, but the infantry that bore the brunt of this new type of warfare were the air-raid wardens and the men who ran about the roofs of London putting out incendiary bombs and the weary squads that dug out people buried under crumpled houses.

When he told his people of the capitulation of France, Churchill foretold the struggle to come:

> What General Weygand called the Battle of France is over. I expect that the Battle of Britain is about to begin. Upon this battle depends the survival of Christian civilization. Upon it depends our own British life and the long continuity of our institutions and our Empire. The whole fury and might of the enemy must very soon be turned on us. Hitler knows that he will have to break us in this Island or lose the war. If we can stand up to him, all Europe may be free and the life of the world may move forward into broad, sunlit uplands. But if we fail, then the whole world, including the United States, including all that we have known and cared for, will sink into the abyss of a new Dark Age made more sinister, and perhaps more protracted by the lights of perverted science. Let us therefore brace ourselves to our duties, and so bear ourselves that, if the British Empire and its Commonwealth last for a thousand years, men will still say: This was their finest hour.

HITLER had continental Europe down, but with England holding out and receiving more and more aid from the U.S. and Canada, and with Stalin a doubtful ally, he could not consolidate his conquests in comfort. Halfheartedly he started to collect shipping for an invasion of England, but before he could risk the Wehrmacht on the channel he had to exterminate the Royal Air Force.

The battle began in early August 1940. Waves of German bombers flying at over 10,000 feet attacked shipping and coastal ports. The Luftwaffe had the weight of numbers, but the R.A.F. had on its side the newly developed radar, the superior armor of the Hurricane and the climbing ability of the Spitfire and a dash and initiative that the Germans for all their discipline and skill just did not have. The Luftwaffe lost two planes to the Royal Air Force's one.

With characteristic recklessness on Aug. 20 when the air battle still teetered in the balance, Winston Churchill was already giving intimations of victory to the Commons:

> The gratitude of every home in our Island, in our Empire, and indeed throughout the world, except in the abodes of the guilty, goes out to the British airmen who, undaunted by odds, unwearied in their constant challenge and mortal danger, are turning the tide of the World War by their prowess and by their devotion. Never in the field of human conflict was so much owed by so many to so few.

In the second and third phases of the battle in August and September, German losses were still unbearably high and the British continued to outclass them in every engagement. By mid-October German planes had been driven out of daytime skies over the southern lands of England. After that the Luftwaffe raided only at night. Their raids were raids of revenge. Though they caused great loss of life and at times crippled transportation in the London area, the life of the island became adjusted to a state of siege. By midwinter, when the German incendiaries set fire to the ancient core of empire, the "City" of London, it was clear to all the world that the Germans had lost the battle and that Hitler would never dare invade. —JOHN DOS PASSOS

TO STOP THE LUFTWAFFE, BRITAIN FORTIFIED THE AIR ITSELF WITH BALLOONS. DURING THE WAR AS MANY AS 2,300 HOVERED OVER THE ISLAND, DANGLING

TO STOP THE NAZI INVASION, PIPES WERE LAID TO SPREAD BURNING OIL ON THE WATER

"SEAFORTS" WERE ESTABLISHED FAR OUT IN THE THAMES

Shore defenses

Shore defenses were erected hastily along Britain's channel coast after the abrupt collapse of France. The British—"democratic idiots," Hitler called them —spurned the dictator's offer of a shameful peace. Overconfident Germans had already marked some divisions for disbanding. Hitler gave no thought to invading England until July 2, when with grave misgivings he approved Operation *Seelöwe* (Sea Lion). As plans were drawn up the German army and navy staffs took to squabbling (the generals wanted to land at many points along the south shore of England; the admirals favored a narrower beachhead near Dover). The 40-division plan was cut back to 13. About 3,500 boats and barges and 168 transports were allotted. Hitler was positive about only one thing: Reichsmarshal Hermann Göring's airmen had to knock out the R.A.F. first. "Utterly determined" Britons got ready to defend their skies and, if need be, their shores.

LONG STEEL CABLES TO ENSNARE LOW-FLYING RAIDERS

ESTUARY TO SHOOT DOWN GERMAN MINE-LAYING PLANES

EARLY COASTAL RADAR STATIONS COULD PICK UP LOW-LEVEL AIR ATTACKERS AT 30 MILES

29

BEGINNING AT SUNSET, THE STRAINED VIGIL OF BRITISH ANTIAIRCRAFT GUN CREWS LENGTHENED STEADILY WITH THE FALL NIGHTS OF 1940

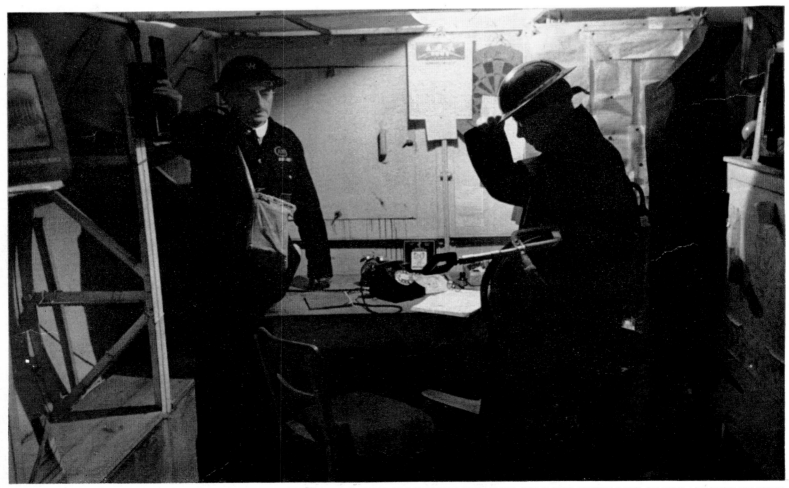

TAKING UP TIN HATS AND FIRE EXTINGUISHERS, THOUSANDS OF ORDINARY BRITONS BEGAN TO LEAD THE NIGHT LIFE OF THE AIR-RAID WARDEN

IN PICCADILLY CIRCUS THE ONLY TRACES OF LIGHT CAME FROM STARS AND DIMMED AUTOMOBILES WHICH MOVED SLOWLY IN THE BLACKOUT

WHEN THEIR HOMES BECAME THE FRONT LINE, 141,000 OF BRITAIN'S CITY-DWELLING CHILDREN WENT TO THE COUNTRY IN BUSSES AND TRAINS

IN AUGUST FIGHTER PILOTS SCRAMBLED TO MEET INCESSANT GERMAN AIR ATTACKS ON SOUTHERN ENGLAND

IN R.A.F. OPERATIONS ROOMS MARKERS ON A MAP PLOTTED THE POSITIONS OF ATTACKING BRITISH PLANES

In the skies

the British could put a daily average of some 600 fighters. The Germans had twice as many planes always available. Göring's first scheme was to draw out and destroy the R.A.F. while attacking ports and shipping. Between Aug. 3 and 17 he lost 305 aircraft to Spitfire and Hurricane pilots, while shooting down 159 of them. The fiercest fight came Aug. 15, when nearly 1,000 Luftwaffe planes made five major strikes over a 500-mile front; 74 were shot down. Most of Britain's 50,000 plane spotters that day saw vapor trails of dog fights like those above. Göring's next big effort aimed to knock out the 15 main airfields of southern England. In this he was almost successful. Many fields were seriously damaged, and the intricate operations system was threatened. By September nearly a quarter of Britain's 1,000 trained pilots were casualties. If Göring had persevered he might have won the Battle of Britain. But he turned to the senseless bombing of London, which gained him nothing but the hatred of Englishmen. On Sept. 27 he admitted the war could not be won by air alone. Since Hitler had specified destruction of the R.A.F. as a prerequisite to a cross-Channel invasion, Operation Sea Lion was hastily called off. In history's first great sky campaign Britain lost 915 planes (Göring had claimed 2,620), and the Germans lost 1,733 (not 2,698, as claimed at that time). The Germans also lost a never-to-be-repeated chance to knock Britain out of the war.

33

THE HURRICANE was the main weapon of R.A.F. fighter command in the Battle of Britain. It went into production some time before the more famous Spitfire, and Air Chief Marshal Hugh Dowding had two "Hurrys" for every "Spit" in his hard-pressed squadrons. Of the two planes, the Spitfire was the star, being able to climb faster and higher. But working as a team, Hurry and Spit scored two-for-one against the Luftwaffe.

MARSHAL GORING'S PLANES WERE FASTER THAN THE R.A.F. FIGHTERS BUT LESS MANEUVERABLE AND LIGHTER ARMED. HERE A GERMAN FIGHTER, CAUGHT FROM

THE HAGGARD HEROES of the R.A.F. fought 'round the operational clock, always against heavy odds, always with cruel losses. Shot down over their homeland, many of them lived to fight many another day, but the fatal gaps in their ranks had to be filled with inexperienced pilots fresh from training schools.

THREE WHO FOUGHT: the pilot at top got the D.F.C., second led Spitfires, third commanded a squadron of Hurricanes.

BEHIND, IS HIT IN THE TAIL (LEFT). UNDER THE HEAVY FIRE OF BRITISH WING GUNS, PIECES OF THE PLANE FLY OFF AND (RIGHT) IT EXPLODES IN FLAMES

London under Fire

OF all the fallacies of World War II, the most widely held was this: people would give up if their relatives were killed and their homes destroyed. It turned out that most people with reasonable hope—and many who had none whatsoever—could take it. This went for Berlin and Hamburg, Tokyo and Osaka. But the residents of these cities had to wait for their mettle to be tested. It was the Englishman who showed them how. In Poland the Germans had supplied a frightening glimpse of their technique of terror-bombing; at Rotterdam the view expanded. But in both these cases the air assaults were part of developing invasions, and targets included military objectives.

When Göring unleashed his bombers on London Sept. 7 with a 300-plane attack, his savagery was simply intended to kill people, however innocent. He underestimated the Briton. Scourged to his subway dungeon (*opposite*), the Londoner lightheartedly cocked his fingers in the V sign. Atop his Anderson shelter, when spring came, he sometimes planted stonecrop and alyssum. One day Winston Churchill went to see damage caused by a heavy raid on humble south London which wrecked 20 or 30 small houses. He found little Union Jacks already fluttering amidst the ruins. The stricken people cheered their leader, who admitted, long afterward, "I was completely undermined, and wept."

A week after he started the heavy bombing of London, Göring found his losses to the R.A.F. becoming unacceptable. He switched from daylight raids and, since London was the easiest place to find in the dark, it became the prime target. With near impunity—since night fighters were still in the primitive stage and antiaircraft guns served mostly as morale boosters—Göring's pilots caused very great damage. For 57 consecutive nights the Germans put an average of 200 bombers over London. Then, on the night of Nov. 3, no German bomber came over. After that raids were sporadic but sometimes very heavy. The great incendiary bombing of Dec. 29 was the worst, with some 1,500 fires. The Guildhall was heavily damaged and eight of Sir Christopher Wren's great churches were totally or partially wrecked. In March 1941 the Mother of Parliaments herself was violated, but it was night and no members of Commons were present when their building was demolished.

The attacks on English cities suddenly stopped on May 10, 1941 as Hitler treacherously prepared to turn eastward on Russia (hoping to enlist these indefatigable Britons in his cause). Luftwaffe pilots had unloaded 57,000 tons of bombs on Britain during 1940–41, killed 42,000 Englishmen. London's share was about half the total. Militarily Hitler's accomplishment was nil: after eight months' intensive bombing British war production was up 40%. Psychologically Hitler had only managed to turn most of the neutral world—particularly mighty America—against himself.

NIGHT: INCENDIARY BOMBS TURN A STATIONERY STORE INTO A WALLED PYRE

MORNING: A SENTRY FIRE PUMP SOAKS DOWN THE STILL-SMOLDERING RUBBLE

THE FIRE RAID OF DEC. 29 LEFT BRUTAL HISTORICAL GAPS IN VENERABLE

"CITY" SECTION OF LONDON. HERE WRECKERS HAVE PILED UP THE DEBRIS INTO AN ORDERED DESOLATION. BARRAGE BALLOONS ARE VISIBLE IN THE DISTANCE

BOMB WHICH HIT THE BALHAM HIGH ROAD BLASTED THE FACADES OFF FOUR STORES AND ENGULFED A DOUBLE-DECK BUS IN ITS HUGE CRATER

WITH LONDON STANDING FIRM, GORING BEGAN AN INCENDIARY TOUR OF THE PROVINCES, PUTTING THE AIRBORNE TORCH TO BRISTOL ON NOV. 24

THE LUFTWAFFE STRUCK AT COVENTRY'S ARMS FACTORIES BY DEVASTATING THE HEART OF THE CITY WHERE WORKERS LIVED AND SHOPPED

IN THE MERSEYSIDE "MAY WEEK" SEVEN CONSECUTIVE RAIDS RUINED CENTER OF LIVERPOOL BUT DID NOT CLOSE ITS GREAT PORT OF ENTRY

THE NAVAL PORT OF PLYMOUTH SUFFERED DAMAGE TO OVER 50,000 HOUSES IN THE ALL-OUT AIR CAMPAIGN TO LOCK BRITAIN'S MARITIME DOORS

VOLUNTEER FIREMEN FOUGHT INCENDIARIES NIGHT AFTER NIGHT

VOLUNTEER WATCHERS, 50,000 STRONG, CHARTED ENEMY FLIGHTS

TELEPHONE OPERATORS KEPT VITAL AIR-DEFENSE CIRCUITS OPEN

BOMBED-OUT CITIZENS STILL GOT THEIR CUP OF TEA AT CANTEENS

RESCUE OF A WOMAN from the basement of her bomb-collapsed house came after 18 hours of digging. This was one of 50,000 bomb "incidents" during the blitz which kept Londoners constantly probing through the rubble to disarm buried land mines, clear streets for the fire engines and repair the mangled underground system of subways, sewers, water mains, gas pipes and telephone cables on which life of the great city depended.

Major weapon

in Britain's lonely and troublous time was the defiant figure of Winston Churchill. Short, blocky, with a bulldog set to his jaw, Churchill personified British bravery and determination. Even in moments of relaxation (*below*) he managed to look indomitable. For years Churchill had warned of disasters to come; after Munich he said: "And do not suppose that this is the end. . . . This is only the first sip, the first foretaste of a bitter cup which will be proffered to us year by year unless . . . we arise again and take our stand for freedom as in the olden time." When the bitter cup overflowed in 1940's fateful spring, Churchill was the inevitable choice for prime minister. Speaking in a slightly lisping, husky voice that exuded confidence in his countrymen and scorn for the "Nozzy" enemy, he rallied not only Britain but the free world. Eighteen months after Dunkerque, with both the U.S. and Russia at war with the Axis, Churchill came to Ottawa and there eloquently reviewed the grim days when England fought alone. With the fall of France, he said, the French generals predicted, "In three weeks England will have her neck wrung like a chicken." Churchill growled, "Some chicken! Some neck!" He did not add what Hitler had long since painfully learned—that neck and chicken were still intact primarily because of a dynamic, articulate little man, "half American and all British," who had taken a stand "for freedom as in the olden time."

Richard Edes Harrison 1950

III
The Axis Strained

Europe: 1941

As the year 1940 came to an end over the smoldering ruins of London, Hitler, like Napoleon before him, found himself the master of continental Europe. But the British seaborne empire remained afloat with Churchill thundering defiance from the quarterdeck. Preparations for the projected invasion of England, Operation Sea Lion, which neither Hitler nor members of his general staff ever really relished, were becoming more and more halfhearted.

With the triumph of Compiègne still tingling in his blood, the question in Hitler's mind was what next. Conquered France was not fitting as smoothly as it should into the schemes of the mighty Reich. The talkative government of the Third Republic had vanished without trace into the restaurants and alleys of Bordeaux. In its place the aged Marshal Pétain, highpriest of the religion of defeat, sat in a small stuffy parlor in a hypochondriacs' hotel at the ancient watering-place of Vichy. In North Africa, Weygand ruled. In other fragments of the French dominion satraps in uniforms indulged themselves in every crotchet of the French military mind which had never been reconciled to the First Republic, much less to the Third. Between these archaistic figures and the office of the occupation authorities under Otto Abetz in Paris there shuttled a number of slippery adventurers with Pierre Laval as their greatest exemplar. Each of these worthies had plans of his own. It was a situation bad for the French, but not too good for the Germans. Men and events kept slipping out of Hitler's hands. For one thing, he could not get hold of the French fleet which still would command the balance of naval power if anybody could be found to put the ships to sea.

In Italy, Mussolini was greeted with the cadenced cries of *Duce! Duce!* by blackshirted Roman crowds whenever he stepped out on his balcony at the Palazzo Venezia, but not all his oratory could properly equip his armies or induce his troops to fight. His defeats by the ragged Greek mountaineers were beginning to make the whole dictatorial idea ridiculous; and in Africa, Wavell's tiny armored columns were cutting Rodolfo Graziani's grandiloquent expedition, which was supposed to take Suez, into shreds. Far to the south other British Empire forces were beginning their dash into Abyssinia. The British army had invented tank warfare. They were beginning to show their mettle in it.

From the days of *Mein Kampf* Hitler had felt that his course of empire lay eastward along the road traced by the Teutonic knights. In order to keep Stalin temporarily quiet while he swung at the West, he had let him subdue the Baltic countries. Now Hitler began to feel the intrigues of Kremlin agents interfering with his own envoys in the Balkans. A concentration of German troops in Eastern Europe would be a guard against Stalin's treacheries. He could crush Soviet Russia while England died slowly of the blockade's strangulation.

The sudden overturn of a pro-Nazi government in Yugoslavia forced Hitler's hand and early in April of 1941 the Wehrmacht started to move in through the zigzag Balkan valleys. German speed forestalled any help to Yugoslavia, but Britain had a venerable alliance with Greece. Risking the ruin of his North African campaign, Churchill threw 53,000 troops into Greece. The British were outflanked and outclassed by the Wehrmacht and, as at Narvik and at Dunkerque, were pushed into the sea. After three weeks of fighting Hitler had assured his control of the Balkans.

Before the battered British forces that had crawled off the ships on the long stony island of Crete had a chance to reform and re-equip, the Luftwaffe overwhelmed them by the first great airborne invasion in history. The invasion was successful but the butcher's bill was so high that Hitler never again had the stomach for a similar maneuver. The British kept precarious hold on Cyprus in the east and, against continual air attack, on Malta in the west, but the empire's Mediterranean artery was threatened.

If Hitler in the summer of 1941 had followed a traditional plan of the German general staff to move toward the Near East he might possibly be ruling in Europe to this day. But he had set his heart on the wheatlands of the Ukraine. The poor showing of the Russian army in Finland had made him unduly scornful of Stalin's military power. If the Wehrmacht could push the barbarous Muscovite into Asia and install the punctual, cleanly German order across the black-soil belt all the way to the Volga and the Caucasian oil fields, Hitler would hold the heartland of the world. The English-speaking peoples could be allowed to disintegrate in peace around its fringes. They must be made to understand that Hitler meant them no real harm. To tell that story to the conservative aristocrats of Britain, Rudolph Hess, Hitler's close friend, set out in May on his solitary flight to Scotland. Churchill promptly shut up the airborne Quixote and made it seem as if his mission had never occurred. After the burning of British cities neither Churchill nor any other islander was in the mood to talk terms with the Germans.

If the British made no peace move Hitler would go it alone against Russia. On June 22, two days before the day on which Napoleon crossed the Niemen in 1812, the armored Wehrmacht started to advance against the multitudinous human masses of the Russian armies. Hitler had decided to stake everything on the knockout blow of a single great campaign. Although Stalin had been warned from various sources, including both Roosevelt and Churchill, that the attack was preparing, the Soviet generals were caught off guard. Army after army was annihilated in a series of giant pincer movements. The Germans advanced fast but not fast enough. The Russians had taken enormous losses but they continued to hold the railroad hub that centered on Moscow and a line to the Baku oil fields. Worse than that, although the Kremlin regime was none too popular in the Ukraine, the Germans, by their brutal tactics against the partisans the Kremlin leaders left behind in the forests and villages, made a reconciliation with the peasant population impossible. In a fury of destruction the Russians, as they retired, wrecked every utility that might fall into German hands. German rule ended within gunshot of their lines. Hitler's supply moved on wheeled trucks rather than on caterpillar vehicles. There were no roads worth the name. In spite of brilliant engineering work in converting and repairing the railroads there was never enough transport.

Winter came early. Like Napoleon, Hitler wore out his armies on the Russian steppe in a battle against the immensities of cold and space. As his failure to knock out England in 1940 had stalled his drive to the west, so his failure to take Moscow in 1941 stalled his drive to the east. He was caught in a trap of his own making. —JOHN DOS PASSOS

LATE IN 1940, ALL THE DUCE'S DONKEYS AND ALL THE DUCE'S MEN MARCHED UP THE HILLS OF GREECE AND MARCHED RIGHT DOWN AGAIN

KILTED GREEK EVZONE CONFRONTS BLACKSHIRT PRISONER

Greece in the fall of 1940 looked like an easy target for a dictator anxious to enhance his military prestige. The Italians struck on Oct. 28, 1940. From Albania, which he had occupied in 1939, Mussolini tried to take Greece with 27 divisions. In this operation he got fearfully scorched; the Greeks knocked him 30 miles back into Albania's mountains and kept him pinned there all winter, a most discredited dictator. Meanwhile fires broke out all over the Mediterranean. The war seesawed across North Africa— General Archibald Wavell captured 130,000 Italians before the Germans under General Erwin Rommel arrived. Admiral Andrew Cunningham caught the Italian fleet at Taranto and put half of Italy's six battleships out of the war for half a year. The Greek government invoked a prewar treaty and Churchill found himself playing fireman in yet another theater. British troops occupied the Greek island of Crete when Mussolini attacked from Albania. In March 1941, 53,051 British Imperial troops were rushed to Greece. But on April 6 Germany jumped into this war too. Marshal Siegmund List's blitz through Yugoslavia and Greece was horrific. The British fell back; warships took off four fifths of the retreating army.

WRECKED ITALIAN PLANES WERE LEFT BEHIND IN HASTY RETREAT

THEIR MOUNTAIN GUNS WERE OLD, BUT GREEKS WERE GOOD SHOTS

WINTER STALLED ITALIAN MOTOR TRANSPORT IN THE MOUNTAINS

COATED WITH FROST, GREEK SUPPLY DONKEY FORAGED IN SNOW

HARDY GREEK FOOT SOLDIERS TOILED OVER THE SNOWY MOUNTAIN PASSES INTO ALBANIA, KEPT LARGER ITALIAN ARMY ON THE DEFENSIVE

GERMAN ARMOR came down into the Balkans like a spring flood and broke the winter impasse of the Axis in Greece. Pushing off from satellite Bulgaria, German tanks twisted through the rough mountain passes of southern Yugoslavia in only four days. Marshal List burst suddenly into Greece from the north, simultaneously flanked both the main Greek army in Albania and the British Expeditionary Force on the east coast.

THE NAZI CONVOYS were not slowed by heavy rains. Along the soggy Greek roads German trucks halted only long enough for advance units to force back the stubborn British rear guard. Despite overwhelming air attacks, the British managed to make a stand at the classic strong point of Thermopylae. But the allies they had come to save were already fallen. Yugoslavia yielded April 17, the exhausted Greeks a week later.

THE BEATEN BRITISH landed on the docks of Alexandria after leaving Greece on April 24. After the Greek surrender on that day the B.E.F. was left alone in the Balkans and once again the Royal Navy was called to the rescue. No air cover was possible, so the transports and warships put into the small ports of the Peloponnesus at night. Allied ships, despite heavy Luftwaffe attacks, successfully evacuated 50,000 soldiers.

GREEKS BADE FAREWELL to their allies when townspeople came down to the shore to watch a flying-boat take off the last British troops. All of their country had fallen to the Germans except for the island of Crete, where 19,000 of the evacuated British landed and dug in. On the mainland the Greeks defied the cruel Nazi occupation by helping some 1,400 British stragglers who were left behind to escape eventually to Egypt.

Crete has long been regarded as the masterpiece of the parachutists' art. Actually, though Hitler gained a spectacular victory, his losses were so severe that he told Colonel General Kurt Student, "The day of parachute troops is over." Britain started the battle with 30,000 men, mostly evacuees from the Greek disaster, many unarmed; there were few tanks and few antiaircraft guns. Operation Mercury, mounted in conquered Greece, began on May 20 with a heavy bombing attack followed by hundreds of Nazi parachutists floating down near Maleme airfield. Many were killed, but more were coming; so were troop-carrying gliders which landed in areas held by the 'chutists. The audacious Germans beat off all counterattacks. On May 28 the British again started rescuing their troops because, said Admiral Cunningham, "It takes the navy three years to build a new ship. It will take 300 years to build a new tradition." At Crete he lost to Nazi bombers three cruisers, six destroyers; 15,000 British soldiers and sailors were killed, wounded or captured. But the tradition lived, and Hitler's costly success decimated his only corps of airborne troops.

COMING IN LOW, NAZI TRANSPORTS SEEDED HERAKLEION AIRFIELD WITH

STUKAS STRUCK THE BRITISH HEADQUARTERS AND NAVAL BASE AT SUDA BAY

SEIZED BY PARATROOPS, MALEME FIELD BECAME AN AERIAL BRIDGEHEAD.

PARATROOPERS AND PARACHUTE-BORNE EQUIPMENT. HIT BY ANTIAIRCRAFT FIRE, ONE PLANE NOSED DOWN IN FLAMES, BUT THE LUFTWAFFE KEPT COMING

DROPPING ON OPEN COUNTRYSIDE, THESE PARATROOPS WERE FIRST OF 14,000

MORE THAN 20 TRANSPORTS LANDED EVERY HOUR WITH REINFORCEMENTS

GERMAN FORCES USED GUNS BROUGHT IN BY PLANE TO STOP BRITISH ATTACKS

MALTA'S PROLONGED PUNISHMENT BY THE AXIS REACHED ALMOST UNBEARABLE INTENSITY IN THE GERMAN RAIDS OF APRIL 1942. BY THEN BOMBS HAD RAVAGED

Malta is a small island (9x18 miles) plunk in the center of the Mediterranean. Although it was separated from Italian air bases on Sicily by only 60 miles, it managed to stay in British hands, where it had reposed since Nelson's time. The Axis powers' failure to capture this British steppingstone was a major blunder. Not that Hitler and Mussolini didn't try—their planes assaulted Malta almost continuously for more than two years. In April 1942 there were 5,715 sorties which dropped 6,728 tons of bombs, but Malta's submarine pens and airfields still functioned. So, despite his experience at Crete, Hitler decided to invade Malta with German parachutists, to be followed by six to eight seaborne Italian divisions. But he called it off; he feared the Italian ships would turn back if the British navy interfered. The bombing went on. Malta's defense cost Britain 568 planes (to the Axis' 1,129), but more always came through. During the time of the gravest crisis the U.S.S. *Wasp* delivered 94 of the saving Spitfires.

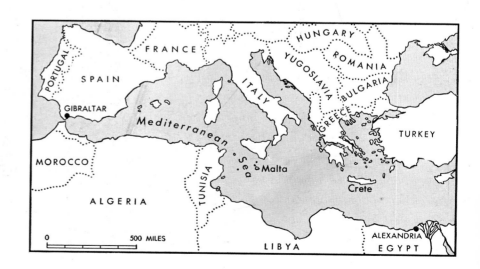

ANTIAIRCRAFT HUNTERS HAD LONG SEASON, CLAIMED 236 PLANES SHOT DOWN

THREE OUT OF FOUR OF THE CAPITAL CITY'S SUN-WEATHERED BUILDINGS

MALTA BEGAN WAR WITH THREE BIPLANES. THIS ONE WAS CALLED "FAITH"

IN THE FALL OF 1941 R.A.F. HURRICANES TOOK OFF FROM THE OLD AIRCRAFT CARRIER ARGUS (LEFT) AND FLEW 400 MILES TO REINFORCE BESIEGED MALTA

FORTIFIED BY THE CRUSADING KNIGHTS OF MALTA, VALLETTA'S "GRAND HARBOR" STANCHLY SERVED THE ROYAL NAVY THROUGHOUT THE WAR

Invasion of Russia

"DRANG NACH OSTEN" BEGAN AT DAWN FROM PRUSSIA'S FORESTS

HITLER'S alliance with Russia was less than one year old when he secretly decided to have done with it. On Dec. 18, 1940 he put his decision in writing: "Crush Soviet Russia in a quick campaign before the end of the war against England." The Nazi dictator had been proceeding for two decades on the theory that Communist Russia must be annihilated. Nonetheless his stubborn insistence on fighting on another front, before he had prevailed over the British, was mad. Operation Barbarossa began at dawn, June 22, 1941, with an attack along a 2,000-mile front, from the White Sea to the Black Sea. Into this biggest campaign of mankind's biggest war Hitler sent 121 divisions and some 3,000 planes, dwarfing Napoleon's effort 129 years earlier. With the troops went a number of German artists, and it is their captured canvases of the early advances which appear on this and the following pages.

Hitler knew the Russians had about 120 divisions facing the German front and he expected to destroy them before reaching the Dnieper River 350 miles away. For a month he seemed likely to succeed; his armies rolled forward as much as 40 miles a day. Stalin, despite a lifetime of intrigue, apparently was caught napping by his partner. But these Russians defending their motherland were not the same people the Finns had made look ridiculous. Deeper and deeper into Russia's awesome, scorched emptiness they drew the Germans. Hitler soon had 200 divisions committed. Winter—the worst in many years—came early. Supply lines began to fail.

BY JULY THE GERMANS HAD MARCHED 400 MILES INTO RUSSIA, BUT THE GLOW OF BATTLE WAS STILL CONSTANT ON THE SOMBER, ENDLESS HORIZON

VICTORY-SEASONED GERMAN ARMOR SHEARED THROUGH THE RUSSIAN FORESTS AND, WITH STUKA SUPPORT, CUT OFF WHOLE ARMIES AT MINSK

LOW-FLYING STUKAS CONSTANTLY HARASSED THE PRIMITIVE, HORSE-DRAWN CARAVANS RETREATING ALONG BLEAK DIRT ROADS TO MOSCOW

ROLLING THROUGH VILLAGES OF THE UKRAINE, NAZI COLUMNS MADE HITLER OVERSEER OF THE "BLACK EARTH," RUSSIA'S HISTORIC WHEATLAND

AFTER THE SMOLENSK BATTLE, WOUNDED RUSSIAN CAPTIVES AND WRECKED ARMOR SWELLED THE NAZIS' BAG TO 300,000 PRISONERS, 3,000 TANKS

AT MOGILEV NAZI TROOPERS DISARMED THE CAPTURED GARRISON. WHEN CUT OFF, RUSSIANS FOUGHT ON STUBBORNLY, SLOWED DOWN THE BLITZ

STILL ON THE ROAD TO MOSCOW, BATTLE-WEARY GERMANS HALTED AT YELNYA, WHERE THE RED ARMY THREW THEM BACK FOR THE FIRST TIME

IN 1941 SOVIET TANKS WERE WEAK, BUT RUSSIA SACRIFICED ENOUGH OF THE STRONG MEN INSIDE THEM TO FINALLY STOP THE NAZI ADVANCE

Blitzkrieg

of unimaginable proportions swirled upon Russia in the north, the center and the south. The first Panzer drives pointed toward the Soviet Union's three greatest cities: Leningrad, Moscow and Kiev. The world's military "experts" gave the Red Army a maximum of 13 weeks—Hitler himself told his generals it would be over in ten. Only a fortnight had passed before it became apparent that something was wrong. The ill-trained Russian soldiers fought back with a contemptuous disregard for death and the Germans found no psychic paralysis anywhere. Two great offensives pierced south and center, von Rundstedt with three armies and four armored divisions, General Fedor von Bock with three armies and ten Panzers. In 25 days von Bock drove 400 miles to Smolensk, then swerved south and joined von Rundstedt's armor beyond Kiev in an envelopment which yielded prisoners to the fantastic number of 665,000. Von Rundstedt swept on to Kharkov and Rostov, but by then it was November, about 20 costly weeks since the attack began. Stalin still had not mentioned surrender. Late in November, Marshal Semion Timoshenko counterattacked savagely at Rostov and took back 40 of the 500 miles von Rundstedt had won.

PANZER TROOPERS CHARGE FROM ARMORED HALF-TRACKS TO BATTLE RED

FROM THE CITADEL OF KIEV NAZIS SURVEYED THE BROKEN DNIEPER BRIDGES

BY OCT. 24 THE GERMANS WERE FIGHTING INSIDE CITY OF KHARKOV

SHARPSHOOTERS IN THE OUTBUILDINGS OF A BURNING FARMHOUSE. IN THE FIRST WEEKS THE INVADING PANZERS MOVED AS FAST AS THEY HAD IN FRANCE

LAST SOUTHERN LUNGE CARRIED NAZI TANKS INTO ROSTOV ON NOV. 21

RUSSIANS RETURNED WITHIN A WEEK AND DROVE NAZIS OUT OF ROSTOV

CHARGING OUT OF RUSSIA'S PAST, SWORD-WIELDING COSSACKS JOINED THE ALL-OUT DEFENSE OF MOSCOW AND FLANKED VON KLUGE'S ARMY

LACKING CAMOUFLAGE FOR WINTER WAR, FOUR SURRENDERING GERMANS STAGGER THROUGH THE DEEP SNOW INTO THE RUSSIAN LINES AROUND MOSCOW.

WINTER-HARDENED RED SKI TROOPS AND TANKMEN COUNTERATTACKED WHILE THE GERMANS WERE HOLED UP IN "HEDGEHOG" POSITIONS

ROAD BLOCKS WERE READY, BUT IT WAS RUSSIAN WINTER THAT CLOSED THE ROAD TO MOSCOW

THE RUSSIAN FROST HAD BIT DEEP INTO NAZI MORALE

Moscow was saved by Hitler's decision to attack first toward Leningrad on the north and the Caucasus on the south. When he changed his mind in September and ordered von Bock to proceed he gave that field marshal 48 additional infantry divisions plus 12 with armor. Von Bock now had 1,500,000 men. His troops jumped off on Oct. 2, with Field Marshal Günther von Kluge in command of two armies and two Panzer groups. Soon snow—in mid-October instead of mid-November—began to cover tanks already mired in Russian mud, and enemy counterattacks grew more frequent, more fierce. Nonetheless the attack carried within 40 miles of Moscow. Hitler's soldiers could see the antiaircraft fire directed at German bombers over the city, and a few patrols actually reached Moscow's suburbs. But it was now December. Snow was falling heavily in the forests and fields around the Soviet capital and the temperature was well below zero. Then, on Dec. 6, General Georgi Zhukov struck von Kluge's shivering soldiers with—of all things—a hundred divisions. The Germans fell back to spend a miserable winter in too-light clothing, harassed by guerrillas, bedeviled by machines and weapons that stuck and froze. These things did not please Hitler, who fired his commander in chief, Field Marshal Walther von Brauchitsch, and Chief of Staff Franz Halder, and took their jobs himself. He also booted out all his top field commanders in Russia, including the ablest, von Rundstedt. Hitler still thought he could turn the Russian trick in 1942. With some reason he could blame his failure in 1941 on the weather—but so could Napoleon in 1812.

Leningrad

which means "Lenin's city" is what the Soviets named Peter the Great's beloved "window to the sea." Leningrad's capture was assigned to another Prussian field marshal, Wilhelm von Leeb, with two armies, four armored divisions and the help of 12 Finnish divisions under old Field Marshal Carl Mannerheim, who wanted to get back what the Kremlin had clumsily taken from him in 1940. But in the north the Russians had near equality, and progress was slow. The heroism of Leningrad's defenders—civilian and military—inspired Composer Dmitri Shostakovich, who was one of them, to write a symphony about the Battle of Leningrad, as Tchaikovsky had memorialized Napoleon's retreat in his classic *1812 Overture*. In October the German news agency, attempting to explain Leningrad's survival, said there was no reason for "a prestige attack on this city, in which probably every cellar is loaded with dynamite."

The Russians' fight for their motherland stood with the R.A.F.'s defense of Britain. Its implications were immediate and worldwide. Winston Churchill, who had battled Communism for a quarter century, sided with Stalin: "If Hitler invaded Hell I would at least make a favorable reference to the Devil in the House of Commons." In the U.S. President Roosevelt received the vociferous support of the Communist party and its organ the *Daily Worker*, which had castigated him since 1939 as an imperialist warmonger. Roosevelt followed Churchill's lead; five weeks after Hitler invaded Russia he sent Harry Hopkins to find out what Stalin needed. (Stalin said antiaircraft guns, aluminum, machine guns, rifles.) Although it was not yet August, the Russian dictator convinced Hopkins his troops could stop Hitler. The Grand Alliance was about to be forged.

FOR 515 DAYS THE NAZIS BOMBARDED LENINGRAD WITH BIG SIEGE GUNS LIKE THIS. HERE, AFTER FIRING, GUNNERS WHEEL UP ANOTHER SHELL

DAY AFTER DAY NAZI SHELLS CRASHED INTO LENINGRAD'S HOMES

COFFIN WAS DRAGGED HOME FOR ONE OF THE CITY'S 1,750,000 DEAD

WITH RESERVOIRS GONE, PEOPLE DREW WATER FROM RIVER NEVA

WORKERS MARCHED OUT TO DIG ENTRENCHMENTS, CLEAN UP RUINS

SOVIET TRUCKS BROUGHT SUPPLIES ACROSS THE WINTER ICE OF LAKE LADOGA AFTER THE GERMANS BLOCKED ALL LAND ROUTES TO LENINGRAD

67

DNIEPER DAM, together with its electric plant, largest in Europe, was dynamited by retreating Reds. Along with this ruined keystone of the **Five Year Plans,** the invaders seized 70% of Russia's coal mines, 75% of her iron ore and 60% of her metalworks. But the Soviets saved whole factories—including 75% of Leningrad's industry—by moving them east of the Ural Mountains where a new industrial complex was building.

RUINS OF MINSK were Russian-made. Before withdrawing from the city the Red Army carefully set fires in these buildings and left not even a roof for the Wehrmacht. Following this ruthless policy everywhere, the Russians reduced their richest lands to scorched earth. The Germans got little from this desolate land except harassment by Soviet partisans, whose number constantly increased as Nazi oppression deepened.

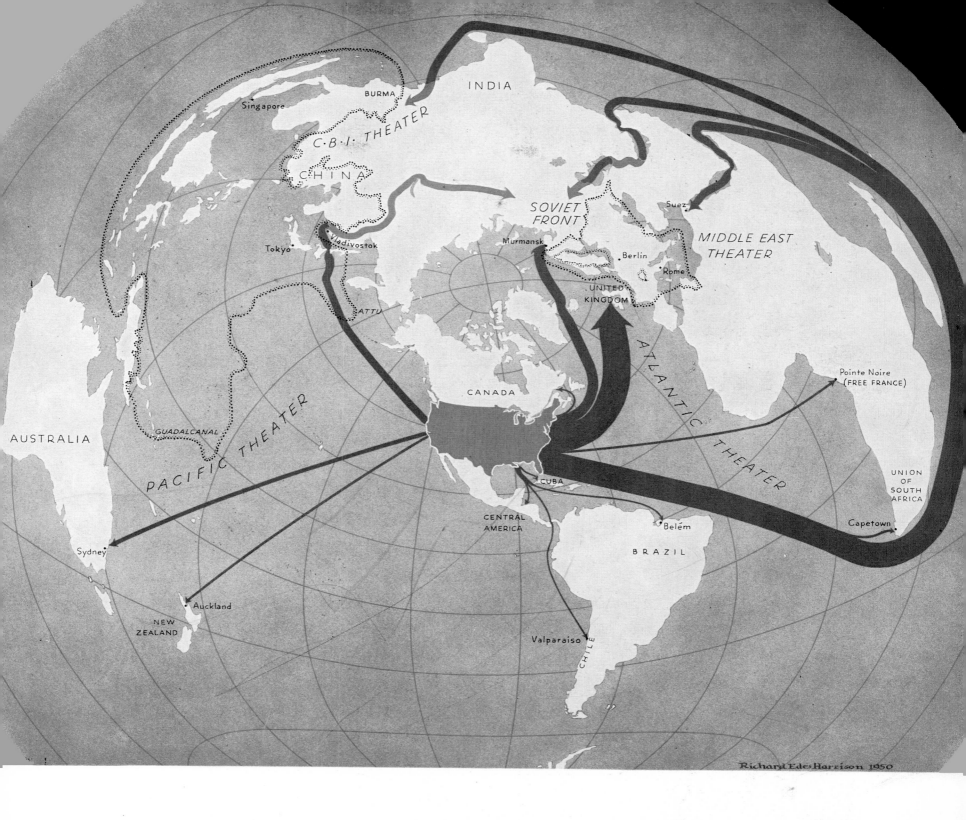

IV
The Arsenal of Democracy

U.S.A.: 1941

HITLER'S faulty estimate of the Soviet Union ruined his hopes of empire; his faulty estimate of the U.S. dug his grave. The dream of a separate future for the New World, so near the heart of the political ideas round which the American nation was built, had, by the end of Franklin D. Roosevelt's second administration, begun to fade. The Wehrmacht's lightning knockout of Western Europe had shaken Washington as profoundly as Westminster. It had shaken the American people even more profoundly than their representatives in Congress. We began to understand that the sink of massacre and ruin we looked out on beyond the seas was the world we lived in. The airplane had changed our map. Our American continent that once had seemed so secure between the oceans on the Mercator projection stood in quite different relation to the other land masses when you looked down from the North Pole at the great circle routes round the globe. We began to awaken to the somber truth that if we wanted peaceful progress at home we would have to take part in the government of mankind.

The cause of isolation had really been lost in the debates of a generation before, but a number of patriotic people had tried to go on believing that there was still a chance for a separate future. They could point out with some justice that American blood and treasure had been lavished on the First World War and that it had brought no peace. Every morning Americans opened their newspapers to be met with some new evidence of Europe's backsliding from the standards that the Christian polity had built up painfully through the centuries. It was obvious that war was not the cure for civilization's sickness, but what the isolationists could not explain was how by standing aloof we could avoid it. Furthermore the advocates of peace were discredited by the adherence to their cause of the Kremlin-led Communists, who during the period of the Stalin-Hitler agreement did their best to hamper American aid to Britain, and of groups who were inspired by Nazi ideas of leadership and race. The people generally were for preparedness, though they were hardly ready to admit how far they were willing to go to sweep the bloody dictators off the earth. In the presidential campaign of 1940, when Roosevelt made his bid for a third term on the basis of leadership of the Western World, the question of aid to Hitler's victims was never in dispute.

THE first objective was clear. Whatever forces were willing to oppose the extension of Hitler's rule must be backed up by American supplies. The niggardly slogan "Cash and Carry" went into the discard and the Administration went to work to find pretexts for circumventing the Johnson Act which forbade loans to nations that had not paid their debts from the first war, and the Neutrality Act of 1939 which went through Congress in a last flare-up of isolationist sentiment. A way had to be found to turn over to the besieged British, in desperate need of small ships to protect their convoys, some of the overage destroyers tied up in American ports. Roosevelt kept all the threads of the delicate deal in his own hands. While Cordell Hull's Department of State carried on the routine of diplomacy, a network of negotiations grew up round the White House. Presidential envoys official, semiofficial and unofficial were sent flitting about the world on special missions. Harry Hopkins flew to London, where he landed in the midst of what the cockneys called "a proper blitz," to discuss with Churchill the swapping of a string of island bases for the destroyers and to size up the chances of Britain's holding out. Admiral William Leahy went to Vichy to stiffen Pétain's aged spine against Laval. Robert Murphy cozied up to Weygand in North Africa. Wendell Willkie started on his travels carrying a cheering quotation from Longfellow copied in the President's hand for Churchill. The intricate machinery of the Grand Alliance was being assembled.

At home the U.S. was taking on the mood of a nation at war. Once it was established through the polite fiction of Lend-Lease that the American taxpayer would pay all bills, industry's throttle was pushed wide open. The boom was on to flabbergast friend and foe alike by the quantity and diversity of America's output. In one of his fireside chats the President tacked up the slogan: Arsenal of Democracy.

With Hitler's attack on Russia the war had effectively become worldwide. Stalin tried to protect his far-eastern rear by an agreement with the Japanese which had the effect of freeing their powerful Manchurian armies for further adventures. The military men who had seized tight hold on the Japanese government felt their turn had come to start a drive for empire. While their shipyards hammered away at troopships and aircraft carriers their ambassadors tried to see how much they could get by blackmail and negotiation. In Washington they got nothing out of long conversations with Cordell Hull but they were more fortunate in Berlin: in return for Tokyo's adherence to the Rome-Berlin Axis, Hitler, hoping to isolate American seapower in the Pacific, bludgeoned Vichy into giving the Japanese army peaceful entrance into Indochina, thereby driving a wedge into the British Empire's eastern arteries. With Japan on the move in the Pacific and Nazi submarines ravaging the Atlantic routes, the English-speaking peoples faced a bleak future.

ROOSEVELT and Churchill were working together but at a distance. They were men of buoyant spirits with a taste for world politics and the resounding phrase. They got along. They agreed to send Harry Hopkins to Moscow where Stalin proved to him that the Russians could and would resist the Wehrmacht. Roosevelt and Churchill felt they were fighting back to back against great odds. Both decided they had to meet to discuss mutual aid and to hear Hopkins' estimate of Russian power.

In meeting at sea in August 1941 the two leaders took a daring and calculated risk. Nazi submarines in the Atlantic were probing farther and farther west. All that summer and fall Washington's attention was concentrated on the shipping lanes that kept Britain supplied. In spite of the aggressive behavior of the Japanese, Navy ships had to be drafted out of the Pacific. Only a few staff officers followed with interest rumors of a movement of Japanese fleet units toward southern Asia. Every Saturday night the battleships of the diminished American force in the Pacific tied up in pairs at their moorings while crews were given liberty in Honolulu. At breakfast time one December Sunday carrier-based Japanese planes came in from the north round the cloudy mountains and bombed the fleet to bits. The radio woke the U.S. to the reality of war: *air raid—Pearl Harbor —this is no drill.* When Churchill got the news that we were in all the way he took a deep breath of relief; from that moment he was certain of victory. —JOHN DOS PASSOS

FITTING OUT IN A CANADIAN HARBOR, THREE VETERAN U.S. DESTROYERS FLEW NEW COLORS

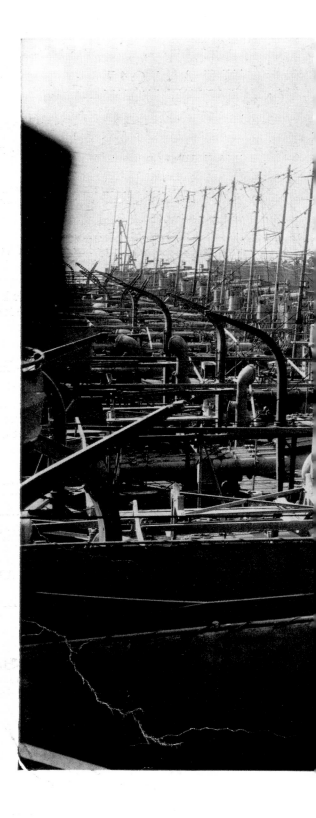

THE PAINT WAS PEELING OFF THE OLD SHIPS AS THEY MADE A STORMY CROSSING TO BRITAIN

Destroyers

were badly needed by the Royal Navy in 1940 to oppose the powerful submarine fleets of Germany and Italy. The U.S., though weak in those untested ships called aircraft carriers, had considerably more destroyers (171 to 98) than potential enemy Japan. The British were understandably eager to obtain some of these small but vital ships. In May, Churchill cabled Franklin D. Roosevelt, pointing out Britain's urgent necessity. Turned down, the Prime Minister became considerably blunter after 11 destroyers were sunk or damaged in a fortnight in July: "Mr. President, with great respect I must tell you that in the long history of the world this is a thing to do *now*." The Nazi avalanche in the spring of 1940 had impressed Roosevelt no less than the American people—a *Fortune* poll showed a leap from 20% to 70% in favor of aid to Hitler's enemies. But under existing law the President couldn't dispose of any military supplies unless they were certified as useless. Admiral Harold Stark had already testified that his World War I destroyers were valuable. Now a way was found: Stark said some ships could be spared if Britain gave in exchange the eight Atlantic bases she had offered. With the secret approval of his political opponent, Wendell Willkie, but without consent of Congress, Roosevelt announced on Sept. 3 that Britain would get 50 of the Navy's 1914-type destroyers. Actually these ships were too old to be of decisive help. But they paved the way for what Churchill wanted most: an alliance. The deal would have justified Germany's declaring war on the U.S., Churchill admitted later. But that was the last thing wanted by Adolf Hitler, who believed that he had the war won anyway.

The Congress met in joint session Jan. 6, 1941 to hear President Roosevelt's "State of the Nation" speech. Steel girders had been installed to bolster the sagging roof of the House of Representatives (*left*). After hearing the President's speech, some congressmen seemed to think that the roof had fallen on them anyway. Mr. Roosevelt, emboldened by re-election to a third term, asked for Lend-Lease ("Suppose my neighbor's house is on fire, and I have a length of garden hose . . ."). The President declared: "The future and the safety of our country and our democracy are overwhelmingly involved in events far beyond our borders. . . . I shall ask this Congress for greatly increased new appropriations . . . to manufacture additional munitions and war supplies of many kinds, to be turned over to those nations which are now in actual war with aggressor nations."

The bitter hearings that followed reflected the indecisions and dissensions that had torn the American people (and their Congress) from the beginning of the war in Europe. Soon after the invasion of Poland the President persuaded a reluctant Congress to lift the arms embargo. In May 1940 as the world shook he asked U.S. factories for 50,000 planes a year (experts in aviation called this impossible). In September the draft act was passed despite violent opposition by isolationists who took the view that the way to stay out of war was to ignore it. The Lend-Lease battle was the fiercest of all, and it was not fought along party lines. Republican Wendell Willkie supported it; Charles A. Lindbergh opposed it and became the hero of America First rallies. Senator Burton K. Wheeler, a western Democrat, charged Lend-Lease meant plowing under every fourth American boy. That was a low blow and a high estimate of the casualties to come. But Wheeler was joined in his dissent by millions of Americans—some dupes of Nazi and Communist propaganda, some frightened pacifists, but mostly plain citizens who shunned war and its consequences.

Nonetheless, Lend-Lease was approved. The U.S. had set out on its "awful mission" (as Production Chief Donald Nelson called it). Three decades earlier Sir Edward Grey had told Winston Churchill: "[The United States] is like a gigantic boiler. Once the fire is lighted under it, there is no limit to the power it can generate." But not even this clairvoyant minister of World War I could have foreseen that the mighty boiler would pour forth $51 billion worth of supplies for the many anti-Axis nations—all freely given.

AT MADISON SQUARE GARDEN ON OCT. 30, 1941, 20,000 AMERICA FIRSTERS RALLIED TO HEAR COLONEL LINDBERGH DENOUNCE AMERICAN LEADERS

BROKEN WINDOWS at the isolationist headquarters in New York were produced by an unknown, but very direct, interventionist. As the U.S. moved closer to war some isolationists were revealed as anti-Semitic.

BROKEN HEADS resulted when U.S. foreign policy was thrashed out in New York streets. Here isolationist (*center*) fights interventionist over a copy of Father Coughlin's *Social Justice*, which backed America First.

IN WASHINGTON A PUBLICITY-CONSCIOUS "MOTHERS' CRUSADE" KNELT ON THE SIDEWALK AND PRAYED FOR DEFEAT OF THE LEND-LEASE BILL

ADMINISTRATOR EDWARD STETTINIUS SHOWS ROUTES OF LEND-LEASE

LONG-RANGE B-24 BOMBERS WITH BRITISH MARKINGS WENT TO THE R.A.F.

BULLDOZERS WERE MASSED IN THRACE TO DIG OUT LIBERATED GREECE

OIL AND WATER FLOWED INTO THE AFRICAN DESERT THROUGH U.S. PIPES

Lend-Lease

supplies were on their way to Hitler's and Hirohito's enemies within a few hours after Roosevelt signed the Lend-Lease Act (dramatically called HR 1776) on March 11, 1941. First transfer (to Britain) included guns for merchant ships, charges for depth bombs, 28 brand-new PT boats (which caused grousing among some U.S. naval officers). The same day Roosevelt also sent 50 artillery pieces and 180,000 shells to the Greeks to shoot at Mussolini's soldiers. (It was too late; they wound up being fired at Rommel by the British in North Africa.) In May the Chinese got some trucks and gasoline for the Burma Road. When Hitler attacked Russia the Soviets were allotted gasoline, shoes, wheat, P-40 planes. The U.S. at first was only a little arsenal. In March 1941 only 16 tanks were made. But eventually supplies gushed forth from U.S. fields and factories in such quantities as to sate the maw of Mars. When wartime Lend-Lease ended in September 1945, Britain had received some 28,000 tanks, Russia 14,795 planes (plus 1,981 locomotives, 345,735 tons of explosives, 15,417,000 army boots). And the jeep had become the most universal vehicle in the history of mankind—a powerful little bug that climbed Italy's mountains, waded New Guinea's rivers and conquered the mud of the Ukraine. Of 630,000 jeeps manufactured, the U.S. gave its allies 183,000.

AMERICAN TRUCKS CARRIED SUPPLIES TO CHINA OVER THE BURMA ROAD

AT A LASHIO DUMP COOLIES LOADED TRUCKS WITH OIL FOR CHUNGKING

UBIQUITOUS LITTLE JEEP HELPED FREE FRENCH ALONG THE ROAD BACK

CASUALTIES OF ALL ALLIED NATIONS RODE IN LEND-LEASE AMBULANCES

MOROCCANS STOCKED THEIR GRANARIES WITH FREE AMERICAN FLOUR

SHIPPED TO IRAN, LOCOMOTIVES HAULED LEND-LEASE NORTH TO RUSSIA

AT DIVINE SERVICE ON THE DECK OF THE "PRINCE OF WALES," ROOSEVELT, CHURCHILL AND THEIR STAFFS SANG "ONWARD, CHRISTIAN SOLDIERS"

AFTER THE LAST MEETING CHURCHILL WATCHED ROOSEVELT'S SHIP DEPART

Meeting of Churchill and Roosevelt, the first of ten historic conferences between the Prime Minister and the President, took place in a quiet Newfoundland bay in August 1941. The "former naval person" (as Churchill called himself in cables to Washington) went on his new battleship *Prince of Wales*, the President on the old cruiser *Augusta*. The meeting produced a far-reaching document called the Atlantic Charter. The charter (a semifinal version with corrections in Churchill's handwriting is shown on the opposite page) laid the foundation for the first international organization since the League of Nations. To Churchill's surprise, the charter was interpreted by Asiatics as rejecting colonialism in specifying "the rights of all peoples to choose the form of government under which they will live." At the time of the meeting U.S. marines had been sent to Iceland and the U.S. Navy, fully blacked out, already was convoying shipments to Hitler's enemies. In pledging "the final destruction of the Nazi tyranny," the charter took the U.S. another long step toward an open rather than covert war against Hitler.

Prime Minister's meeting with President Roosevelt - Aug. 1941
Draft of Joint Declaration —

COPY NO: 1

M O S T   S E C R E T

NOTE: This document should not be left lying about and, if it is unnecessary to retain, should be returned to the Private Office.

P R O P O S E D   D E C L A R A T I O N

The President of the United States of America and the Prime Minister, Mr. Churchill, representing His Majesty's Government in the United Kingdom, being met together, deem it right to make known certain common principles in the national policies of their respective countries on which they base their hopes for a better future for the world.

First, their countries seek no aggrandisement, territorial or other;

Second, they desire to see no territorial changes that do not accord with the freely expressed wishes of the peoples concerned.

Third, they respect the right of all peoples to choose the form of government under which they will live; and they wish to see self-government restored to those from whom it has been forcibly removed.

Fourth, they will endeavour, with due respect to their existing obligations, to further the enjoyment by all peoples of access, on equal terms, to the trade and to the raw materials of the world which are needed for their economic prosperity.

Fifth, they support, fullest collaboration between Nations in economic field with the object of securing for all peoples freedom from want, improved labour standards, economic advancement and social security.

Sixth, they hope to see established a peace, after the final destruction of the Nazi tyranny, which will afford to all nations the means of dwelling in security within their own boundaries, and which will afford assurance to all peoples that they may live out their lives in freedom from fear.

Seventh, they desire such a peace to establish for all safety on the high seas and oceans.

Eighth, they believe that all of the nations of the world must be guided in spirit to the abandonment of the use of force. Because no future peace can be maintained if land, sea or air armaments continue to be employed by nations which threaten, or may threaten, aggression outside of their frontiers, they believe that the disarmament of such nations is essential pending the establishment of a wider and more permanent system of general security. They will further the adoption of all other practicable measures which will lighten for peace-loving peoples the crushing burden of armaments.

Private Office
August   1941.

Pearl Harbor

Pearl Harbor was aware of the possibility of war in January 1941 when the Japanese began planning their sneak attack. But by September, when details of the plan were perfected in Tokyo, the U.S. had dropped its guard. Curiously enough, the Japanese navy shared the American view that a war with the U.S. was unlikely to be profitable. Admiral Isoroku Yamamoto said he could run wild for six months or a year, but had no confidence in the second or third years. In 1941, however, hot-headed army leaders were in control and they told Yamamoto to get on with the attack, even after he cautioned that to win "We would have to march into Washington and sign the treaty in the White House." (Propagandists twisted this dire warning into a boast.)

The attack came from six carriers and contemplated no invasion—Yamamoto's transports were busy carrying troops to Malaya, Siam, the Philippines, Guam and Wake Island. It was this southward surge that helped deceive the nodding admirals and generals in Hawaii. They couldn't believe the Japanese capable of striking eastward too. Decoded Japanese messages didn't indicate it. If the U.S. went to war, the admirals and generals thought, it would be over Manila or Siam, not Pearl Harbor.

Ironically, the first blood spilled on that red Sunday, Dec. 7, was Japanese: an hour before the first planes hit Pearl the U.S. destroyer *Ward* sank a midget sub which was lurking outside the harbor entrance. The destroyer's warning was fumbled, and an Army radar operator's report of incoming planes was laughed off by his superior. The Japanese victory, in consequence, was overwhelmingly lopsided: against the loss of one large sub and five midgets and only 29 of the 360 attacking planes, they sank six battleships, burned up 164 planes and killed 2,008 sailors (five times as many as the Navy lost in World War I), plus 218 soldiers, 109 marines and 68 civilians. More than 1,178 other men lay wounded. Americans were not alone in their surprise. Tojo didn't even tell his "peace" negotiators in Washington—or his ally, Hitler.

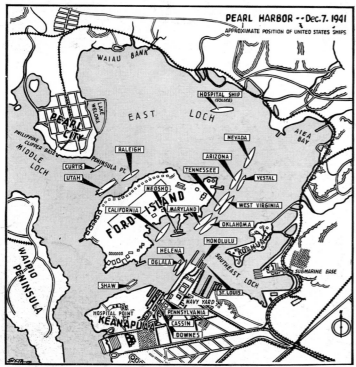

FORD ISLAND'S "BATTLESHIP ROW" WAS MAIN JAPANESE TARGET

AT 6 A.M., WITH A RINGING "BANZAI!" FROM OFFICERS AND CREW, JAPANESE

FIRST JAPANESE BOMBERS APPEARED OVER PEARL HARBOR AT 7:55 A.M.

FORMAL JAP "PEACE" ENVOYS WERE INTERNED

AN INFORMAL JAP ATTACHE BURNED HIS PAPERS

CARRIERS LAUNCHED THEIR FIRST WAVE OF 183 PLANES TO ATTACK PEARL HARBOR, 275 MILES AWAY

PLANES BANK AS GEYSER RISES FROM A HIT ON "OKLAHOMA" (CENTER)

TORPEDO TRACKS SHOW AS THE WAVES SPREAD FROM HIT BATTLESHIPS

SWIRLING PILLARS OF SMOKE ENVELOP BATTLESHIP "MARYLAND" (CENTER) AS A FIREBOAT (RIGHT) SKIRTS PATCHES OF BLAZING OIL ON THE SURFACE OF PEARL HARBOR

AT THE NAVAL AIR STATION ON FORD ISLAND STUNNED SAILORS WATCH THE EXPLOSION OF THE BATTLESHIP "ARIZONA," DIVE BOMBERS DESTROYED 33 PLANES ON FIELD

BOMBED INSIDE THE FLOATING DRY DOCK, THE DESTROYER "SHAW" BLOWS UP IN A FIERY THUNDERCLOUD. AT RIGHT, FIRES OUTLINE TURRETS OF BATTLESHIP "NEVADA"

LAUNCH RESCUES A MAN WHO JUMPED OVERBOARD FROM THE TORPEDOED BATTLESHIP "WEST VIRGINIA" WHICH, WITH DECKS AWASH, IS SINKING ALONGSIDE "TENNESSEE"

Anger

was America's first reaction to the attack on Pearl Harbor: "Why, the yellow bastards!" Thousands rushed out to enlist; others offered to work in factories all night. President Roosevelt called Dec. 7 "a date which will live in infamy," and within three days Congress had declared war on the whole Axis (Hirohito had "declared" war on the U.S. an hour after the Pearl Harbor bombers returned to their carriers, and Germany and Italy quickly followed suit). After anger came overconfidence—the U.S. would show 'em! (A songwriter dashed off a tune: *We did it before and we can do it again.*) High-hearted Americans noted with satisfaction that never before in its 165 years had the nation presented so solid a union. People who had worried about the $55 billion national debt were dismayed when the chairman of the Senate Finance Committee predicted that war might raise the debt to $150 billion (it reached $258 billion before the Japanese surrendered).

In retrospect Pearl Harbor seemed clearly the best thing that could have happened to the U.S. The nation was not ready for war in 1941, but it probably was as close as this democracy could get before the shooting started. Discontent in the training camps had been running high, and there had been threats of mass desertion. (O.H.I.O. was what the boys were writing on their barracks walls in the summer of 1941: "Over the hill in October.") Only 16 weeks before the Pearl Harbor attack, Congress extended the draft by a single vote. At the actual scene of adversity a few jewels sparkled in the rubble: three aircraft carriers—all there were in the Pacific—were absent on missions and therefore unharmed. Had the battleships been caught at sea, they probably would have been sunk in a thousand fathoms. Instead, all but two—raised from Pearl's mud—fired their big guns in bombardments when the U.S. fleet was ready to take the offensive in the Pacific. Lack of battleships excused the Navy from relieving the faraway Philippines, which, considering the caliber of U.S. ships and planes, were indefensible anyway. For that improbable task it would have been necessary to divert strength from the Atlantic, where, sentiment aside, it was necessary to beat Hitler first.

FLAGSHIP "PENNSYLVANIA" WAS STILL AFLOAT AMID THE WRECKAGE

AT 12:30 P.M. ON DEC. 8 ROOSEVELT ASKED CONGRESS TO DECLARE WAR

V
Japanese Conquests

Pacific: 1941-42

Japan's attempt to knock out our fleet at Pearl Harbor was, strategically, a diversion. While Vice Admiral Nagumo's carriers were launching their planes from pitching decks into a gray Pacific dawn, the warships and transports of the main expeditionary forces were steaming southward to conquer the oil and the rice and the rubber of the East Indies. For a hundred years the Japanese had been studying the techniques that gave the unruly nations of Europe ascendancy over the world. Of all the agricultural peoples whose civilizations fringed the coast of Asia, the Japanese had proved themselves the most capable of prompt adaptation to the discordant currents of European energy that poured into every Oriental port with the trading ships and the missionaries of the West.

As far back as the records go, although the writings and traditions on which their culture was based were Chinese, the Japanese islands had lived a separate life from that of the Asiatic mainland. Their culture probably was equal in its way to that of 16th Century Europe and, as occasionally happens to peoples living off the main paths of history, had developed an odd elaboration. The simplest acts—drinking tea, picking flowers, visiting a feudal lord—had become encased in complicated rituals, half esthetic and half religious. The early European explorers found the Japanese a friendly and resourceful people of dominant military tradition, tillers of the soil but also traders and artisans and fishermen. The first mechanical invention that stimulated their interest was an arquebus that some shipwrecked Portuguese brought ashore with them in 1542. Immediately Japanese artisans took it apart and started to copy each part so that soon gunpowder began to play a role in the wars between feudal leaders that were the main occupation of the islanders at that time. So cordially had the Portuguese been received that ships soon returned with a mission led by St. Francis Xavier to preach the gospel to these amiable heathen. The Christian doctrine made such headway that the lords in their castles began to fear for the ascendancy of their military caste. The Tokugawa shoguns butchered native Christian converts by the thousands and drove out their Spanish and Portuguese mentors, and for two centuries Japanese feudalism carried on its highly stylized affairs walled off from the rest of mankind. During these years only one small Dutch trading post was allowed to subsist as a carefully screened conduit to the fast-evolving world outside. But by the mid-19th Century the waters around Japan were too full of American whalers and clipper ships on the China run and British traders and Russian explorers for isolation to continue feasible.

When the feudal lords allowed Commodore Perry to open up the islands to foreign trade in 1854, the immediate result was the collapse of the feudal system and the reorganization of the government into a centralized monarchy. The nobles of the warrior caste, forced to give up the luxury of internal war, turned their military bent outward according to the accepted 19th Century scheme of nationalist expansion. They fought the Chinese leviathan, already strangling in the coils of change as the traditions of the Manchu empire crumbled under the impact of the West. They soon defeated backward Korea and conducted an impressive and successful war against Czarist Russia.

When Germany started to batter Europe in World War I the Japanese took advantage of the mental confusion of the Western Allies to obtain for themselves a string of bases across the Pacific. In the years between the European wars they smashed Manchuria, conquered large parts of China and occupied Shanghai. They dumped cheap goods on the world's market, but still they could not manage to balance their industrial economy. Chinese resistance continued. Japanese armies advanced into China's vast spaces and added further to the disorganization of its multitudinous populations, but there was little money in it for Tokyo.

The breakup of Europe under Hitler's sledge hammer and the absorption of Anglo-American seapower in the battle of the Atlantic seemed to the war party in Tokyo the golden moment for which their people had waited long. They followed eagerly every development of sea-air warfare and learned from the campaigns in Norway and Crete that fighting ships were very nearly helpless against land-based planes. Their people were clever with machine tools. Their factories were producing fighters and bombers. The mandated islands furnished a string of airstrips across the Pacific. Their plan was to sweep south into the Indonesian archipelago and the Malay Peninsula. There, firmly based on an immense reservoir of raw materials, they could balance their economy while repulsing Allied counterattacks.

The Japanese planners believed that naval power was dependent on fixed bases. They could prove on paper with mathematical certainty that with Pearl Harbor and Ceylon open to carrier raids, America and Britain could never mount a sufficient bridge of ships to supply expeditions of necessary fighting power into a region nearly 10,000 miles away from bases in either direction. In the eventual peace the Japanese might have to make concessions of some outlying islands but the core of empire, their Greater East Asia Co-Prosperity Sphere (so the name is translated), would be firmly established. The plan looked unbeatable, on paper.

For five months they had it all their own way. While the burial squads were still doing their work at Pearl Harbor the Japanese were attacking Wake; they were softening up the Philippine Islands for invasion; they were landing in Guam and in Borneo and Hong Kong; their soldiers were trotting into Bangkok without pressing a trigger and, in obscure Malay ports, were getting ready to rush the great naval fortress of Singapore from its lightly held jungle side. After Christmas, General MacArthur declared Manila an open city and retired to Australia. The trapped American troops in the Philippines had been driven into Corregidor and Bataan, where, fighting back stubbornly but hopelessly, they were to tie up a very sizable Japanese force for months before they surrendered. By January, Japanese forces from Truk were bombing the Australians in Rabaul. On Feb. 19 carrier-based planes wrecked Allied shipping at Darwin. On Feb. 27 the Allies lost the battle of the Java Sea. By March all Indonesia and New Guinea lay open to Japanese occupation. In April, Vice Admiral Nagumo's carriers smashed up the British naval base at Colombo in Ceylon and sank two heavy cruisers and a carrier at sea. In that same month Halsey's task force, to prove that the flag was still flying, launched Doolittle's raid on Tokyo. It didn't do the Japanese much harm, but it did the U.S. a great deal of good.   —JOHN DOS PASSOS

In China

war was a story more than four years old. Following a clash at the Marco Polo Bridge near Peking in 1937, the Japanese determined to make a vassal out of sprawling China. The Japanese won the coastal cities, but the Chinese retreated inland, often carrying their few factories on their backs. Not many battles were fought, but in those few, Japanese steel massacred tens of thousands of Chinese. Chiang Kai-shek's capital, Nanking, and thousands of its people were raped in late 1937; the government moved 400 miles to Hankow. A year later it moved 500 miles farther inland to ancient, hill-crested Chungking, which was nearly impervious to assault from land or from the mighty Yangtze, which flowed swiftly below its cliffs. Chungking could, however, be bombed. Beginning May 3, 1939, its million Chinese were subjected to all-out assault from the air (*above*). But Chungking could take it. Its hillside dugouts sheltered much of the population. Long before London, Chungking had a blackout—made effective by sentries who simply shot at every light. Japan almost made China into a united nation. And China, by her stubborn resistance, contributed greatly to Japan's decision to turn east across the Pacific.

RAIDS DROVE MOBS OF CHINESE INTO CHUNGKING'S CAVE SHELTERS

AFTER A PANIC A TUNNEL SHELTER YIELDED 4,000 TRAMPLED BODIES

JAP MULE TRAIN proved useful in moving military supplies over the primitive roads of China. Japanese learned their war lessons in China, just as the Axis did in Spain. Some of these techniques—including mules —were abandoned; others served as guides for the duration. In 1945 an officer on Chichi Jima ordered his troops to eat shot-down American flyers—he had heard that in China such gestures improved morale.

JAP OFFICER BLOODED HIS SWORD ON A DYING CHINESE PRISONER

JAP INFANTRYMAN CONTINUED "WAR GAMES" WITH HIS BAYONET

CHINESE WEIGHTED WOVEN PIERS WITH STONES TO BUILD A BRIDGE

ANCIENT BASKET CARRIERS WERE USED TO CLEAN UP BOMB RUBBLE

CHINESE SOLDIERS, poorly armed, snuggled close to the land as their camouflaged caps indicate. Throughout the war Allied commanders wistfully eyed great Chinese manpower reserve. With proper supply and training Chinese proved good soldiers in Burma, but under their own inept command they were starved, underpaid and wasted. Nonetheless, the slow war in China managed to tie down a million Japanese.

Guam was the outpost island of America's slender overseas defenses and the subject of some fancy debate in Congress in 1939. The Navy asked for $5 million to dredge a harbor at this Pacific base which had been American territory since the war with Spain in 1898. "A dagger at the throat of Japan!" cried New York's Hamilton Fish. "A small kumquat in the hand of Japan," said Wisconsin's Stephen Bolles. When the House turned down the authorization New York's Bruce Barton gleefully sang, "Guam, Guam with the wind." On Dec. 10, 1941, 5,000 Japanese troops proved Bolles right. They landed near Agana (*above*), the capital of the 200-square-mile island, opposed by only 365 U.S. marines and 308 native Chamorros. Heaviest U.S. arms were .30-cal. machine guns. The island's Navy governor surrendered after a brief fight costing 17 U.S. casualties. When Guam was recaptured in 1944 it became fleet headquarters, was thoroughly dredged. Eventual cost of installations on Guam: $281 million.

Wake was a lonely sentinel in the central Pacific, 1,000 miles west of Midway. It was defended by 452 marines who arrived a short time before Pearl Harbor. On Dec. 10 Wake gave the U.S. its only victory of 1941: as the enemy tried to land destroyers *Hayate* and *Kisaragi* were sunk by Marine guns and air. When Pearl Harbor sent a radio message asking what supplies Wake needed, a radio operator padded out his coded reply with the wry suggestion, "Send us more Japs!" This American bravado thrilled the nation. What Pearl Harbor actually did send was a relief force under Rear Admiral Frank Jack Fletcher. On Dec. 22, as he neared the island, Fletcher unaccountably paused to refuel his ships, and the next day Wake was overwhelmed. In Washington Navy Secretary Frank Knox groaned to Churchill: "What would you do?" The flag was hauled down until 1945, but nearly 1,000 Japanese had gone to join their ancestors.

FROM KOWLOON ON THE CHINESE MAINLAND, JAPANESE SOLDIERS WATCH THEIR SHELLS FALLING ON HONG KONG'S CAPITAL BELOW "THE PEAK"

Hong Kong had been ruled by the British from their great houses on "the peak" for just a century when the Japanese struck. Within a few hours of Pearl Harbor bombers launched from China proper were dropping death on the lovely island and the British mainland strip called Kowloon. Unlike the optimistic Americans in the Philippines, the British knew from the start that their Oriental outpost was doomed—although Churchill had reluctantly reinforced the garrison. Without hope of further aid, six Imperial battalions (two Canadian) and a 2,000-man civilian volunteer corps fought well against three Japanese divisions. In the wake of heavy bombing and bombardment the enemy began landing on the island the night of Dec. 18. On Christmas Day, after casualties amounting to more than one third of the Imperial forces, the British surrendered. By the war's end, some 10,000 Allied subjects had been executed in Hong Kong prisons.

THE ASIATIC CONQUERORS PARADED DOWN STREETS OF VICTORIA

VAST FUEL AND AMMUNITION DUMPS IN SINGAPORE WERE SET AFIRE BY JAPANESE ARTILLERY BASED ON THE TIP OF THE MALAY PENINSULA

JAPS ENJOYED TELLING U.S. PRISONERS ABOUT SINGAPORE'S FALL

Singapore was defended by 70,000 troops, 332 planes and the newly arrived battleship *Prince of Wales* and battle cruiser *Repulse*. More than $200 million had been spent arming the "mightiest fortress in the world," much of it for 15-inch coastal guns to cover the sea approaches. Some 45,000 Japanese troops sailed Dec. 4, 1941 from Hainan, went ashore a few hours after Pearl Harbor, not on Singapore Island but 400 miles north on the Malay Peninsula. Vice Admiral Tom Phillips moved out to sink the transports. Within three hours after the first Japanese torpedo planes struck, the *Prince of Wales*, the *Repulse* and Admiral Phillips were on the bottom of the South China Sea. Lieut. General Tomoyuki Yamashita's army invaders pressed relentlessly through the "impenetrable" Malay jungle. On Feb. 8, 1942, under artillery cover, they landed on Singapore's northern side, behind the big coastal batteries. A week later Singapore surrendered.

97

IN BURMA THE WHITE MAN'S RICH BURDEN WAS ASSUMED EAGERLY BY THE JAPANESE, SHOWN PUSHING ACROSS THE YENANGYAUNG OIL FIELD

Empires which had required centuries to build toppled in weeks before the Japanese avalanche. Burma, Asia's biggest rice exporter, went through a tortuous campaign before an American general-come-lately called "Vinegar Joe" Stilwell delivered its epitaph: "I claim we took a hell of a licking." The Japanese rushed through Siam into Burma in January 1942, captured Moulmein, then Rangoon, and turned to the north. The British scorched Burma's big oil fields but at burning Mandalay they lost the campaign and retreated into India in May. The Japanese drove on to capture the Burma Road and thus cut off China from the outside world except by air. Action was more spectacular in the rich Netherlands East Indies; results just as inevitable. When the Japanese landed Jan. 24, 1942 on Borneo in Makassar Strait, four U.S. Asiatic fleet destroyers plowed in and sank four of Rear Admiral S. Nishimura's transports (not 11 as claimed). In a series of violent naval clashes the Japanese overpowered the Allies, sinking 30 warships, including the U.S. cruiser *Houston* and the world's oldest aircraft carrier, *Langley*. Japan's prime target—Java—surrendered March 9, 1942.

BOMBS BLACKED OUT THE ALLIED NAVAL BASE AT SOERABAJA, JAVA

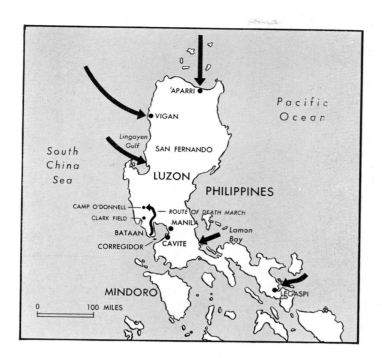

Philippines

got ten hours of grace after the Pearl Harbor attack when bad weather at Formosa delayed the Japanese aerial task force. But even so, when the enemy bombed airfields near Manila at noon of Dec. 8, 1941, about half the 123 combat aircraft in the Philippines were destroyed, mostly on the ground. Two days later the Cavite Navy base was smashed. The Japanese also landed in the north, capturing the airstrip at Aparri. The communiqué that day said Pilot Colin Kelly set afire the battleship *Haruna*. Actually this famous ship was not present but was covering the landings on Malaya, although a Navy plane also claimed sinking her 12 days later. Japanese forces closed in on Manila from the north and southeast; on Dec. 26 General Douglas MacArthur declared it an open city. His Luzon troops—U.S. Army (18,000), Navy and Marine Corps (2,500), Philippine Scouts (8,000), Philippine Army (60,000, poorly equipped)—withdrew, according to a 20-year-old plan, to Bataan Peninsula and Corregidor Island. The Navy's Asiatic fleet (except submarines) retreated to East Indies waters and the last 14 (of 35) Flying Fortresses to Australia. In February, General MacArthur himself was ordered to Melbourne to command the groggy Allied forces.

ON LUZON ARMOR WAS LANDED BY THE JAPANESE AND, LIGHTLY CAMOUFLAGED WITH PALM FRONDS, ROLLED SWIFTLY SOUTH TOWARD MANILA

JAPANESE HERDED CORREGIDOR'S EXHAUSTED DEFENDERS OUT OF THE FORTRESS TUNNELS WHERE THEY HAD BEEN BESIEGED FOR 28 DAYS

GENERAL WAINWRIGHT (LEFT) SURRENDERED TO GENERAL HOMMA (RIGHT)

Bataan became a U.S. rallying cry, but the Army's reward for its hopeless, heroic defense of this corner of Luzon was bitterness and torture. Major General Edward King's 78,000 troops were down to one-third rations when the enemy began a push on April 3, 1942. Although Major General Jonathan Wainwright (who succeeded MacArthur) forbade it, King surrendered his starving remnants on April 9. Then began the Death March out of Bataan. The Japanese brought down big guns to shell Corregidor, began their landings the night of May 5. Two days later Wainwright surrendered Corregidor's 10,000. Troops in the southern Philippines refused his orders to quit. Nonetheless on June 9, having lost only 4,100 killed in half a year's fighting, the Japanese could announce that organized resistance had ended.

MASS OF AMERICANS STARTED THEIR LONG HIKE TO PRISON CAMPS

PRISONERS, CARRYING THOSE WHO FELL, STRAGGLED INTO CAMP

WITHOUT FOOD OR WATER, HANDS TIED BEHIND THEM, THE PRISONERS WERE BEATEN ALONG THE 85 MILES OF THE INFAMOUS "DEATH MARCH"

ON APRIL 18, IN ROUGH WEATHER, DOOLITTLE'S BIG B-25s WERE READIED FOR TAKE-OFF FROM THE PITCHING DECK OF THE CARRIER "HORNET"

Tokyo Raid by Colonel Jimmy Doolittle's Army bombers furnished the U.S. its first real revenge for the mauling the Japs had administered. After special training for short take-offs, 16 B-25s were loaded aboard the aircraft carrier *Hornet*, flagship of a special task force. Planes were to be launched within 500 nautical miles of Japan; after dropping bombs they were to proceed 1,100 miles farther and land in China. But on April 18, 1942 the force was spotted by two picket boats 650 miles from Japan and the planes had to be launched at once. Though forewarned, the Japanese did not expect the attack until the next day. All planes dropped their bombs, but they ran into foul weather and airmen had to crash-land or bail out. Of 80 fliers, 71 survived. Three were executed. Morale-wise the Japanese were not notably depressed, but Americans got a big boost from what Vice Admiral William Halsey, the task force commander, called "one of the most courageous deeds in all military history."

THE BOMBERS CAME IN LOW OVER THE NAVAL BASE IN TOKYO BAY

DOOLITTLE'S OWN BOMBER CRASHED IN ALLIED CHINA AFTER THE MEN BAILED OUT. TWO OF THE B-25s FELL INSIDE JAP LINES, ONE IN SIBERIA

CHINESE SOLDIERS PROUDLY ESCORTED FOUR LUCKY TOKYO RAIDERS DOWN THE MAIN STREET OF THE VILLAGE NEAR WHICH THEY CRASHED

Midway was shelled by the destroyers *Akebono* and *Ushio* the night after Pearl Harbor, but only four men were killed. The ships retired when one of them was hit by shore batteries. After that the lonely sandspit, only 1,136 miles northwest of Pearl Harbor, stood a feverish alert. But seizure of Midway was not contemplated in Japan's original plans —which chiefly entailed knocking out all obstacles to the riches of the Indies, then waiting for soft America to make a reasonable peace. Never damaged and rarely sighted, the carrier task force which started the war returned to Japan in mid-April, having sown destruction a third of the way around the world, from Hawaii to Ceylon. It hadn't even been needed at any of the invasions. All this made Tojo and Yamamoto understandably optimistic. Meanwhile Admiral Chester Nimitz rushed strong reinforcements to Midway, the last sentry between Japan and Pearl, and the only one left north of the equator.

LOOKOUT TOWERS (LEFT) ROSE ABOVE LONELY SANDS OF MIDWAY

DAWN WAS BEAUTIFUL OVER MIDWAY IN 1942, BUT AMERICANS STATIONED ON THE ISLAND SCANNED THE SOFT PACIFIC SKY CHIEFLY FOR JAPS

VI
The Axis Contained

World Battlefronts: 1942

CHURCHILL spent the dismal Christmas of 1941 with President Roosevelt in Washington. Across the hall from his quarters at the White House he set up his traveling map room. There the President in his wheel chair and the Prime Minister, smoking his long cigar, passed hours together during the wintry nights, when they were free from protracted meetings with the Chiefs of Staff, trying to chart clearly in their own heads the course of the worldwide war. Though both men were indefatigable optimists, the picture must have seemed to them dark indeed.

When their eyes turned to the tiny ragged shapes of the British Isles snuggling into the bight of the North Sea, their first thought must have been of sunken ships. Britain had withstood the air assault; war production was holding up tolerably well, but the protection of her Atlantic supply lines against the daily improvement of German submarine tactics was far from sure. The Irish were sticking to their neutrality with fanatic stubbornness: it was agreed that American troops would be tactfully substituted for British in Northern Ireland. Sight of the promontories and the great bay of the French coast must have brought painful thoughts of Nazi occupation and of Dover dominated by German heavy batteries. Spain was an enigma but not a pressing one. Malta held out. But the threat to Britain's Mediterranean artery had been brutally brought home by the damaging in Alexandria harbor one December night of two British battleships by some nervy Italians using "human torpedoes." With the Axis partners controlling the sky and submarines lying on the bottom, those narrow seas were proving a deadly trap for the Royal Navy.

In North Africa, Churchill promised a victory very soon on the Egyptian front, but emphasized that every effort must be made to keep the west African ports from falling to Hitler. The Near East was at that moment the crux of the war. There things didn't look too bad. The British were managing to keep hold of Suez and of the oil of Iraq and of the Persian Gulf, and to start a few boxcars of supplies for Russia moving up the tortuous mountain railroad that rambled across the highlands and deserts of Iran. With the Mediterranean threatened, the supply line round the Cape of Good Hope to Suez and the Persian Gulf was vital. This route had already been made hazardous by the westward sweep of the Japanese fleets toward the Indian Ocean.

IN Russia, so the reports said, the Soviet armies were making good use of an intensely cold winter for which the Wehrmacht was insufficiently prepared, but no one could foresee what direction Hitler's spring offensive would take or what it would accomplish.

Looking eastward: India was none too secure, the battle in the East Indies was only a forlorn hope; Australia and New Zealand were in danger of being cut off. The British Empire now lay in shattered fragments round the globe. Only North America stood firm. It was up to the U.S. to make good the President's promise: Arsenal of Democracy.

There had been many plans sketched out in Washington for mobilization, but it had been the Japanese who had picked the date, and now the brave paper schemes had been overwhelmed by realities where the needs of each theater cried out for priority over the next. During the first months of 1942 every day seemed to bring a fresh disaster.

While Washington, all at once become the capital of an embattled world, struggled with the toughest problems of organization in the history of mankind, the Japanese continued their mushroom advance south, east and west. They had taken a great gamble in spreading their forces so thin but they had won. Now they had to consolidate their victory by sealing off Australia, by investing Pearl Harbor and by cleaning up what was left of our Pacific fleet.

Their first objectives were Port Moresby in New Guinea and Tulagi in the Solomons to establish bases for command of the Coral Sea and the east coast of Australia. In the fighting during the first days of May 1942 in the Coral Sea the Japanese thrust was blunted and turned. A month later, off Midway, the western outpost of our Hawaiian defenses, the U.S. Navy really gave Admiral Yamamoto a beating. The Japanese suffered losses of carriers and planes which they were never able to make up. In consequence the landings in the Aleutians proved to be a barren victory. With Australia and Port Moresby safeguarded, firm ground was assured from which MacArthur's army could start its long climb back through jungle-clad islands to the Philippines. From Midway on, though there were difficult and bloody months ahead, the offensive was ours in the Pacific.

MEANWHILE as summer advanced, the victory Churchill had so confidently promised in North Africa turned into a series of defeats. The British, after losing their last bout with Rommel in the desert, managed to hold, at the point where Rommel's supply problems became too difficult for him to advance farther into Egypt, a defensive line that ran south from the Mediterranean to the Qattara Depression. While the Germans were growing weaker the British were growing stronger. By October, Montgomery was receiving enough new Sherman tanks from the U.S. and enough fresh planes by air across central Africa to be able to mount a powerful offensive and to start rolling the Germans and Italians back 1,400 miles to Tripoli.

One reason why Rommel lost El Alamein was that Hitler was beginning to neglect him. He could think only of the Russian campaign. Hitler had fallen into the error of fighting a war on two fronts—an error he had sworn to avoid. Already it was costing him dear. Not only was he fighting a war on two fronts, but those fronts were each more than 1,500 miles away from the industrial heart of Germany. It was the expense—in terms of gasoline and transport vehicles—of keeping him in supplies that ruined Rommel. In Russia the armies were much larger and the supply problem was immensely more difficult. Hitler's armies reached Stalingrad and looked across the sluggish river, but they got no farther. Russian resistance grew instead of weakening. Hitler had knocked out their war production in Europe but the Soviets had factories beyond the Urals. The tools of war were coming in from America through Persia. Blockade runners from England and America were beginning to unload in the White Sea. The failure of this summer's campaign in Russia left the mass of German offensive strength strewn over the south Russian plain, open to flank attacks from the center of communications still in Soviet hands round impregnable Moscow. In Washington and London, Roosevelt and Churchill blessed Moscow as they waited anxiously for the outcome of Operation Torch—their first large-scale amphibious attack.　　—JOHN DOS PASSOS

CREWMEN OF TORPEDOED CARRIER "LEXINGTON" ABANDONED SHIP BY SLIDING DOWN ROPES INTO THE WATER, WHILE IN THE SMOKE DESTROYER "MORRIS"

THE "LEXINGTON" SURVIVED TORPEDO HITS BUT AN HOUR LATER SUFFERED A FATAL SERIES OF EXPLOSIONS WHEN GASOLINE VAPOR IGNITED BETWEEN DECKS

Coral Sea

was the first naval battle in which no surface ship engaged another. It was also the opening phase of the Japanese warlords' ambitious expansion of their original program. Finding conquest tasty, they decided to have some more. Phase 1 (Operation Mo) called for capture of Port Moresby on the New Guinea side of the Coral Sea, and Tulagi, the Solomons' capital, on the east. Phase 2, the capture of Midway and the western Aleutians, was Admiral Yamamoto's special project for annihilating the U.S. fleet. Phase 3 entailed seizure of New Caledonia, Fiji and Samoa, to cut the lifeline to Australia (whose invasion was never intended). Yamamoto's greatest trouble was that the Allies had been breaking his code. When, in April of 1942, Japan's Vice Admiral S. Inouye began moving his forces south into the Coral Sea, Admiral Nimitz already knew the U.S. Navy would have to fight the Battle of Midway a month later. He decided to make a stand in both places. Nimitz ordered Admiral Fletcher to Tulagi. On May 7 Vice Admiral T. Takagi's carrier force found the destroyer *Sims* and the tanker *Neosho*, sank both. Fletcher's fliers spotted the 12,000-ton light carrier *Shoho* and sent it under. Still the principal forces had not met. But next day war birds from the giants—*Zuikaku* and *Shokaku* (30,000 tons each) *vs. Lexington* (33,000) and *Yorktown* (20,000)—attacked each others' nests simultaneously. Three SBD Navy dive bombers damaged *Shokaku* so badly she couldn't go to Midway; *Zuikaku* lost so many planes she stayed out too. Both U.S. carriers were hit—the old *Lexington* fatally. The Japanese had outscored the Americans, but Admiral Takagi reviewed his losses and turned back. Vital Port Moresby was saved.

TOOK OFF WOUNDED. WHEN "LADY LEX" WENT DOWN HER SURVIVORS WEPT

HER OWN EXPLODING TORPEDOES BLEW A PLANE OFF "LEXINGTON'S" STERN

THE "LEX" LOST 216 MEN, BUT 2,735 WERE PULLED ABOARD DESTROYERS

109

ON MAY 7 JAP CARRIER "SHOHO" WAS SMOTHERED BY FLIGHT OF 93 U.S. PLANES. ONE VEERS AWAY (RIGHT) AFTER DROPPING TORPEDO (SPLASH)

ATTACKING U.S. BOMBER IS SILHOUETTED AGAINST THE SMOKE AS IT BANKS ASTERN OF BURNING "SHOHO," NOW LYING DEAD IN THE WATER

DEMISE OF THE EXPLODING "SHOHO" WAS REPORTED BACK TO THE U.S. TASK FORCE BY AN EXUBERANT FLASH: "SCRATCH ONE FLATTOP!"

THE NEXT DAY U.S. PLANES FOUND THEIR MAIN TARGET—THE BIG CARRIER "SHOKAKU." HERE A HEAVY BOMB HITS WATER JUST OFF THE BOW

TWISTING AT TOP SPEED TO AVOID BOMBS, "SHOKAKU" CHURNS UP S-SHAPED WAKE AS GEYSER OF SPRAY RISES FROM NEAR-MISS TO STARBOARD

"SHOKAKU" WAS HIT BY ONLY THREE BOMBS, BUT ONE OF THEM SET FIRE TO HER BOW (LEFT) AND SHE WAS OUT OF ACTION FOR TWO MONTHS

North Africa

meant control of the Mediterranean Sea —Mussolini's *mare nostrum* and Britain's imperial lifeline. With all of North Africa in his hands Hitler certainly would have enticed Franco into the war and might have made connections with his Japanese ally. In 1940 Great Britain's prospects of holding the Mediterranean were so slim that, as Churchill remarked eight years later, "Writing about it afterwards makes one shiver." At first Hitler left the Mediterranean to his Italian ally, ignoring his observer General Wilhelm Ritter von Thoma, who told him, "One British soldier is better than 12 Italians." Mussolini had 415,000 troops in Africa, plus a Mediterranean fleet of six battleships, 19 modern cruisers and over 100 submarines. The British had only 82,775 soldiers spread from Egypt to Palestine, four battleships, seven cruisers. Even as Britain strained under the Nazi air blitz, her General Wavell captured 130,000 Italians in North Africa, never using more than two divisions, and a whole army of 220,000 in East Africa. He had only 4,000 men killed. After Marshal Rodolfo Graziani's North African army was so ignobly routed Hitler finally (March 1941) sent General Rommel to be his "hero in the sun." With only one German armored division and two Italian divisions Rommel captured Bengasi

and forced the British to hole up in Tobruk. German planes raided Tobruk 437 times but its "rats" held. In August the British Western Desert force became the Eighth Army of two corps; Rommel now had seven Italian divisions and four German (two of them Panzers). In late 1941 the British forced Rommel all the way back to El Agheila, but in January 1942 he bounced back, recovering 350 desert miles in 17 days. In May he staged a real blitzkrieg. The "desert fox" was outnumbered in men, tanks and planes—125,000 to 113,000, 740 to 570, 700 to 500—but he drove to Tobruk, capturing 30,000 men and immense supplies; then crossed the border into Egypt. (In this June of 1942, with the Russians apparently collapsing, and 115 ships sinking in the Atlantic, the only light shining through the Allied blackness was the Battle of Midway.) His forces exhausted, his available tanks down to 125, Rommel had to stop at El Alamein, 65 miles short of Alexandria. Then the German navy lost control of the Mediterranean and the new Eighth Army commander, General Sir Bernard Montgomery, struck back at El Alamein in October with overpowering strength: 150,000 men, 1,114 tanks, vastly superior aviation. With "Monty" in hot pursuit, Rommel fled across half the breadth of North Africa until he stopped in February 1943 at Mareth in Tunisia.

MONTGOMERY, THE VICTOR OF EL ALAMEIN

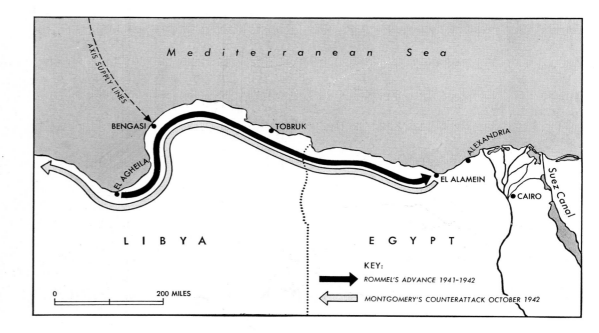

THE BATTLE BEGAN AT NIGHT WITH A BARRAGE FROM 1,000 BRITISH GUNS

SHELL CASES PILED UP AS ARTILLERY COVERED MINE-DETECTOR SQUADS

THE HUSTLING R.A.F. TOOK OFF, WHOLE FIGHTER SQUADRONS AT A TIME

TANKS FOLLOWED THE LANES CLEARED THROUGH ROMMEL'S MINE FIELDS

FIELD GUN WENT ON POUNDING ENEMY WHILE WOUNDED MAN GOT AID

FROM THEIR STONE FOXHOLES RIFLEMEN WATCHED AXIS ARMOR BURN

IMPERIAL INFANTRY RUSHED A DISABLED ENEMY TANK FROM BEHIND

AUSTRALIANS CHARGED NAZI STRONGPOINT WITH BAYONET AND PISTOL

THE SIGNPOSTS OF VICTORY: AFRIKA KORPS WENT THE OTHER WAY—FAST

IN A U.S. TANK EIGHTH ARMY MEN MOVED UP THROUGH LITTER OF BATTLE

R.A.F. STRAFED A JU-52 TRANSPORT. UNDER THE WING IS A FALLEN NAZI

LOW-FLYING EMPIRE PLANES USED CANNON TO RAKE AXIS SUPPLY TRAIN

GROTESQUE SCRAP IRON OF WAR MARKED ROUTE OF ROMMEL'S RETREAT

IN EGYPT THESE TWO GERMANS FINALLY FOUND THEIR PLACE IN THE SUN

114

AFRIKA KORPS'S 88-MM. GUNS NO LONGER COULD STOP THE EIGHTH ARMY

BRITISH TRUCKS WERE SLOWED IN PURSUIT BY RAINS AND NAZI MINES

A BRITISH SNIPER PICKED OFF THIS GERMAN STRAGGLER AS HE WAS PEDALING ALONG THE LIBYAN COASTAL ROAD TO CATCH UP WITH ROMMEL'S RETREAT

SUPPLYING THE EIGHTH ARMY IN ITS 1,400-MILE ADVANCE, AN ENDLESS COLUMN OF TRUCKS CHURNED THROUGH HALFAYA ("HELLFIRE") PASS

INFANTRYMEN PAUSED OUTSIDE TOBRUK AS THEY SWEPT BACK OVER FAMOUS GROUND WHERE DESERT WAR HAD SEESAWED FOR TWO YEARS

GERMAN AND ITALIAN PRISONERS WERE MARCHED BACK FROM THE FRONT TO BARBED-WIRE STOCKADES AROUND ALEXANDRIA. THE EIGHTH ARMY CAPTURED

ENEMY PRISONER COLLAPSED OF THIRST

BRITISH FOUND THEIR AIRMEN'S GRAVES

MORE THAN 30,000 OF ROMMEL'S TROOPS AT EL ALAMEIN

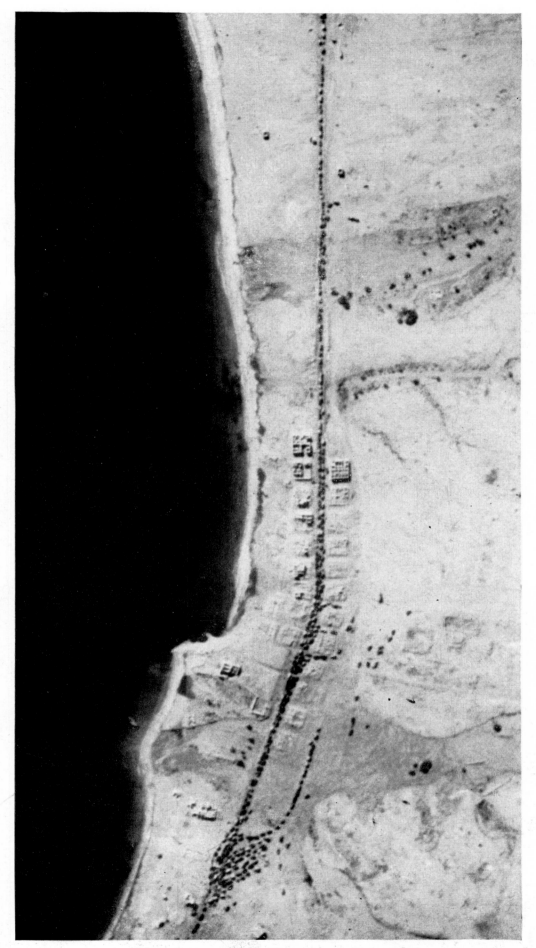

IN HIS RETREAT Rommel left behind 500 tanks, 400 guns and thousands of trucks to create one of history's worst traffic jams. Of his 96,000 troops, 59,000 were killed, wounded or imprisoned. The British lost some 13,500 men and 432 tanks. As Rommel fled American and British troops were landing in the path of his retreat at the western end of the Mediterranean. Incongruously, war in the desert depended on control of the sea. At their lowest ebb the British dared not risk sending supplies to Egypt through the Mediterranean, had to route them around the continent of Africa.

117

The Atlantic

more than any other theater illustrated the axiom that war is a series of blunders. Hitler committed a major error in neglecting his submarines: in September 1939 he had 43 U-boats, of which only 18 were big enough to be effective. Britain began the war with 12 battleships and three battle cruisers (which generally succeeded in bottling up Germany's three pocket battleships and two battle cruisers), but the British were pitifully short of long-range patrol aircraft and the sub-killing destroyers, corvettes and frigates. During the first year Rear Admiral Karl Doenitz had no more than ten submarines at a time operating around the British Isles—one third the 1918 rate—yet sinkings per U-boat shot sky-high. Impressed by this record and finally aware that Britain would fight, Hitler belatedly ordered a program to deliver 300 submarines by 1942 and 900 by 1944. If Hitler had failed to foresee the importance of the submarine, the U.S. Navy was even more derelict. The Navy was caught in December 1941 without even a school to teach antisubmarine tactics. U.S. citizens on the East Coast became accustomed to the sickening sight of their own ships burning offshore. The first (and partial) answer was the convoy system. Thousands of cargo ships in groups averaging some 50 each and making only about 9 knots in "fast" convoys plowed across the Atlantic (*right*), surrounded by destroyers and other escort ships equipped with sound gear which could detect submerged submarines. Even so, in the first half of 1942 the Allies sank only 21 Nazi U-boats while losing 506 ships totaling three million tons.

NAZI U-BOAT OFFICER PREPARES TO TORPEDO AN ALLIED SHIP

IN FEBRUARY OF 1942 A GERMAN SUBMARINE TORPEDOED THE AMERICAN TANKER "R.P. RESOR" ONLY 20 MILES OFF THE COAST OF NEW JERSEY

Convoy duty was frequently cold and invariably unpleasant and boresome—until the Nazi torpedoes struck. Then it was a matter of praying, swimming in slimy oil or drowning. More suicidal than sailing over the Atlantic or up the American coast was the northern run to Russia, undertaken to prove the Americans and Britons meant their pledges to succor the Soviets. These convoys to ice-free Murmansk ran above the Scandinavian peninsula, and they encountered not only submarine and destroyer torpedoes but also bombs dropped by German planes based in Norway. Of 33 ships in convoy PQ-17 (July 1942), 22 were sunk, including 15 American. These losses and those in the western Atlantic and Caribbean could not be endured (5,579 U.S. merchant seamen were killed during the war and 487 taken prisoner). Allied scientists worked frantically on antisubmarine devices. Civilians with small spotting planes tried to help by patrolling the offshore waters. The Navy in desperation called on the Army Air Forces. In the fight against the submarine what paid off in the long run was better weapons, more experience and additional land-based and carrier aircraft (whose radar-equipped planes could find the U-boats), plus American industry, which built ships much faster than the Nazis could sink them. Production rose from one million tons in 1941 to eight in 1942 to 19 in 1943; the British built about two million tons of shipping each year. German submarine losses jumped from 21 in the first half of 1942 to 241 in 1944. Late in the war the Germans produced the snorkel submarine, which did not have to surface and expose itself to radar, but it wasn't available in time. The British sank 524 Nazi subs, the Americans 174 (including 12 by the Air Forces, which also destroyed 42 in the construction pens). Eighty-three were sunk by mines or untraceable agents. Mussolini's fine fleet of submarines went under, 68 to the British, four to the U.S.

IN 1940 CREW MEMBERS OF THE BELGIAN FREIGHTER "VILLE DE NAMUR" TOOK TO THE LIFEBOATS AFTER SHIP FELL VICTIM TO GERMAN U-BOAT

IN 1941 BEFORE THE U.S. WAS AT WAR NAZIS TORPEDOED AMERICAN FREIGHTER "ROBIN MOOR." THESE ARE SOME OF HER RESCUED CREWMEN

121

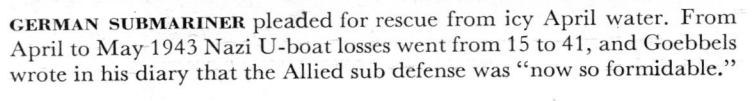

FROM THE DECK OF THE CUTTER "SPENCER" U.S. COAST GUARDSMEN WATCH ONE OF THEIR DEPTH CHARGES BLOW THE U-175 TO THE SURFACE

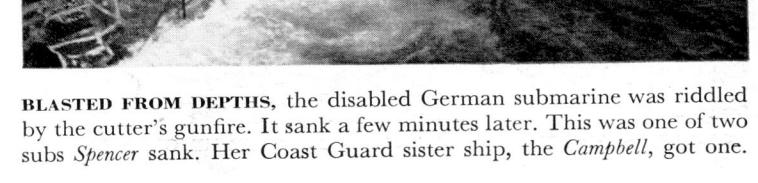

BLASTED FROM DEPTHS, the disabled German submarine was riddled by the cutter's gunfire. It sank a few minutes later. This was one of two subs *Spencer* sank. Her Coast Guard sister ship, the *Campbell*, got one.

GERMAN SUBMARINER pleaded for rescue from icy April water. From April to May 1943 Nazi U-boat losses went from 15 to 41, and Goebbels wrote in his diary that the Allied sub defense was "now so formidable."

Stalingrad

like its contemporary, Guadalcanal, had not been envisioned as a point at which a decisive battle would be fought. By the summer of 1942 Field Marshal von Bock had 225 German divisions in Russia, plus 43 belonging to uneasy satellites. About 50 of them were armored. Supreme Commander Hitler put everything except holding forces into the drive south of Moscow. First, Field Marshal Fritz von Manstein slammed into the Crimea and captured Sevastopol. Then von Bock attacked Voronezh on the Don, southeast of Moscow. Von Bock left a single army group to contain Voronezh and carried all before him southeastward. His objective now was control of the Volga and of the oil fields of the Caucasus. In August the German armies were 300 miles deeper in Russia. The Fourth Panzer Army could have taken Stalingrad earlier, but it was sent south to help Field Marshal Paul von Kleist cross the Don. When it turned north two weeks later the

Russians had reinforced Stalin's city of half a million and Colonel General Friedrich Paulus' Sixth Army had to blast its way forward to help in the siege. Eleven divisions struck at Stalingrad, then six more, then eight more. Late in August more reinforcements fell upon it from the northwest. By mid-September there was hand-to-hand fighting inside the city, which was also undergoing massive air raids. The depleted Russian divisions within fought back more fiercely than ever; every yard of ground was defended from the rubble, from trenches, from the windows of remaining buildings. Halder, chief of the general staff, suggested that with winter coming on again, withdrawal made sense. Hitler dismissed him. Now the advances were cut to 50 yards and Nazi losses were 1,000 to 4,000 men per day. Paulus was in the city with 22 divisions in mid-November and there he was encircled and soon reduced to eating his horses. He surrendered early in 1943 not long after Hitler had promoted him to field marshal.

IN SEPTEMBER NAZIS PUSHED ARTILLERY INTO STALINGRAD'S SUBURBS

HOUSE-TO-HOUSE FIGHTING LEFT STALIN'S CITY DESOLATE BATTLEFIELD

NAZI EXECUTED PEASANT FIGHTER ON THE EDGE OF A PREDUG GRAVE

GERMANS BATTLED INTO A POWER PLANT; REDS DUG IN AGAIN BEHIND IT

BOMBS DROVE CITIZENS OUT OF STALINGRAD TO PLAINS EAST OF VOLGA

WORKERS DUG LAST-DITCH FORTIFICATIONS ALONG THE VOLGA BLUFFS

ON NOV. 19 RED RESERVES ATTACKED NORTH AND SOUTH OF THE CITY

RUSSIAN REPLACEMENTS MOVED IN STEADILY, KEPT GARRISON AT 40,000

RUSSIAN STREET FIGHTERS CHARGED THE NAZIS AMID BURNING RUBBLE

DEFENDERS EMBRACED RED SOLDIERS WHO LIFTED THE SIEGE JAN. 27

FIELD MARSHAL PAULUS WAS CAPTURED ALONG WITH HIS TRAPPED ARMY

RED OFFICERS (TOP) REVIEWED SLOGGING PARADE OF NAZI PRISONERS

THIS PHOTOGRAPH WAS MADE FROM THE CARRIER "YORKTOWN" AS TWO JAPANESE TORPEDO PLANES BORED IN THROUGH A BARRAGE OF ANTIAIRCRAFT FIRE

THE 13,000-TON JAPANESE CRUISER "MIKUMA" WAS REDUCED TO A LISTING, BURNING HULK BY U.S. PLANES, ONE OF WHICH CRASHED ON A TURRET

SHIP'S GUNNERS ALSO FIRED INTO THE SEA TO RAISE A SCREEN OF WATER, BUT THE ENEMY PLANES GOT THROUGH AND HIT "YORKTOWN" WITH TWO "FISH"

U.S. DIVE BOMBERS PEEL OFF OVER A FLAMING JAPANESE WARSHIP

ONE JAPANESE BOMBER HIT THE SEA INSTEAD OF THE "YORKTOWN"

Midway was the Stalingrad of the Pacific. Here for the first—and almost the last—time U.S. forces won against overwhelming odds. The Japanese were under the command of Admiral Yamamoto himself, in the 63,700-ton battleship *Yamato*. Numbers reveal his impressive superiority: five aircraft carriers against the Americans' three, seven battleships to none, 13 cruisers against eight, 45 destroyers against 20. Yamamoto also brought along 12 transports carrying 5,000 soldiers and marines—he intended to take Midway Island as well as the U.S. fleet. But Yamamoto committed a grievous error: he divided his fleet, assuming Nimitz would run north to oppose his Aleutians landing at Attu and Kiska. Nimitz didn't; he had the great advantage of intercepting and decoding Yamamoto's messages. He was not decoyed; he sent Rear Admirals Raymond Spruance and Fletcher to Midway. At 4:30 a.m. June 4, 1942, Vice Admiral Chuichi Nagumo launched 108 planes against the island. They were met by 26 Marine Corps fighters, mostly old Buffaloes, which were slaughtered. From the three American carriers (*Enterprise, Hornet, Yorktown*) 41 torpedo planes went out first, but 35 of them were shot down; no hits. Midway-based Marine bombers and high-level Flying Fortresses also missed. Then Spruance's SBDs fell out of the sky in 70° dives against Nagumo's carriers. *Soryu* was hit, then *Akagi*, then *Kaga*. That afternoon two Japanese torpedoes disemboweled the *Yorktown*, but four *Enterprise* dive bombers holed *Hiryu*. The balance in the Pacific was restored and would not be upset again. In the U.S. there was jubilation, but some weird conclusions. First pilots back to Pearl Harbor were Army fliers who reported their 25 planes had won the victory. Editorial writers pronounced the demise of the aircraft carrier as a weapon—little knowing that all four of Nagumo's ships had been sunk by dive bombers from these same dodoes.

127

AERIAL TORPEDO BREACHES "YORKTOWN'S" PORT SIDE. SLOWED BY BOMB HITS, THE CARRIER COULD NOT DODGE FOLLOWING TORPEDO ATTACK

FIRE DETAIL FOUGHT STUBBORNLY ON THE SMOKING FLIGHT DECK

SALVAGE CREW TROD LISTING DECKS IN LIFE PRESERVERS (RIGHT)

HIT BY TWO MORE TORPEDOES FROM SUB, "YORKTOWN" ROLLS OVER

DESTROYER "HAMMANN" GOES DOWN, A VICTIM OF THE SAME SUB

THE U.S. Navy was tormented by its own shortcomings in the first 18 months of war. The gravest of these was faulty torpedoes, which upon failing to explode caused sub skippers and bomber pilots to curse and cry aloud. Radar was inadequate and was operated by men who didn't know how. Until late in 1942, when the 40-mm. arrived, the fleet had no accurate medium-range AA guns. Ships which should have been saved were lost because poor damage control allowed fires to spread. The Japanese knew better how to fight at night; they had superior patrol planes and torpedo bombers. None of these things was known to the public, which remembered 1942 as a year of flaming oil and splintered steel bulkheads, of burning gasoline and crumpled carrier decks, of drowning sailors and unparalleled heroism—which it was. In August the U.S. lost its only surface ship from which no man survived (the destroyer *Jarvis;* it vanished after Savo Island). Of 51 torpedo planes sent into the Midway battle, only nine returned. Only ten men survived the *Juneau.* It was a great period for the sharks which infest the Pacific seas—and for the militarists in Tokyo whose dreams seemed to be coming true.

BURNING) WITH THREE TORPEDOES, SIX BOMBS, TWO SUICIDE CRASHES ON HER FLIGHT DECK

CARRIER "ENTERPRISE" (CENTER) TOOK THREE HITS FORWARD, BUT NEW 40-MM. ANTIAIRCRAFT (AS AT LEFT) SMOTHERED MOST OF HER ATTACKERS

CARRIER "WASP" BLEW UP IN THE WATERS BELOW GUADALCANAL A HALF-HOUR AFTER TAKING THREE TORPEDOES FROM A JAPANESE SUBMARINE

IN THE CORAL SEA A U.S. DIVE BOMBER SWOOPS UP AFTER ANOTHER HIT ON THE JAPANESE CARRIER "SHOHO," ALREADY BURNING IN HER OWN OIL

VII
The Axis Reversed

World Battlefronts: 1942-43

WHILE Montgomery's troops were pressing hard on Rommel's retreat from El Alamein along the dusty roads of the Mediterranean shore in November of 1942, two convoys, one from Britain and one from the U.S., were zigzagging toward North Africa's beaches. The British Admiral Cunningham was in command of landings in Oran and Algiers, and Rear Admiral Henry K. Hewitt of those at Casablanca. Eisenhower superintended the invasion from a tunnel under the Rock of Gibraltar. At the same time Allied staff men were trying to fit into their complicated political schemes the French General Henri Giraud, who had mysteriously escaped from a German prisoner-of-war camp and whom State Department agents had enticed out of France by promises of great things in North Africa. President Roosevelt had insisted on this Operation Torch against the opinion of some of his advisers, but it turned out to be a risk worth taking.

The Germans were caught asleep. The worst they had expected from the reported concentration of ships was an attempt to relieve Malta. Hitler's answer was an immediate rush of German troops into Vichy France. The disappearance of the fiction of Marshal Pétain's independence made it easier for the wavering French officials in North Africa to collaborate with Allied forces. Pétain's deputy in Algiers, Admiral Jean Darlan, was induced by Eisenhower to order French commanders to cease resistance against the Allied landings. He also ordered the French fleet out of Toulon, but instead of obeying the crews scuttled their ships and went home. He tried to deliver Tunisia but the Germans got to the French commander there ahead of him. The British made landings at Bougie and took Bône but the weather turned bad. The Germans attacked Allied transport vigorously from the air. It was just not possible for Eisenhower to organize his newly landed forces in time to forestall an airborne invasion that gave the Germans a safe defensive position to receive Rommel's columns streaming in from the east with Montgomery hot on their heels. It was only after months of bloody fighting and a destructive counterattack that the Germans were ejected from North Africa.

WASHINGTON hardly had time to digest the success of the landings in North Africa before reports from the Pacific told of several naval engagements off Guadalcanal that, costly as they were to us in ships and men, repulsed the last great Japanese effort to reinforce their troops on that green malaria-smitten hell. Meanwhile in that same fortunate month of November 1942 the Soviet armies, well trained for winter fighting and reinforced with armor and firepower from their own factories and from Britain and the U.S., started the counteroffensives which by nipping off the Stalingrad salient were soon to bring about enormous German losses of men and materials. Refusal to admit early reverses turned Hitler's Russian adventure into disaster compounded on disaster. As Winston Churchill remarked, "It is not even the beginning of the end. But it is, perhaps, the end of the beginning."

President Roosevelt loved a trip. He was not a man to worry about his own personal safety. F.D.R. hadn't had a chance to ride in a plane since he'd flown out to Chicago to receive the Democratic nomination in 1932. His advisers military and medical were something less than easy in their minds when he broached the plan to fly to a meeting with Churchill and, if possible, with Stalin, in North Africa. Early in January he set out by clipper from Miami across the busy air route of the military transport planes and the ferry service via the bulge of Brazil and Bathurst in West Africa. There were good hotel and airfield facilities at Casablanca, so the Atlantic port was chosen as the place. Stalin said no thank you he was much too busy killing Germans. Churchill came with such an array of high-ranking generals that the President hastily had to send for some extra brass to garnish our side of the table. The Prime Minister brought his son Randolph and had a paintbox along to indulge his hobby in his spare time. Roosevelt had his crony Hopkins and two of his sons. The air was dry and sunny. The villas they occupied were full of stately furnishings and draped on the outside with bougainvillea and oleander. The food was good. There was plenty to drink. The luncheons and dinners were gay. The success of Operation Torch proved that the U.S. could supply an expedition 5,000 miles from home and that British and American troops could cooperate in a difficult and delicate operation.

The first problem on the table was Russia. Russian prestige was rising daily. Stalin's emissaries were clamoring for a second front in Europe. Harry Hopkins was putting in an occasional word for Operation Roundup, a project for landing in northern France during 1943. The President and the Prime Minister agreed that it was essential that Stalin be kept in the war, but the British were all for a landing in Sicily first: Operation Husky. Sicily in Allied hands would guarantee the empire's Mediterranean artery. Roundup became Overlord, a project for landing in France in '44. Meanwhile flocks of escort vessels were needed to protect Atlantic ship lanes. American shipyards were increasing their tempo, but there was still not enough tonnage at sea. At that moment we were especially short of landing craft.

WHILE the Combined Chiefs of Staff plugged away on grand strategy the President and the Prime Minister were preoccupied with the anfractuosities of the French military character. Roosevelt and Churchill thought that General Giraud and General Charles de Gaulle should work together for the future of France, but each of these gentlemen wanted to be boss. A great deal of time was spent in arranging a meeting. The President as usual thought that differences could be smoothed out by a friendly exchange. Finally he prevailed on the two generals to meet. Before they knew it they found themselves being photographed shaking hands outside the President's villa. The time had come to make the news releases.

Afterward Roosevelt told Hopkins that the trouble they had getting the French generals together had made him think of what Lee's and Grant's aides had gone through getting that pair into the same room at Appomattox. U.S. Grant's nickname was Unconditional Surrender. Once the phrase got in the President's head he tried it on Churchill. Churchill raised his glass to the words as a toast. Some sounding phrase had to be broadcast to the world to make memorable this daring conference so near the fighting lines that celebrated the first joint victory. When the newspapermen trooped in the President offered a summary, to which the Prime Minister assented: the only terms for the enemy were to be unconditional surrender. —JOHN DOS PASSOS

Torch was the code name given to the British-American invasion of French North Africa. Its purpose was to crush Rommel's desert army between the invaders in the west and General Montgomery's forces in the east, and to clear the Mediterranean in preparation for the later assault on *Festung Europa*. To accomplish the landings the Allies sent across the submarine-infested Atlantic "the greatest armada in military history" —which miraculously went unharmed. Objectives were Casablanca on Africa's west coast and Oran and Algiers on the north coast. D-Day was Nov. 8, 1942.

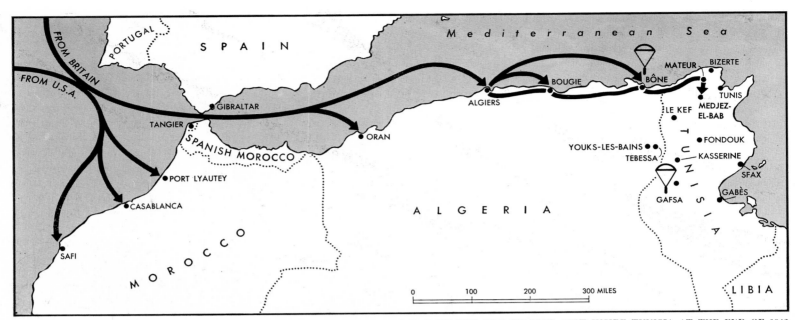

THE ALLIED EXPEDITION OVERRAN BOTH MOROCCO AND ALGERIA IN FOUR DAYS BUT WAS STALLED JUST INSIDE TUNISIA AT THE END OF 1942

U.S. FLEET BOMBED AND SHELLED THE FORTIFIED HARBOR OF CASABLANCA, ENGAGED FRENCH WARSHIPS WHILE LANDINGS WERE IN PROGRESS

Casablanca was defended by French colonial troops steadfastly loyal to their Vichy officers. When they recovered from their initial astonishment at the landing by an American task force at Fedala (close to Casablanca), Safi and Port Lyautey, these troops fought with whatever military resources they could command. The first two towns fell to Major General George Patton's forces in less than ten hours. But fierce fighting developed at Port Lyautey, where the prize was an airfield the Americans needed. Meanwhile U.S. battleship and cruiser guns off Casablanca were directed against the coast artillery batteries that harassed the invasion fleet. They also shot up the new French battleship *Jean Bart*, which was unfinished but able to use her guns. During the exchange of naval fire some units of the French fleet which sortied out of the harbor to attack the transports of the task force met with 5- to 16-inch shells from the American warships and never reached the transport area. All were sunk or beached, excepting one which scurried back into harbor.

UNDER U.S. FIRE, A MERCHANT SHIP CAPSIZED AT HER MOORINGS

OFF SAFI A U.S. TRANSPORT DEBARKED TROOPS INTO CIRCLING LANDING CRAFT. INTRICATE LANDINGS WERE CARRIED OUT BY GREEN CREWS

TROOPS CAME ASHORE THROUGH THE SURF (CENTER). CRISSCROSS OF TRACKS ON SAND WAS LEFT BY FIRST ATTACK WAVE AS IT MOVED INLAND

NEAR ALGIERS "TORCH" TROOPS HIT THE BEACHES BEHIND A LARGE AMERICAN FLAG (LEFT), HOPING THAT THE FRENCH WOULD NOT FIRE ON IT

AS THEY NEARED THE ALGERIAN COAST, SOLDIERS IN LIFE JACKETS CROWDED THE DECKS OF TRANSPORTS CARRYING 39,000 AMERICANS TO ORAN

DESPITE BAD WEATHER LANDINGS WENT OFF SMOOTHLY ON BOTH SIDES OF ORAN AND U.S. COLUMNS QUICKLY ENCIRCLED THE FRENCH CITY

ALGERIANS HELPED TO UNLOAD CANS OF GASOLINE FOR U.S. FORCES

FRENCH PRISONER WAS QUERIED DURING BRIEF FIGHT FOR ORAN

AMERICANS STROLLED THROUGH ORAN AFTER CITY'S SURRENDER

Oran was the target of the center task force. Initial objectives there were vital airfields and a highway system that curved along the Mediterranean coast. Oran's French commander vacillated between cooperation and resistance, finally made up his mind to fight. American Rangers were fired on at Arzeu after landing unopposed in darkness; infantrymen took Les Andalouses despite some artillery fire and the movement inland began. At Oran itself the casualties were heavier. Two British-operated cutters carrying American troops and special antisabotage units bravely crashed the port's protective booms, broke into the harbor. There they met an intense crossfire from warships and guns ashore, which flamed and sank both of the cutters. Two hundred and fifty Americans were killed and the 200 survivors were taken prisoner. But this dubious French "victory" had little effect. Two days later, after the invaders had surrounded the city, a general attack was ordered, and at 12:30 p.m., Nov. 10, Major General Lloyd R. Fredendall accepted Oran's formal surrender.

Algiers provoked heated debate in the planning stage—the British rightly judged it the most important of the three assaults; the Americans feared to get so far into the Mediterranean. The landing force which attacked it comprised 23,000 British and 10,000 American troops staged from Great Britain. As at Oran and Casablanca, the American flag was displayed prominently, on the theory that the French would welcome the invaders as liberators. Even U.S. soldiers serving in British Commando units wore American flags as armbands. Although Britain contributed more than half the naval units at Oran and Algiers, every effort was made to provide an American facade to the operations, since the French were still bitterly aware of earlier clashes with the British at Dakar and in Syria. In spite of this attempted deception, the only effective resistance was encountered by the Americans at Casablanca and Oran. Algiers turned out to be, as Churchill predicted, "the most friendly and hopeful spot where the political reaction would be the most decisive." Capitulation was quick and complete. The assault phase of Torch was a success, fatal to only 770 Americans and 240 Britons; three days after the initial landings almost all of French North Africa was in Allied hands. But unforeseen political problems soon threatened to spoil the military fruits.

SMOKE SHROUDS SCREENED THE WATERFRONT AT ALGIERS FROM NAZI AIR ATTACKS WHICH STARTED AS SOON AS FRENCH RESISTANCE CEASED

WITH BIG PORTS LIKE ALGIERS IN ALLIED HANDS, TRANSPORTS WERE ABLE TO LAND MEN AND MATERIALS IN BULK FOR THE AFRICAN CAMPAIGN

142

Politics

among Frenchmen are complicated far beyond the comprehension of the non-Gallic mind. The North African landings were badly ensnarled in French politics from the outset. British and Americans had not brought along the Free French General Charles de Gaulle, who was vastly unpopular with his brother officers, nor had they even informed him of the plan to invade his country's territory. To take charge of French forces they imported an aged general named Henri Giraud who was received with supreme contempt. Upon landing, the forces of Lieut. General Dwight Eisenhower discovered the powerful Vichyite Admiral Jean Darlan. He commanded

great respect among French admirals and generals, though he was at heart a Nazi sympathizer who detested the British. But Darlan was also an opportunist. When he heard that the Germans had invaded Unoccupied France he cast his lot with the Allies, ordered the cease fire—saving hundreds of lives—and even tried to snag the French fleet out of its base at Toulon. Five days after the invasion General Eisenhower arrived from Gibraltar and confirmed the "Darlan deal," placed the admiral in charge of French affairs (*above*). This "sordid alliance" stirred anger throughout the democracies. Darlan served the Allied purpose until he was assassinated by a young compatriot in Algiers on Christmas Eve.

SCUTTLED BY HER CREW, CRUISER "ALGERIE" RESTS ON BOTTOM

Toulon

was the home base of the French fleet and Darlan was its hero. Here were three battle cruisers, seven cruisers, 25 destroyers, 26 submarines, plus auxiliaries. At Alexandria a battleship, three cruisers, four destroyers and one submarine had languished since 1940; Dakar held the battleship *Richelieu* and three cruisers; the aircraft carrier *Bearn* and a heavy cruiser were immobilized at Martinique across the Atlantic. This navy, still the world's fourth largest, was coveted by Hitler and feared by the British who were determined he shouldn't get it. When Hitler ordered Operation Attila (the occupation of Vichy France) on Nov. 10, 1942 his troops pointed straight for Toulon. Before they arrived Darlan messaged the fleet: sail out and join the Allies. But Vice Admiral Jean de Laborde at Toulon not only despised the British-hater Darlan; he detested the British too. When the Germans demanded that he withdraw his guard around the port, De Laborde signaled, "Carry out Order B!" Roar followed roar as ships were detonated. With the scuttling of 225,000 tons of the French fleet De Laborde had carried out one of Darlan's oft-repeated promises to Churchill: the Germans would never get that fleet. Admirals commanding units at Alexandria and Dakar first adopted a wait-and-see attitude, but finally came over to the Allies after Tunisia was conquered, when no doubt about the victory remained.

THIS GERMAN TANK REACHED TOULON TOO LATE: SMOKE ERUPTS FROM EXPLODING WARSHIPS AND A DESTROYER HAS ALREADY HEELED OVER

144

FRENCH CRUISERS BURNED, BATTLESHIP "STRASBOURG" SANK UPRIGHT IN SHALLOW WATER (TOP) AND ROW OF DESTROYERS CAPSIZED (CENTER)

145

ROOSEVELT BROUGHT GIRAUD AND DE GAULLE TOGETHER FOR MEETING WITH CHURCHILL

THE TWO HIGH COMMANDS MET AT ONE TABLE. FROM

CHURCHILL AND F.D.R. GAVE CORRESPONDENTS A HEADLINE: "UNCONDITIONAL SURRENDER"

LEFT: ARNOLD, KING, CHURCHILL, ROOSEVELT, BROOKE, POUND, MARSHALL.   STANDING: JACOB, ISMAY, MOUNTBATTEN, DEANE, DILL, PORTAL AND HOPKINS

Conference at Casablanca in January 1943 brought the war's most far-reaching military decisions. The Allied leaders reaffirmed their intent to beat Hitler first, despite pressure from a large segment of the American public which wanted to get back at the Oriental enemy in a hurry. Looking beyond North Africa, the conference approved plans for Operation Husky, the Sicily invasion. Thus the Americans abandoned—without admitting it—the possibility of invading France in 1943 and yielded to Churchill's urge to pierce "the soft underbelly" of Europe. "Security of sea communications" got top priority, meaning the Nazi submarines were yet to be licked. To keep the Germans engaged in the east, all possible supplies for Stalin were ordered. The skeptical British, who noted that the B-17s hadn't dropped a bomb on Germany

in half a year, reluctantly approved the daylight bombing of Europe, although its cost in manpower and equipment seemed to them absurdly high. Pacific affairs were handed over to the Americans as their exclusive province with the provision that the Europe-first priority not be overridden. It was expected that this would mean concentrated submarine warfare against Japanese shipping, plus strikes against enemy supply lines by Army bombers based in China. The eventual effect was to let Admiral Ernest King have the "leftovers" like the big *Essex*-class carriers which became the indispensable striking force of the Pacific war. Most spectacular, if unforeseen, result of Casablanca came from Roosevelt's casual remark that nothing less than unconditional surrender would be accepted from the Axis. Enemy propagandists seized upon this phrase as a rallying cry for Axis resistance.

147

President

took time during the Casablanca Conference to pay a surprise visit to units of Lieut. General Mark Clark's newly activated Fifth Army training at Rabat, about 85 miles to the northeast. GIs were startled to see their commander in chief in Africa. So was the press, which knew nothing of the ten-day conference until it was over. No less excited was Franklin Roosevelt, who had an absorbing sense of the historically dramatic. No President in 78 years had visited a battle theater. None had ever left the U.S. in wartime. None had ever been to Africa, or traveled by air. Mr. Roosevelt was happily shattering all four precedents simultaneously—and on soil that so recently had been a battleground. Slipping away from Washington and the mountainous volume of detail work connected with prosecution of the war gave the surprise-loving President a soaring thrill. After his review of the troops the President and his military hosts sat down to a not-very-typical field mess. They dined on boiled ham, sweet potatoes, string beans, fruit salad, bread, butter and jam, and washed it all down with black coffee. The 3rd Division artillery band drew homesick sighs by playing *The Missouri Waltz*, *Deep in the Heart of Texas* and *Chattanooga Choo Choo*.

VISITING IN THE FIELD, ROOSEVELT SHOOK HANDS WITH A CORPORAL

THE FIRST PRESIDENT SINCE LINCOLN TO ENTER A BATTLE AREA, ROOSEVELT INSPECTED THE U.S. SOLDIERS WITH LIEUT. GENERAL MARK CLARK

FLYING FORTRESSES SEEMED ALMOST LOST IN THE VAST, HEAT-HAZY LEVELNESS OF THE DESERT. THESE PLANES BOMBED ITALY AS WELL AS TUNISIAN TARGETS

-OF DUST, THE TELL-TALE AERIAL TRAIL OF ANY MOVEMENT ON THE DESERT FLOOR

TANK BATTLES IN OPEN DESERT WERE SUDDEN, SHARP AND COSTLY

151

DESERTED BY NAZIS, ITALIAN CAPTIVES CALMLY PLAY CARDS

EARLY January found the Allies thinly stretched along a 250-mile Tunisian front. On the right flank, far to the south, French patrols roamed the desert on camels. American paratroopers, who had been dropped in the race for Tunis, trudged the wastelands around Gafsa and Faïd Pass. The lightly armed French XIX Corps, having finally decided to go over to the Allies, controlled the Ousseltia valley in the center of the line, but it refused to serve under British command. Eisenhower had to coordinate its front-line activities as best he could from his command post in the rear. The British First Army—still an army in name only—held the rest of the front north to the sea at Cape Serrat. Nearing Tunisia from the east in his retreat before the British Eighth Army, Field Marshal Rommel guessed that his enemy on the western front "probably lacks cohesion and suffers from inherent weaknesses of an Allied command." The estimate given by the Desert Fox was verified when Colonel General Jürgen von Arnim hit French positions at Fondouk on Jan. 2 and the garrison fell easily. On Jan. 18, at the junction point of the British and French sectors, the Germans used the Mark VI Tiger tank to drive a wedge into the Allied line. The small but determined Axis thrusts revealed how precarious was the Allied position. Up and down the Anglo-American line all eyes anxiously looked east, wondering what might come next.

AT A CAPTURED AXIS AIRDROME AMERICANS LOOKED OVER THE HENSCHEL 129, A GERMAN ANTITANK PLANE CAMOUFLAGED FOR THE DESERT WAR

AMERICAN P-38 FIGHTERS FLEW INTO TUNISIA TO JOIN THE ALLIED TACTICAL AIR FORCE IN ITS CONSTANT SUPPORT OF THE GROUND FIGHTING

African air was filled with planes as Britain's experienced Desert Air Force chased Rommel along the Mediterranean. In the west, however, the newly arrived U.S. Twelfth Air Force was bedeviled with short supplies, overcasts and inexperience. On Dec. 17 Major General Doolittle could report only 200 of his 600 planes operating effectively. Planes were based too far behind in Algeria to help much in the race for Tunis (whose failure Anderson blamed on lack of airpower). When forward airfields began operating they became so muddy that steel mats only sank in the quagmire; meanwhile Axis planes flew from all-weather fields at Tunis. During the Kasserine battle a flight of B-17s got lost and bombed an Arab village 100 miles inside Allied lines. After the Casablanca Conference all aviation in Africa was put under Britain's Air Chief Marshal Sir Arthur Tedder, with Major General Carl Spaatz his deputy for northwest Africa and Air Chief Marshal Sir Sholto Douglas for the Middle East. The merger paid off as the Allies closed in on the Axis force (*map*). In the April 18 "Palm Sunday massacre" Allied fighters shot down more than 50 Junker transports bringing Hitler's reinforcements. In Tunisian harbors many hulks of ships were found, nine sunk and 31 damaged by air attacks. Surrendered Nazi generals awarded this tactical aviation team much of the credit for their defeat.

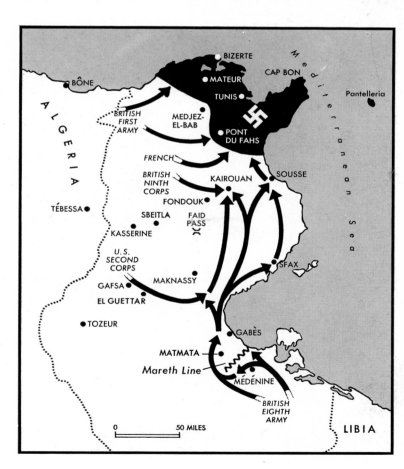

Rommel was reaching the end of his long retreat from El Alamein, pressed relentlessly by General Montgomery's Eighth Army and constantly harried by the Western Desert Air Force, which by early 1943 was about 10% American, 90% British. In February, Rommel holed up behind the strongly fortified Mareth line the French had built on the Tunisia-Libya border. There Rommel had the Gulf of Gabès on his north, the desert on his south. To the west elements of three American divisions, organized as a section of Anderson's army, were strung out between Sbeitla and Gafsa, and Montgomery was drawing near in the east. To gain time the Nazi field marshal decided to have a go at the Americans. At St. Valentine's dawn the 10th and 21st Panzer divisions broke through the weakly held line at Kasserine Pass. What resulted was both disastrous and humiliating. In their first important combat more than 2,400 U.S. soldiers surrendered; only 192 were killed; 2,500 wounded. The repercussions were worldwide: the British bandied disparaging remarks about Americans' fighting qualities; so did Joseph Goebbels, who noted in Berlin that the "big-mouthed Yankees" hadn't even met select troops. General Sir Harold Alexander, by now Eisenhower's operational deputy,

sent over veteran British officers to train the Americans for war, and Churchill assured Britons there would be no need to worry once the ally's soldiers got some experience. Most of this fuss was nonsense; the troops were badly disposed (by their British commander), in some cases badly led, and they had exhibited some stage fright. The defeat only served to make them mad (they called their British instructors "nursemaids"); after Kasserine they fought well. Rommel's success lasted a few days longer; he captured Sbeitla and the Thelepte airfields. But the Panzers were overextended and U.S. artillery near Tébessa cut them up. Other failures forced them back through Kasserine on Feb. 23. That day Rommel was made army group commander, but his African career was nearing its end. On March 6 he made four attacks against Médénine, lost 52 tanks, attacked no more. This was Rommel's last gesture on the continent that gave him the fame of a Hannibal. About March 15 he left his cornered forces in Tunisia. To save his own skin, guessed Eisenhower. Because Mussolini demanded he be removed, said Goebbels. Both of them were wrong. Rommel made one last desperate appeal to Hitler to rescue his troops. Hitler called him a coward (which Rommel certainly never was) and lost the troops as well as North Africa.

THREE OF ROMMEL'S MARK III TANKS WERE KNOCKED OUT BY BRITISH 6-POUNDER GUNS WHEN THE EIGHTH ARMY STOPPED HIM AT MEDENINE

ROMMEL: THE NAZI DESERT FOX WAS BROUGHT TO BAY IN TUNISIA

NAZI INFANTRY WAITS FOR COMMAND TO FOLLOW A TANK ATTACK

AMERICAN HALF-TRACK (LEFT) WAS A CASUALTY OF ROMMEL'S RAID THROUGH KASSERINE PASS. RIGHT: A U.S. COLUMN RE-ENTERS THE PASS

GENERAL PATTON (*right*), wearing a pearl-handled pistol on either hip, watches his tanks advance at El Guettar. He took over command of the U.S. II Corps after the defeat at Kasserine Pass. After six weeks he was relieved by Major General Omar Bradley and sent back to plan the Sicilian invasion. All Allied forces came under Eisenhower as top commander in North Africa, but British held air, navy and ground-force commands.

AMERICANS CHARGE into a barrage laid down by Italian artillery and the Luftwaffe's Ju-88 bombers in front of the oasis of Sened. Many sharp local actions like this were fought in February and March as Americans pressed toward the sea along the Gafsa front. This probing of Rommel's right flank was intended to keep him squeezed into his southern corner until Montgomery's Eighth Army was ready to attack the Mareth line.

WITH NAZI SHELLS OVERHEAD, MEN QUIT JEEPS FOR GROUND COVER

SURVIVORS OF A HALF-TRACK GET AID AFTER STRAFING BY ME-109s

TANK-BUSTING HOWITZER ON HALF-TRACK SHELLS TOWN OF SENED

BOMBING FORCED TANK-DESTROYER UNIT TO DIG IN AT EL GUETTAR

157

EIGHTH ARMY GUN JOINED IN LAYING DOWN HEAVY ARTILLERY BARRAGE AROUND PALM TREES CONCEALING MARETH LINE FORTIFICATIONS

THE TACTICAL AIR FORCE BATTERED THE MARETH FRONT WITH BOMBS

Mareth line

attack was called Operation Pugilist. March 20 Montgomery was ready with approximately eight crack divisions (which included not only British troops but also New Zealanders, Australians, Indians, Nepalese Gurkhas, Poles, Czechs, French, South Africans). This fine army, which firmly believed—as all good armies do —that it was the best in the world, was at its peak and Britain was crying for a victory. As New Zealanders and an armored division swung wide to the left, "Monty's" XXX Corps butted directly into the 20-mile-long Mareth line's pillboxes and anti-tank ditches. A powerful German counterattack threw back this attempt, so the marshal shifted weight by sending two more divisions on the end run. With 22 British and eight American squadrons bombing ahead of them, these troops broke through. The Mareth line was almost surrounded and the Axis forces hurriedly withdrew northward toward Tunis, lest they be cut off. But Rommel was gone, evacuated sick to Germany, they said. Rommel's troops were pushed northward to join von Arnim's. Hitler intemperately threw more thousands into this fast-closing trap and had some 150 transport planes shot down in the process.

RECOILING GUNS SNAPPED BACK AND FORTH AS BARRAGE MOUNTED

INFANTRY STORMED THE WADI ZIGZAOU TO PIN DOWN NAZI ARMY

GUNS CLEARED PATH AROUND ROMMEL'S FLANK FOR TANKS (RIGHT)

BRITISH ARMOR REACHED EL HAMMA BEHIND THE MARETH LINE

FLANKING FORCE HAD FREE FRENCH MORTAR MEN FROM LAKE CHAD

BRITISH CELEBRATED ATOP CAMOUFLAGED MARETH LINE PILLBOX

RETREATING GERMANS LEFT A GRAVE AND A FEW MINES ON SLOPES OF HILL 609

Hill 609

restored American prestige and morale which had suffered so badly at Kasserine Pass. The Axis, now backed against the sea, held a big pocket in northeastern Tunisia. Its defense line swung from west of Bizerte to Enfidaville. As part of a great Allied offensive April 21, Major General Bradley's American II Corps, numbering 100,000 troops, was moved 150 miles northward over mountains and across the supply lines of the British First Army. The Americans took up positions facing the enemy at Mateur, the major gateway to the port of Bizerte. Between them and their objective, however, was a formidable belt of rugged hills ranging from 15 to 20 miles in depth. One of these, Hill 609, which rose like a flat-topped fortress above the lower hills (*right*), dominated the highway and railroad leading into Mateur. The 34th Division was given the difficult job of reducing the heavily-defended enemy stronghold. After two days of hard fighting along its approaches, the troops reached the base of 609. Then two days later, reinforced and supported by medium tanks, the 34th battled its way to the summit. The Germans hastily reorganized and the following dawn launched a determined counterattack. The Americans held their fire until the enemy advanced to within 200 yards. General Bradley reported the subsequent action tersely: "A strong enemy attack was repulsed. Fighting was intense and bloody. The enemy was engaged with bayonet and grenade, and there were many cases of outstanding bravery." On May 3 the 1st Armored Division entered Mateur. The way was now open for the final drive to squeeze Axis forces off the African continent.

THE CITIZENS OF TUNIS HAILED ENTERING BRITISH WITH CHURCHILL'S V SIGN

Conquest of Tunisia when it finally came in May was quick and complete. The knockout blow followed General Alexander's order for continued pressure along the whole 130-mile front. The Germans reckoned that their old enemy, the Eighth Army, would deliver the blow. But when the attack was launched it was in the center of the line. The objective was Tunis. Two infantry divisions of the British First Army advanced behind a 1,000-gun barrage and Allied planes flew more than 2,000 supporting sorties. Within eight hours the troops had broken the line. Two armored divisions poured into the gap and raced 30 miles in 36 hours to occupy Tunis May 7. One armored division turned northward; the other headed southeast toward Bon Peninsula. At the same time the American II Corps pushed north and captured Bizerte. The Axis collapse was complete. By May 13 it was all over. Herded into prisoner-of-war pens (*left*) were some 250,000 Axis soldiers, among them Colonel General von Arnim. To forestall an Axis sea rescue, the British navy stood offshore. Clearing the Mediterranean meant saving 9,000 miles from the Middle East route—equivalent to acquiring 240 extra ships. In May the first unmolested convoy since 1940 sailed from Gibraltar to Alexandria. In Tunisia much more had been lost than the last of Rommel's desert army; the Axis had poured in 620,000 men, all gone now. Although the Americans never used more than four divisions, they learned well the indispensable lessons of combat. By furnishing 13 divisions, east and west, the British carried most of the load in winning their first decisive victory in nearly four long years of war.

IN THE CAUCASUS MOUNTAINS RED ARMY MORTAR SQUADS HARASSED PROBING NAZI COLUMNS, NOW OVEREXTENDED AND SHORT OF GASOLINE

Russians

complained bitterly about their Allies' failure to open a second front in Europe. Stalin was only slightly mollified by the invasion of North Africa, which never engaged more than a tenth the ground forces fighting in Russia at the time. Nor was Stalin consoled with the knowledge that Britons and Americans were grappling with half Hitler's Luftwaffe and all his seapower. The Russian dictator never let Roosevelt and Churchill forget their reckless promise to invade France in 1942 or, at the latest, in spring 1943. But despite his Allies' haunting fears, and despite tremendous casualties (after the war the Russians claimed they had 17 million killed, of which ten million were civilians), Stalin did not collapse. Instead he fell upon the long, slender Stalingrad salient to begin an offensive that eventually drove the Germans out of Russia (*map*). In its sheer, overpowering effect this great Soviet counterattack had no precedent in land warfare and comparisons must be sought halfway around the world in other elements—in the U.S. Navy's mighty surge across the Pacific and the Army Air Forces' fire bombing of Japan in the last five months of war. But neither of these loosed a torrent of blood such as flowed from the Caucasus to the Baltic.

RED GUARDS DIVISION COUNTERATTACKED AT MOZDOK, FARTHEST POINT OF THE GERMAN ADVANCE WHICH WAS AIMED AT GROZNY OIL FIELD

IN FALL OF 1943 BARGES EVACUATED LAST GERMANS RETREATING FROM THE CAUCASUS, FERRYING THEIR GEAR ACROSS THE STRAIT TO CRIMEA

ON KIEV FRONT BEATEN GERMANS WITHOUT BARGES TRIED TO ESCAPE ACROSS TETEREV RIVER ON AN ICE FLOE, WERE PICKED OFF BY SNIPERS

GERMAN ARMOR was a formidable weapon both offensively and defensively. In top picture, taken in 1943 near Novorossisk, Germans, backed up by a 62-ton Tiger tank, await Red attack. Below: an advancing Nazi tank hits a mine.

TANK DEFENSE found Russians using an antitank rifle against Nazi armor. The best they could do with this weapon was blow off a tread, leaving the tank a sitting duck for 100-mm. guns. By 1943 Soviets had plenty of these.

PANZER GIANTS were the Tiger and Panther (*right*), here abandoned with guns swung to the rear to cover the Nazi retreat. Although these were powerful war machines, the Nazis never had enough of them. In 1942 only 4,000 tanks were built in Germany, and Panzer divisions were cut from 400 to 250 each. Meanwhile the Russians had learned much about tank warfare and in mid-1943 produced the T-34, probably the best medium tank in the world at that time.

IN COMMAND POST underground, Red officers confer during night fighting on northern front. Caliber of Soviet commanders in second and third years of war surprised Western experts as much as improved quality of troops.

TANK-BORNE INFANTRY (*top*) dismounts from one T-34 for ground attack on Germans while another provides covering fire. These tactics are common to all armies. Below: captured Nazi vehicles are repaired at a Soviet factory.

RUSSIAN ARTILLERY moved forward at night on the Leningrad front early in 1944. In January of 1943 the Soviets had broken the terrible starvation blockade of the city, but the great counteroffensive did not begin for another year. When it did the Russians attacked westward over the ice of Lake Ilmen and along a 100-mile front extending from Novgorod to Leningrad. By March, 60 Soviet divisions had hammered 27 reeling German divisions back to Estonia.

NAZIS TAKE COVER as a Russian shell explodes during Kursk battle, 500 miles northwest of Stalingrad, in July 1943. This battle, involving 1,500 tanks, brought Hitler his worst defeat in the Russian offensive.

NAZIS SURRENDER readily after suffering heavy casualties, despite the fear of torture. From the outset Hitler declared that international law didn't apply to the Russians, who reciprocated his destructive attitude.

NAZI PRISONERS WERE NUMB WITH COLD DESPITE GREATCOATS AND DAZED BY CONSTANT DEFEAT UNDER THE WEIGHT OF THE RED OFFENSIVE

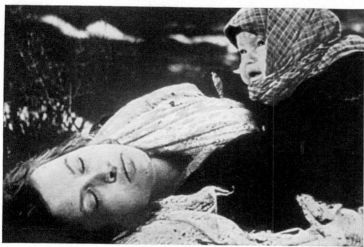

THE RUSSIAN PEOPLE in Nazi areas were dealt with ruthlessly by the Gestapo. Partisans and hostages went to the gallows (*top*); ordinary citizens suffered casual brutality, like this dead mother and her child.

RETURNING REDS mounted guard around a church still standing in recaptured Yelnya and stared at surrounding ruins. During counter-offensive Russians found hundreds of towns virtually uninhabitable.

MOSCOW WOMEN HELPED FILL HOME-FRONT JOBS IN FACTORIES AND TRANSPORTATION, RESTED BETWEEN SHIFTS IN STARK, CROWDED QUARTERS

Aleutians

had belonged to the U.S. ever since Seward's "folly" of 1867. Insofar as most Americans were concerned, Attu and Kiska might have been the names of craters on the moon—until Yamamoto's diversionary force occupied those islands during the Midway battle. Then it was recalled with alarm that the aviator general, Billy Mitchell, had predicted 18 years earlier that America would one day be invaded from that direction. Yamamoto had no such intention; reading Billy Mitchell had given him a hunch that the U.S. might invade *his* country from the north, and he was only taking precautions against that. By April 1943, the month Yamamoto was shot down by a P-38 in the Solomons, there were 2,500 Japanese on bleak, treeless Attu and 5,400 on equally inhospitable Kiska. On May 11, 1943 the Army's 7th Division invaded Attu and won it after 20 frostbitten days of fighting that took 700 American lives; 1,500 were wounded. Two months later 35,000 U.S. and Canadian troops assaulted Kiska and got the surprise of their lives: the enemy was gone, evacuated 19 days earlier by a task force that slipped through the Navy's screen.

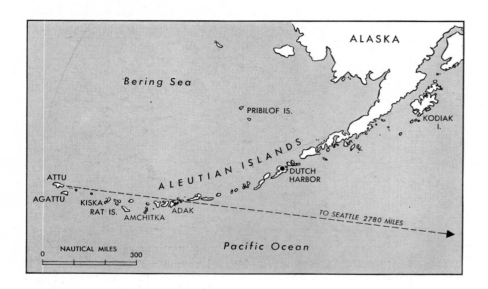

EVEN IN THE RARE INTERVALS OF SUNSHINE ADAK'S VOLCANIC

AT ATTU A DESTROYER SEARCHLIGHT GUIDED BOATS LANDING THROUGH THE DENSE FOG

U.S. INFANTRY FOUGHT UPHILL THROUGH SNOW DRIFTS

170

LANDSCAPE WAS FORBIDDING. THESE TRAILS WERE LEFT BY TRACKED VEHICLES, THE ONLY KIND THAT COULD MOVE ON THE ISLAND UNTIL ROADS WERE BUILT

A MACHINE-GUN TEAM FIRED ON JAPANESE DUG IN BEHIND THE CRAGS

GROUPS OF SURVIVING JAPANESE COMMITTED HARA-KIRI WITH GRENADES

171

MASSACRE VALLEY held a quiet Army encampment after conquest of Attu, but during the invasion it was the snow-covered scene of an American drive that trapped the Japanese near Chichagof Harbor. Refusing to surrender, the enemy made a suicidal banzai charge into the U.S. lines. With this mass spurt of blood the fight on Attu against the Japanese ended, but the fight against weather and terrain lasted for the duration.

QUONSET HUT on Adak, biggest U.S. base in the Aleutians, was papered with photographs of far-away females by Army fliers. From Adak bombers flew 1,000 miles south to bomb the Japanese base on Paramushiro, northernmost of the Kurile Islands. Of nine transports, three destroyers and five subs lost by Japan in the Aleutians, Army and Navy fliers sank ten, but their 14-month bombing of Kiska killed only 5% of the garrison.

AIRFIELDS AND ROADS were built on desolate Adak by Army Engineers and Seabees, whose steam shovels first removed the tundra, a spongy layer of dead grass and muck that sometimes was 4 feet deep.

PBY FLYING BOATS took off from Amchitka's airfield in weather so bad one pilot swore that a discouraged seagull hooked a ride on his wing. For every plane shot down by the enemy, six were lost in subarctic weather.

173

U.S.S. "SPOT" WAS ONE OF THE 156 NEW SUBMARINES BUILT DURING THE WAR. ON THE SURFACE THESE SLEEK, 1,500-TON BOATS DROVE THROUGH THE WATER AT 20

SUBMARINER REPORTS BY INTERCOM FROM THE COMPACT ENGINE ROOM

TWO SAILORS STAND WATCH IN THE AFTER TORPEDO ROOM AS SHIP DIVES

Submarines

operated throughout the war in such secrecy that their exploits never got the public recognition they deserved. Despite their long, dangerous missions (average: 47 days at sea) in cramped quarters, the submariners' morale was high, and their designation as a *corps d'élite* was never disputed. The U.S. started the war with 111 boats, mostly 1,500-tonners carrying crews of about 80, along with 24 to 28 torpedoes costing more than $10,000 each. Beyond brief missions by a few boats, U.S. submariners stayed out of the barren Atlantic and found their best hunting grounds in the far Pacific. They got off to a bad start: five submarines in Lingayen Gulf sank only one Japanese ship of the 80 that invaded the Philippines. U.S. submarines sank only seven ships during January 1942, five in February and 11 in March. During all of 1942 their bag amounted to 151 Japanese vessels—and probably would have been twice as big but for defective torpedoes which ran too deep or failed to explode. After 19 months this bedevilment was corrected, and from late 1943 until the end of the war the 14,000 American submariners did damage to Japan out of all proportion to their numbers. The "co-prosperity sphere" was doomed by the sinking of a staggering 8,141,591 tons of Japanese shipping—no less than 55% of it (1,100 ships) by U.S. subs, which also sent under nearly a third of Japan's navy (only the carrier planes accounted for more naval tonnage). Of the 288 subs employed against the enemy, the U.S. lost 52. One submariner in seven lost his life.

KNOTS; SUBMERGED FOR TORPEDO ATTACK, THEY MADE 9 KNOTS

CONTROL ROOM DIRECTS INTRICATE DIVING, SURFACING

SUBMERGED, MEN IN CONTROL ROOM KEEP THEIR EYES FIXED ON SUB'S DEPTH GAUGES

PERISCOPE'S-EYE VIEW of the war ranged from peaceful sailboats in the South China Sea (*top left*) to burning, exploding tankers, merchantmen and warships, and even to a 1943 view of Japan's sacred Mt. Fuji (*bottom right*). Most of these pictures were taken through U.S. submarine periscopes a few minutes after the U-boats' one-ton torpedoes had been sent running "hot, true and normal" for the target, 700 yards to 5 miles away.

STILWELL MAPPED THE LEDO ROAD AND RECONQUEST OF BURMA

WINGATE LED AIRBORNE RAIDERS IN THRUSTS BEHIND JAP LINES

C.B.I. stood for China-Burma-India, but the initials might very well have meant "constant bickering inside." No other theater of the war produced more recrimination. The disagreement started at the top: Roosevelt insisted that China's half-billion people could contribute much to victory; Churchill refused to be impressed by numbers and turned his share of the campaign toward recapturing Singapore, Hong Kong and Rangoon for the empire. In 1944 cooperation reached a wartime low and the theater was split: India-Burma and China. Dissension was even sharper among Americans. General Stilwell wanted to fight overland; Major General Claire Chennault, the air commander, had such exaggerated faith in combat aviation that he promised Roosevelt in 1942 to "accomplish the downfall of Japan" if given 147 planes. Chennault and Stilwell despised each other. Stilwell also hated the British and Generalissimo Chiang Kai-shek (whose chief of staff he was); Chennault liked Chiang but he had contempt for his own superiors in the Air Forces. For seven months of 1944–45 the B-29s attempted to bomb Japan from Chinese bases, but the distance was too great to make the raids effective. But if the C.B.I. produced many failures, it had one notable success: the Hump airlift (*map*), which kept China in the war during the long months the Burma and Ledo Roads were building.

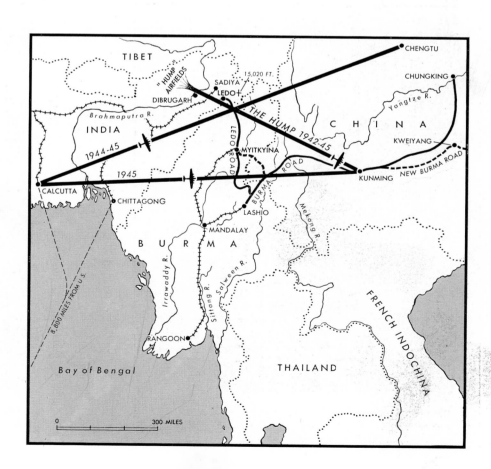

The Hump

was the nickname of the soaring peaks of the Himalayas over which transports flew in order to supply China. Ten airline C-47s borrowed from Africa flew the first mission in April 1942, taking 30,000 gallons of gasoline to China for Doolittle's raiders. Four months later the goal of air supply from India and Burma to China bases was set at 5,000 tons per month—K-rations, bombs, gasoline, ammunition, trucks and typewriters. Nothing could enter China by sea until the Navy won its way across the Pacific, nothing by land until the Japanese were pushed out of north Burma and a 478-mile road built. By January 1943 Hump air deliveries had risen to 1,208 tons; by November to five times that much, and the new schedule adopted at Quebec called for 16 times as much. In the last month of 1943 the Air Transport Command flew more than 12,000 tons into Kunming and Chungking—four fifths as much as the prewar Burma Road could deliver. This was expensive transportation: AAF statisticians have not yet been able to compute the cost of landing a gallon of gasoline in China. Crossing the mighty Himalayas, many an airman went to his death—the final number killed was 850; planes lost amounted to 250. But the tonnage delivered was beyond the most fantastic dreams: 24,000 tons in August 1944, to 44,000 in the next January, to 69,365 in July, the last full month of war. The Hump was not the only operation which demonstrated that jungles and mountains are best conquered by air supply. In May 1943, British Brigadier Orde Wingate, the fabulous onetime leader of guerrillas in Abyssinia, harassed the Japanese behind their lines in Burma for three months, almost entirely dependent on air supply. Lord Louis Mountbatten's armies in Burma were furnished by air: 615,000 tons of cargo, 315,000 reinforcements flown in, 110,000 casualties flown out—the whole project divided about 60% American, 40% British. Nowhere else was the arrival of the age of air transport more conclusively proved.

TAKING OFF, PILOTS SAW BARGES HAULING SUPPLIES UP THE BRAHMAPUTRA

PLANES USED EITHER SIDE OF "W" PASS TO CROSS THE CROWN OF THE HUMP

IN INDIA COOLIES HELP LOAD A CHINA-BOUND TRANSPORT PLANE

OVER CHINA FLIERS LOOKED DOWN AT THE AWESOME GORGE OF THE YANGTZE

PLANES PASSED OVER DUST RISING FROM TRUCKS ON THE LEDO ROAD (BOTTOM, LEFT), THEN BORED INTO ICE CLOUDS AT 22,000 FEET, ABOVE THE HUMP ITSELF

LOADED C-46 CLIMBED TOWARD 18,000-FOOT PEAKS AROUND SALWEEN RIVER. FOREST FIRES (RIGHT) CONFUSED PLANES SEARCHING FOR CRASHED TRANSPORTS

NEAR THE END OF THE RUN PLANES PASSED OVER OLD BURMA ROAD (LEFT), CLOSED BY JAPS, THEN SETTLED DOWN OVER RICE PADDIES TO KUNMING AIRFIELD

179

THE C.B.I. ROADS—the Burma and Ledo—were bulldozed 1,044 miles through jungle by U.S. Army Engineers. The comprehensive project was called—in tribute to its principal advocate—the Stilwell Road.

CHINESE SOLDIERS from Stilwell's army heaved logs into place on one of 600 bridges built along the roads. U.S. Engineers also drew heavily on natives, employing 20,000 coolies to grade one airfield.

TRUCK CONVOY moved along Ledo Road, which joined old Burma Road (it also had to be rebuilt) at Lungling in China. The road supplied airfields at Kunming, eventually reached almost to Hong Kong.

ENGINEERING MASTERPIECE, the road was built despite incessant rains, malaria, leeches and Jap snipers. But when war ended airlift still was carrying three times as much cargo as could be moved by land.

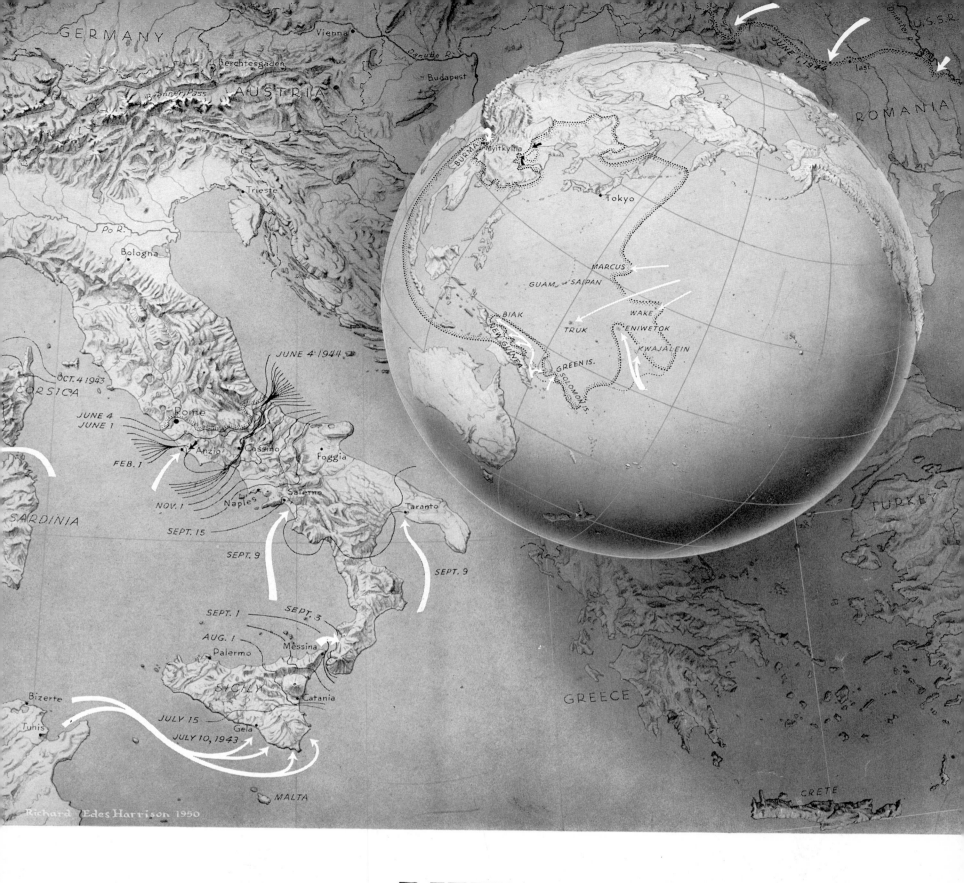

VIII
The Axis Broken

World Battlefronts: 1943

NINETEEN hundred and forty-three was a year of conferences. While sailors drowned in the oily seas and airmen met flaming deaths and the dogfaces ground their bellies into the Mediterranean beaches, war leaders shuttling from conference to conference crowded the air routes. With the glimmer of victory dissensions as to plans and aims increased among the Allies. At a time when Free French and British and American troops were working as a team to drive the Afrika Korps into prisoner-of-war pens in Tunisia, the President and the Prime Minister were presiding in Washington in May over the greatest assemblage yet of braid and brass. Even with all the visual helps of the great map room at the White House it was hard for the leadership to keep in focus fronts that stretched in a broad belt of violence round the globe.

The American people, exerting one of the greatest coordinated efforts in history, were learning the desperate game of war. In the strenuous school of the channels and jungles of the bloody Solomons the armed forces in the Pacific had been learning all the past winter to use the products of shipyard and factory to master climate and disease and break the enemy's will. Nimitz' fleet was developing into that self-contained unit, an airforce afloat, which was to nullify all the calculations of the Japanese. In Australia, Aussies and Americans were building the basis of teamwork which would result in MacArthur's campaign to the Philippines. In the Near East the pipelines and the routes of the tankers were secure. To the north on the plains of Russia the counterattacks of the Soviet armies were becoming potential thrusts into Europe. As Hitler's propaganda began to shift its emphasis from *lebensraum* to the defense of *Festung Europa*, Stalin's men in the Kremlin began to plan their offensive. No dissensions there. They knew what their aims were: to destroy the old order, and to rule in its place. As they felt their power growing the Western Allies were finding them increasingly hard to deal with.

When Churchill and Roosevelt studied Atlantic charts they agreed that more bases were needed for air and sea patrolling of the shipping which was building up the British Isles as a supply base for the coming assault on Hitler's Reich. There was still some disaccord as to the form the assault should take. Churchill, constantly mindful of political problems, was still very strong for attacking "the soft underbelly" of Europe, while the American staff, thinking in terms of logistics, was for landing in Normandy. Though the Normandy invasion was decided upon, this conference broke up leaving many other questions unanswered.

THE success of Operation Husky again confronted the U.S. and its Allies with a need for decisions. In July 1943 our armies had made seaborne and airborne landings in Sicily. The Germans thrown in to keep the Italians at their guns put up a sturdy defense, but the Allies overran the island in barely six weeks of hard fighting. The fall of Sicily not only affirmed Allied control of the Mediterranean; it knocked Italy right out of the war. All through the Fascist regime the King of Italy had quietly devoted himself to his numismatic collections in the Quirinal Palace. Suddenly alerted into action by the Allied "precision bombing" of nearby marshaling yards, the aging remnant of the House of Savoy joined in a movement to oust Mussolini after a meeting of the Fascist Grand Council had raised a storm against the dictator. Mussolini was arrested and old Marshal Pietro Badoglio was appointed prime minister with instructions to get Italy out of the war no matter how. Immediately an Italian representative turned up at the British Embassy in Madrid for discussions of peace terms.

These events raised new problems at the Quadrant Conference in Quebec in August. There were others, relating to the Pacific war. General MacArthur had long believed the defeat of Japan could best be accomplished by a systematic advance from New Guinea to the Philippine Islands and beyond; other strategists favored an attack westward across the wide Pacific from Pearl Harbor. The Quadrant Conference decided to utilize both approaches to Japan. The Gilbert Islands were chosen as the first target of the new cross-Pacific offensive, and Admiral Spruance was sent down to New Zealand to tell the 2nd Marine Division to prepare to capture an unheard-of atoll called Tarawa.

Meanwhile Roosevelt and Churchill decided to supplement the Normandy landings with another in southern France. The soft underbelly of Europe was proving hard and scaly. The landing at Salerno was finally accomplished by Sept. 9, 1943, and on Sept. 27 the British occupied the airfields at Foggia. But the Germans weren't beaten yet. In Italy, having seized control of communications, they were withdrawing northward. They were fighting too hard in Russia to try more than a series of holding operations, but they held. The new situation demanded a new conference.

THE President set out for Oran in November on the new battleship *Iowa*, which was almost hit on the way when a torpedo was joggled loose from one of her escorting destroyers. From Tunis, where he inspected the ruins of Carthage with General Eisenhower, whom he was considering for commander of Overlord, the C-54 *Sacred Cow* took him by night to Cairo. There he met Churchill and Chiang Kai-shek and struggled for a while with the welter of conflicting interests that arose every time the C.B.I. was mentioned. There was nothing to tell the press because the real news at Cairo was that Roosevelt and Churchill were on their way to Teheran to meet Stalin.

The day after Roosevelt arrived in the dusty Iranian capital for the conference which had been given the enthusiastic code name Eureka, Stalin politely invited him to stay in the armored compound of the Russian Embassy. Roosevelt was no man to worry about his own safety, but hoping, no doubt, for an opportunity for friendly chats with the mysterious master of the Kremlin, he accepted. Stalin and his men said very little about what they wanted but they were explicit about what they didn't want. They didn't want the Allies to mess with Turkey or to enter the Balkans. Like the Americans, they were for a second front in France; Stalin was insistent that the second front could not be a reality until a commander for Overlord had been appointed. At dinner one night he unbent sufficiently over his vodka to gloat over executing the German leaders when Germany was conquered. According to the President's son Elliott, Churchill jumped to his feet, red in the face, and said there would be no executions without proper trial. Roosevelt passed the matter of executions off with a wisecrack. When the Americans went home they talked of their diplomatic victory, Eureka. —JOHN DOS PASSOS

OFF GELA A U.S. AMMUNITION SHIP BLOWS UP AFTER BEING BOMBED BY GERMAN FLIERS ATTACKING THE SEVENTH ARMY INVASION CONVOY

BRITISH EIGHTH ARMY STEPPED ON THE TOE OF ITALY SEPT. 3, 1943

Sicily lies athwart the narrow waters separating North Africa and the toe of Italy. On July 10–11, 1943, 80,000 Allied soldiers moved adroitly onto the Sicilian beaches, Montgomery's Eighth Army on the east coast and Lieut. General Patton's Seventh on the south. Although the amphibious operation went off smoothly, its airborne accompaniment encountered tragic difficulties. High winds blew gliders into the sea and parachutists far off their targets. Two nights later American airborne reinforcements arrived in the midst of a German bombing attack. Badly confused, both ship and shore-based guns opened fire and shot down 23 of the 144 transport planes, killing 410 soldiers. Despite these misadventures Patton's and Montgomery's soldiers finally converged on Mt. Etna, overcame sharp resistance there and drove to Messina on Aug. 17. But they were too late to stop 35,000 Germans from crossing the narrow strait to Italy, where they would fight again. Of 167,000 lost by the enemy, 130,000 were Italians. Allied casualties—4,801 killed, 13,366 wounded—were almost evenly divided between the Seventh and Eighth Armies.

Surrender

of war-weary Italy was the immediate consequence of the Sicilian invasion. On July 25, 1943 Italy's little king, Victor Emmanuel III, abruptly imprisoned Benito Mussolini and appointed as premier old Marshal Pietro Badoglio, who soon began dickering for peace. Mussolini's sun had set, though he was daringly rescued by German paratroopers and lived on 19 months longer as Hitler's pensioner (*below*), until partisans executed him with his mistress in northern Italy. Eisenhower finally announced Sept. 8 that Italy had surrendered. A more important result of Sicily stemmed from an agreement Churchill had skillfully extracted from the Americans four months earlier: if Sicily went well, Italy should be invaded next. General George Marshall, the U.S. Chief of Staff, and Eisenhower reluctantly agreed. Thus one of history's toughest campaigns was launched.

Sua Maestà il Re e Imperatore ha rivolto agli Italiani il seguente proclama:

Italiani,

Assumo da oggi il comando di tutte le Forze Armate. Nell'ora solenne che incombe sui destini della Patria ognuno riprenda il suo posto di dovere, di fede e di combattimento: nessuna deviazione deve essere tollerata, nessuna recriminazione può essere consentita.

Ogni italiano si inchini dinanzi alle gravi ferite che hanno lacerato il sacro suolo della Patria.

L'Italia per il valore delle sue Forze Armate, per la decisa volontà di tutti i cittadini, ritroverà nel rispetto delle Istituzioni che ne hanno sempre confortata l'ascesa, la via della riscossa.

Italiani,

sono oggi più che mai indissolubilmente unito a voi dall'incrollabile fede nell'immortalità della Patria.

Firmato: **VITTORIO EMANUELE**
Controfirmata: **BADOGLIO**

Roma, li 25 luglio 1943

ON JULY 25 THE KING PROCLAIMED HIMSELF COMMANDER IN CHIEF

HITLER GREETED MUSSOLINI AFTER HIS RESCUE FROM JAIL AND SET HIM TO ORGANIZING, OF ALL THINGS, A "REPUBLIC" IN NORTHERN ITALY

AMERICAN COMBAT TEAMS OF THE FIFTH ARMY WADED ONTO THE ITALIAN MAINLAND AT SALERNO WHILE EMPTY BOATS (LEFT, BACKGROUND) PLOWED BACK

NAVY MEDICAL MEN COULD NOT HELP THIS SOLDIER HIT BY NAZI 88 SHELL

FOXHOLES WERE DUG ALONG SHORE TO SHELTER MEN FROM GERMAN

Salerno notched the narrow Italian coastal plain 185 miles north of Sicily—the most distant target Sicilian-based fighter aircraft could provide with effective cover during a landing. So Salerno it was, and a leathery piece of underbelly it turned out to be. Lieut. General Mark Clark's Fifth Army—100,000 British, 69,000 Americans—got ashore Sept. 9, 1943 after a brief, sharp fight. Real trouble arrived shortly when German reinforcements counterattacked from the north. The U.S. VI Corps was endangered when six battalions near the weak center were surrounded or severely mauled. In the crisis Eisenhower ordered the Strategic Air Force to lay off railroads and help the beachhead. Its very heavy attacks, plus tactical air and naval gunfire, helped turn the tide. On Oct. 1 British troops entered Naples, and the Germans withdrew behind the Volturno River, having suffered 8,000 casualties in one month (the Americans lost 4,947 in killed, captured and wounded, the British 7,272). Meanwhile Montgomery's Eighth Army—landing at Reggio Calabria on Italy's toe and Taranto on the heel—drove up and across to capture Foggia's prized airfields.

O THE FLEET FOR MORE TROOPS BOMB BURSTS BEHIND AMERICANS WHO WERE PINNED DOWN ON A WIRE LANDING MAT BY STRAFING PLANES

BOMBING AND SHELLING. LIMITED FLEET OF LANDING CRAFT WAS STRAINED TO BUILD UP THE ALLIED FORCE AGAINST STEADY GERMAN COUNTERATTACKS

GERMAN FLAK IN ITALY CLIPPED THE WING OF THIS CAREENING B-24

Ploesti was a great oil center 35 miles north of Bucharest, home of ten major refineries of the Romanian fields which produced 60% of Germany's crude oil. The Army Air Forces considered it Europe's prime strategic target and began planning the month after Pearl Harbor to bomb it out of the war. Some favored a small, high-altitude attack, but Operation Soapsuds finally evolved as a low-altitude massed raid. Just after dawn on Aug. 1, 1943, 177 four-engined B-24s took off from Bengasi, flying southeast of Italy's heel and across parts of Greece, Albania and Yugoslavia. Some of the five groups were detected but all courageously bored in at treetop height, through intense flak, balloon cables and high chimneys, as well as Messerschmitt fighters. Total losses were grave: 54 planes, 532 airmen; but about 42% of Ploesti's refining capacity was temporarily destroyed. This was indecisive, however, because the raid was not followed up; the Nazis rebuilt quickly and activated hitherto idle units.

CHIMNEY-HOPPING OVER PLOESTI'S REFINERIES, A BIG LIBERATOR BOMBER DIPS THROUGH THE TURBULENT SMOKE OF BURNING ROMANIAN OIL

A TIME EXPOSURE RECORDED THE FIREFLY PATTERN OF SHELLS BURSTING ON MT. TROCCHIO AS U.S. 105-MM. HOWITZERS (LEFT) RAKED THE PEAK

Winter line defenses of 1943–44, hastily built by the Germans 85 miles south of Rome, forced a long, dismal and costly campaign. It was a fight over mountain peaks like Camino, Trocchio and Sammucro—giant milestones along the road to Rome. General Alexander's tactics entailed a double envelopment of the Germans, by the Fifth Army on the left flank, the Eighth on the right. But Montgomery's attack bogged down after the Sangro crossing. The Fifth Army punched only 8 miles in a 61-day campaign ending Jan. 15, 1944 and costing 15,930 casualties. Field Marshal Albert Kesselring could choose the peaks and slopes which he wished to defend. Allied infantrymen (whose priority in Italy had always been second to strategic air) had seen Eisenhower, Tedder, Bradley and Montgomery leave Italy Dec. 24, 1943 (they were off to plot the favored Normandy invasion). "The forgotten war" was what foot soldiers in Italy began to call the most important event in their lives.

NEAR MIGNANO ARTILLERYMEN SWAB GUN AIMED AT MT. TROCCHIO

189

GERMAN-HELD MOUNTAINSIDE WAS SPLASHED WITH PHOSPHORUS SHELLS BY FIFTH ARMY ARTILLERY TO COVER THE RETURN OF A U.S. PATROL

THE HISTORIC ABBEY OF MONTE CASSINO WAS ENGULFED BY EXPLODING AMERICAN BOMBS DURING THE FIRST BIG SATURATION RAID ON FEB. 15

Cassino is a small town that lies at the entrance to the Liri Valley 75 miles below Rome on Highway 6. The first, probing attack upon it was launched on Jan. 15, 1944 by American troops, who were thrown back. Allied commanders decided that the 6th Century Benedictine abbey was being used by the Germans as an observation post and therefore must be destroyed. On Feb. 15 the first wave of 255 Allied bombers struck the famous religious sanctuary, and thousands of rounds of artillery helped blast it to bits. But as New Zealanders and Indians advanced up the hill it became clear that the scattered rubble only made the Germans' defense easier. A tremendous try one month later sent 388 heavy bombers and 176 mediums with 1,110 tons of bombs, and artillery fired 195,969 rounds against Cassino, but the German 1st Parachute Division proved again that well-dug-in soldiers with steel nerves don't break under excessive noise. Some of the bombing was bad; French corps headquarters, 12 miles from Cassino, was shattered by an entire formation of badly navigated heavy bombers. "A sobering shock" was what Lieut. General Jacob L. Devers, Alexander's deputy, called aviation's failure. After eight days the Allies conceded the imperturbable Nazi parachutists' victory. In May 1944 the Germans withdrew from Cassino, their supply lines having been effectively severed by the same planes which failed to drive them from the hillsides.

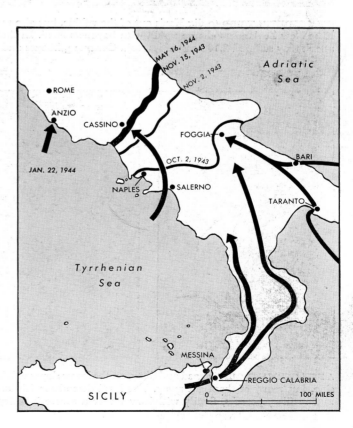

191

THE TANKMEN TRIED to blast their way into Cassino, but like aviation, artillery shells and most other modern inventions, the tanks proved relatively ineffective against the stouthearted defenders of the Nazi position.

INFANTRYMEN TRIED to dig Nazis out of the rubble, but also to no avail. Here New Zealanders charge uphill with bayonets fixed. In their second attack they suffered 2,106 casualties from German pillboxes and dugouts.

A FEW GERMANS QUIT, dazed and dirty, on the lower slopes of Monte Cassino, but many of them got away. The Nazi defenders withstood all air and artillery attacks, finally withdrew under a severe infantry assault.

CASSINO WAS A FIELD OF GRANULATED RUBBLE WHEN ALLIED ARMIES FINALLY

ENTERED. ABOVE THE TOWN THE FAMED MOUNT WAS BARE EXCEPT FOR SKELETON TREES AND A CROWN OF RUINS WHERE THE ANCIENT ABBEY HAD STOOD

A GERMAN SHELL SPLASHES DANGEROUSLY CLOSE TO A FLOTILLA OF DUKWs (AMPHIBIOUS TRUCKS) SHUTTLING IN AND OUT OF ANZIO BEACH AREA

Anzio was the Allies' gamble to relieve the forces stalled before Cassino. Although Churchill estimated the outflanking movement (120 miles up the coast from Salerno) would require only two divisions, 50,000 troops were aboard when the transports arrived off Anzio's shores Jan. 22, 1944. Surprise was achieved, and there was a brief opportunity to break through and disrupt German supply lines. But the U.S. corps commander stopped to consolidate his beachhead, and Kesselring—acting on Hitler's personal orders to lance the "abscess" that threatened Rome—rushed more than five crack divisions to Anzio. The counterattacking Germans slashed through the Allied lines almost to the beachhead defenses, but superior artillery and aviation helped check disaster. The offensive turned to grim holding-on. The slugging around the 35-mile perimeter continued for 123 days. What started as a three-division operation expanded finally to seven. Then on May 23 the troops broke through and joined the advancing Fifth Army for the march on Rome, justifying the whole overoptimistic operation.

SMOKE GENERATORS were used to make up for the lack of natural cover. Right flank of the beachhead was flat farmland created when the ancient, malarial Pontine Marshes were drained. In this reclaimed land foxholes were always wet.

AS U.S. FORCES STRUGGLED INLAND FROM ANZIO, SMOKE SHELLS WERE FIRED TO HIDE THEM FROM GERMAN GUNS IN THE SURROUNDING HILLS

SOLDIERS CROUCH behind road embankment to avoid enemy observation. Omnipresent German artillery led to the stooping "Anzio gait" and one of the war's highest psychoneurosis rates.

ANZIO EXPRESS was the nickname Americans gave this formidable 280-mm. railroad rifle which the Germans brought up during the latter part of the campaign. After it was pulled back "the big one" was knocked out by U.S. planes.

DEAD SOLDIERS were laid out on stretchers in muddy Anzio streets during February crisis. The awful month cost the American assault force 17% casualties. The British rate was 27%.

ANZIO'S CASUALTIES were 30,000 for Allies, nearly 30,000 for Germans. U.S. dead were 2,800, wounded 11,000. Third Infantry Division, which was most decorated U.S. outfit in World War II (39 Medals of Honor), was hit hardest.

GENERAL CLARK RODE IN TRIUMPH DOWN THE AVENUE FROM ST. PETER'S

Rome fell to the Allies June 4, 1944. "Why have you been so long in coming?" inquired the Italians. The GIs were no more amused than they were when the home folks asked how things were in "sunny Italy." But Rome was a happy rendezvous (*below*) after the mud, misery and chill of the previous 275 days in Italy. Was it all necessary? The richest prize, the Foggia airfields, had fallen to the Allies soon after Salerno. After that the most they could hope for was to pin down forces Hitler needed elsewhere. Instead of adjusting to that objective, the Allies kept trying the offensive, though the high command never committed sufficient troops to make the going in Italy anything but slow and costly. The Allied armies kept beating against German strongpoints almost to the end, 11 months after the political obligation was discharged at Rome. The cost: 21,389 American lives, 30,782 British.

THE ETERNAL CITY CHEERED ITS ALLIED CONQUERORS IN FRONT OF MONUMENT TO VICTOR EMMANUEL II, THE FIRST KING OF MODERN ITALY

War in the Mountains

FRENCH COLUMNS FOUGHT ACROSS THESE MOUNTAINS TO ESPERIA, HIDDEN IN THE BLUE HAZE AT THE BASE OF CONE-SHAPED MONTE D'ORO (LEFT)

MANY pleasant things have been said, written and sung about mountains, but not by the men who fought in Italy. From the landing beaches to the Gothic line and beyond, the Italian boot offered a succession of cruel, heavily defended coruscations often sheathed in snow, ice or numbing mud. General Alexander's Fifteenth Army Group, which included the U.S. Fifth and British Eighth Armies, fell heir to this grueling campaign. The group was a patchwork of United Nations forces—at one time or another its ranks included Americans, British, Canadians, French, New Zealanders, South Africans, Greeks, Indians, Brazilians, Italians, Poles, Algerians, Arabs, Goumiers and Senegalese. Among the U.S. troops were the Nisei—Americans of Japanese ancestry—who fought with great valor (and 30% casualties). The only real variety in Italy was in nationalities. All of Alexander's men knew the bitterness of a war that dragged on and on, from peak to bloodied peak.

RIDING INTO BATTLE, POILUS DISPLAYED THE SKEPTICAL GRINS OF VETERANS

197

BEYOND ESPERIA, FRENCH WERE CAUGHT IN SUDDEN ENEMY FIRE AND FELL BACK PAST A DISABLED TRUCK

IN LESS THAN A MINUTE NAZI SHELLS IGNITED

THESE photographs show what happened to some French troops one day in May 1944 along a road in the fortified hills between Cassino and the Tyrrhenian Sea. This was the setting: on May 11 General Alexander's order of the day was given to the French Expeditionary Corps. It specified the objective—to break the long stalemate along the Gustav line and in front of the Anzio beachhead. The French commander, General Alphonse Juin, read the order to his troops, many of them colonials, then added the touch of emotion which particularly appeals to French soldiers: "Having the honor of carrying our flag, you will achieve victory, as you have already done before, thinking of martyred France awaiting you and looking toward you. Forward into battle!" H-hour was scheduled one hour before midnight. Suddenly the night flared with a barrage of 1,000 guns thundering from Cassino to the sea. Moving out ahead of the other troops—the British on the right with orders to take Cassino, the Americans on their left attempting to open the way to Anzio—were the French and their Goumiers, Senegalese and Algerians. Some Americans went with them to man Sherman medium tanks. Allied warplanes rendered powerful support with attacks on supply lines and gun batteries. Within two days the attack led by the French had broken the Gustav line and pushed on to the Hitler line, which was turned quickly in the great sweep toward Rome. The road on which these pictures were made on May 18 is near the little town of Esperia, a cluster of stone houses at the foot of formidable Monte d'Oro on the Hitler line. The Germans were retreating, but as the French approached Esperia a sharp counterattack was launched which utilized 88-mm. guns, tanks and other tracked vehicles. One of the first German shells blew up a French light tank. A hundred shells followed in quick succession and seemed to lift the hill into the air. Then another hundred poured down on other vehicles. Finally the Algerians attacked and drove into the village, flushing the Germans out of the houses at bayonet point and taking many of them prisoner.

U.S. TANK PAUSED BY BODY OF A GERMAN WITH HIS LEFT ARM BLOWN OFF

VEHICLES ABANDONED AS FRENCH TOOK COVER   AFTER THE SHELLING STOPPED FRENCH OFFICER WITH A CANE RECONNOITERED THE SMOKY NO-MAN'S-ROAD

FRENCH CHAPLAIN STAYED BEHIND TO HELP MEN WOUNDED BY NAZI SHELLS   CHAPLAIN'S MEN CARRIED A CASUALTY TO SHELTER UNDER WRECKED VEHICLE

AFTER conquering Esperia, General Juin stood in the town square and told his men: "Now at last we are beginning to pay them back for 1940." As these photographs indicate, the price of redemption came high. In the Italian fighting the four French divisions and their attached units had 27,671 casualties—5,241 killed and 20,847 wounded, with 1,583 missing. Their losses amounted to one fourth as many as the Americans had suffered, and about half as many as those of British units which served in the Fifth Army. Juin's troops were about 20% French and 80% colonial.

Guadalcanal

inaugurated the Pacific "defensive-offensive." As a part of their drive south to sever the U.S.-Australian lifeline the Japanese started building an airfield at the edge of the Guadalcanal jungle. Alarmed Navy strategists convinced the Joint Chiefs of Staff, over vigorous objection by General MacArthur, who wanted to strike directly at Rabaul, that this island at the bottom of the Solomons ladder must be retaken first. The result was six months' savage fighting under fearful hardship, replete with malaria, snipers, air battles, dysentery, bombs and bombardment. The only trained amphibious troops in the Pacific—20,000 tough marines, most of them from the 1st Division—went ashore early in August 1942. Eventually the Japanese committed 36,000 troops against them and lost 600 planes; the U.S. used four divisions and much of its Navy. Three times the Japanese came within an inch of winning, but they never attacked full-scale until it was too late. In February 1943, after losing 24,000 men, they skillfully evacuated by ship the last 12,000. U.S. dead numbered 1,202 marines, 550 soldiers.

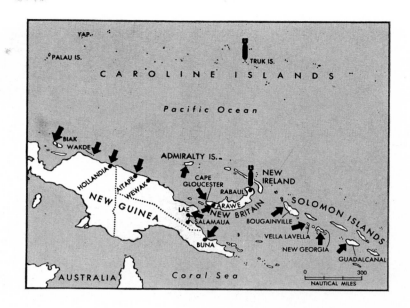

ON THE SHORE OF GUADALCANAL JAPANESE TRANSPORTS BRINGING IN REINFORCEMENTS WERE SET ABLAZE BY FLIERS FROM HENDERSON FIELD

MARINE COMMANDER on Guadalcanal was Major General A. A. Vandegrift. His troops made the first landings, held out in cut-and-thrust fighting until the Army came.

MATANIKAU RIVER was the marines' defense line west of the island's vital airstrip, Henderson Field. From Oct. 23 to 26 they killed more than 3,000 attacking Japanese and destroyed 10 light tanks which tried to cross the mouth of the river on a sand bar.

ARMY LANDED MASSES OF MEN AND MATERIAL AT LUNGA POINT IN DECEMBER WHEN MAJOR GENERAL ALEXANDER PATCH ASSUMED COMMAND

1ST MARINE DIVISION, RELIEVED AT LAST, WAITED FOR ITS TRANSPORTS. RIDDLED WITH MALARIA, DIVISION DID NOT FIGHT AGAIN FOR A YEAR

JAPANESE DEAD lie near the Tenaru River. They were part of first reinforcements landed by destroyers from Rabaul. Jap naval forces came south so regularly the marines nicknamed them the Tokyo Express.

JAPANESE TRANSPORT was bombed and beached while landing troops at Tassafaronga. Beyond wreck Savo Island can be seen across Iron Bottom Bay, so named because of many U.S. and enemy ships sunk there.

203

U.S. DESTROYERS SANK THREE ENEMY "CANS" IN A SHARP NIGHT BATTLE IN VELLA GULF. HERE "STERETT" FIRES ON AVENGING JAP BOMBERS

SOLDIER AIMS GRENADE AT JAP PILLBOX ON BOUGAINVILLE

Solomons

ladder to Rabaul took more than a year to climb. After Guadalcanal there was a five-month lull during which Japan's General Hitoshi Imamura strengthened his defenses until he had eight airfields. But U.S. strength was growing too, June 30–July 2, 1943 Admiral Halsey, the Solomons commander, landed troops on Rendova and New Georgia Islands. Unseasoned soldiers took five weeks to push five miles through New Georgia's jungle and capture Munda airstrip. On Aug. 15 U.S. Army and New Zealand troops performed the first island hopping in the South Pacific when they by-passed Kolombangara to land on Vella Lavella. Japanese attempts to reinforce, then evacuate, New Georgia and Kolombangara brought on two fierce night naval battles in which the enemy sank the cruiser *Helena* and two destroyers and put three more U.S. cruisers out of action for months. The Japanese lost only three ships. Only in the air was Allied superiority conclusive: in 1943 Halsey's Solomons fliers—Marine, Army, Navy, New Zealand—were better than the Japanese in every respect, and by December they had twice as many planes. It was by air, therefore, that the strategists decided to beat Rabaul. The Bougainville landing Nov. 1 put U.S. airfields on the top rung of the ladder, only 225 miles from Fortress Rabaul; now fighter cover could be provided for bombers which would neutralize Japan's greatest overseas bastion.

MARINES LANDED ON BOUGAINVILLE AT EMPRESS AUGUSTA BAY AND SEIZED JUST ENOUGH OF THE MUCKY ISLAND TO BUILD THREE AIRSTRIPS

SHIELDED BY A TANK INFANTRYMEN PUSHED SLOWLY THROUGH ROTTING, JAP-INFESTED JUNGLES AROUND THE BOUGAINVILLE BEACHHEAD

New Guinea

got a second scare in July 1942, two months after the Coral Sea battle, when the Japanese landed troops at Buna-Gona on the northeast coast. They marched over the towering Owen Stanley range toward Port Moresby, but Australians stopped their patrols 32 miles away. In October, Americans and Australians themselves started across the high mountains. The Buna-Gona campaign was fought in miasmic jungles. When green U.S. soldiers failed to take Buna in six weeks MacArthur sent a new general, Robert L. Eichelberger, to "take Buna or don't come back alive." He took it in January. The Japanese lost about 8,000 men. Allied dead (1,731 Australians, 787 Americans) outnumbered Guadalcanal's. In March of 1943 Army planes smashed a convoy in the Bismarck Sea, sinking 12 of 16 ships and drowning 3,600 intended reinforcements. Substantial progress up the New Guinea coast had to wait another year, until Rabaul was taken out.

EICHELBERGER AND AUSTRALIA'S GENERAL BLAMEY ENTER BUNA

FIRST ALLIED TANKS WERE LANDED NEAR BUNA IN DECEMBER AND LED AUSTRALIAN TROOPS AGAINST JAP BUNKERS IN THE COCONUT GROVES

TRYING TO ESCAPE BY SEA, LAST OF THE TRAPPED JAPANESE WERE KILLED ON THE BEACHES WHERE THEY HAD LANDED SIX MONTHS BEFORE

ONE OF THE FIRST PICTURES OF AMERICAN WAR DEAD TO BE RELEASED, THIS GRIM VIEW OF THE BEACH AT BUNA SHOCKED THE U.S. HOME FRONT

Rabaul was the keystone of the Japanese defense of both South and Southwest Pacific, and Rabaul died hard. Nippon's admirals even pulled their best pilots and planes off carriers and based them at Rabaul. Already there were stirrings in the Central Pacific, but after a brief foray into those waters the admirals reconsidered and decided to stake almost everything on Rabaul's defense (thereby taking the heat off the Gilberts). In October 1943 the all-out air assault on Rabaul began. Southwest Pacific bombers flattened most of the town, but otherwise produced only some wildly exaggerated claims (415 planes, 27 ships against an actual 80 and five). On Nov. 5 the Navy sent a carrier force that caught and crippled six cruisers which had come down from the fleet base at Truk to attack the Bougainville beachhead. Bougainville's airfields in December spawned strikes which destroyed 230 planes (700 were claimed) in the next two months and sank 12 transports. By Feb. 20, 1944 Rabaul was impotent and its last 120 planes were withdrawn. Landings on the other end of New Britain (Arawe, Cape Gloucester) and on Emirau, the Admiralties and Green Island completed the circle from which Rabaul was pounded the rest of the war. MacArthur now could push toward the Philippines and Nimitz could devote himself to the spectacular Central Pacific campaign.

CARRIER STRIKE AT RABAUL IN NOVEMBER SENT JAPANESE CRUISERS AND DESTROYERS STREAKING OUT OF THE HARBOR INTO THE OPEN SEA. U.S. PILOTS

AT BEACHLESS CAPE GLOUCESTER THE MARINES LANDED RIGHT IN THE JUNGLE

SHOT DOWN 25 JAP PLANES THAT ROSE FROM THE AIRSTRIP (RIGHT)

LSTs FED DECKLOADS OF SUPPLIES TO THE TROOPS SECURING CAPE GLOUCESTER

JAPANESE PLANE WITH TORPEDO SLUNG UNDER ITS BELLY SKIMS A SPLASH-BARRAGE IN ITS HEAD-ON FLIGHT TOWARD A U.S. CARRIER OFF TRUK

WOUNDED MAN IS HELPED FROM HIS PLANE AFTER CARRIER STRIKE

Truk was the most secret of all of Japan's many "islands of mystery"—the overseas home of the combined fleet, the Japanese Pearl Harbor. Scuttlebutt (later proved unfounded) said Truk had been fortified for 20 years. Part of the mystery was dispelled Feb. 4, 1944, when two Marine Corps Liberators got over the base and photographed it in all its strength: four battleships, including two mighty 64,000-tonners, four carriers, 11 cruisers, many destroyers and hundreds of land-based aircraft. Admiral Spruance immediately was ordered to take his Fifth Fleet 1,100 miles west from the newly captured Marshalls to trap this concentration of Japanese power. Spruance struck on Feb. 16–17 with 700 planes (the Fifth Fleet by now had 12 aircraft carriers), but Japan's Admiral Mineichi Koga, frightened by the photo planes, had scurried away with his battle fleet. Nevertheless Spruance's raid changed the course of the war. This most modest of admirals claimed only 200 Japanese planes and 23 ships—his actual total was 264 planes and 37 ships totaling 209,848 tons. The Joint Chiefs in Washington decided the planned five-division assault on Truk was unnecessary and substituted a landing in the Marianas, only 1,300 miles from Japan itself.

TORPEDO RAIDER trying to hit the new *Yorktown* disintegrates in flames under carrier's antiaircraft fire, then (*right*) splashes into the sea. This action occurred off Kwajalein a few weeks before daring February 1944

raid on Truk. The Truk raid was one of the war's most productive (in tonnage), but other early 1944 forays by the new carriers pounded enemy bases in the Palaus and Marianas, paved way for advance across Pacific.

NAVY YARD AT TRUK WAS FIRED (LEFT) DURING THE AMERICAN FOLLOW-UP RAID IN APRIL 1944 WHICH CLEARED THE BASE OF SHIPS AND PLANES

IN FEBRUARY 1944 STRIKE AT TRUK, U.S. AVENGER CIRCLES OVER A WEAVING JAP DESTROYER, ALREADY STRADDLED BY STRAFING (SPLASHES)

HELLCAT FIGHTER PUNISHES ANOTHER STRICKEN DESTROYER WHICH HAS BEEN RUN AGROUND ON A CORAL REEF TO KEEP HER FROM SINKING

War in the Jungle

SOME of the battles of World War II were fought in the hot desert, some in snow and some atop forbidding mountains. But none of these natural miseries could quite compare with the primeval jungles of Asia and the Pacific. More than a million Americans, British, Indians, Australians, New Zealanders, Fijians, Chinese—and Japanese—fought in the jungles, and the survivors will never forget its smell and feel and noise. At the beginning of the war only the never-seen enemy seemed able to master the brooding terrain. Learning came hard, but by the time Aaron Bohrod painted *Still Life Guadalcanal* (*above*), Japan's enemies had begun to learn, and Japanese bones and gas masks mingled with riddled American helmets around tree-root dugouts. Troops found that the white man could exist—and triumph—with the help of mosquito nets, atabrine and patient courage.

The Allied offensive in the Pacific followed two roughly parallel courses through some of Earth's densest jungles: Nimitz' South Pacific drive began in August 1942 at Guadalcanal, continued up the Solomons and was completed at Bougainville. MacArthur started three months later at Buna on the northern shore of the world's second largest island, New Guinea, moved up its coastal jungles and jumped to Morotai and the Philippines. In the early stages of both campaigns disease was as great an enemy as the Japanese. MacArthur's 41st Division, which spent the whole war in one jungle or another, had a malaria ratio of 361 cases per 1,000 men in New Guinea in 1942. By 1945, in the Philippines, the division ratio was reduced to 25 per 1,000 men. At the end it was the Japanese themselves who were left, cut off from civilization and resupply, to rot and starve in a hundred jungle settlements.

THE jungle is as inhospitable as the desert or the southeast corner of hell. The term "jungle" sometimes has been applied to landscape as innocuous as coconut groves or swatches of sharp *kunai* grass, but worst of all is the true rain forest. There the tropic sun cannot penetrate the overhead branches of the giant trees, and in the twilight there is a sliminess and an aura of decay that sours the nostrils. The jungle's great trees may be rotten to the core; on Cape Gloucester in New Britain 25 marines were killed by falling trees. When such a giant crashes the delicate balance of nature is upset. The sunlight which breaks through the gap quickly raises up huge clusters of shrubs, herbs and young trees. Then the great vines from the forest's upper reaches snake downward, joining the growth below to close the wet, green roof again. In such surroundings man is an unwelcome intruder. His blood is sucked by leeches, and he is set upon by scorpions, centipedes, fire ants and giant mosquitoes. His clothing mildews, his shoes rot, and so do patches of his own fungus-laden skin. His jackknife rusts in a single day. Even the mound of his grave is soon leveled by the unceasing rain.

THESE paintings (the one at left is the work of Japanese Artist Fukusei Aujita, the one below was done at Bougainville by the late Kerr Eby) convey the feeling of imprisonment which every man experienced in the jungle. Nature seemed to conspire with the enemy to trap the advancing force. Hidden in the vines, the Japanese could kill a man without detection from a distance of 15 feet. Hallucinations were common: a regiment on New Georgia lost 360 men to combat fatigue in one day—a fatigue born of the horror of the jungle itself and the menace of the unseen, undiscoverable enemy.

HUDDLED IN A CLEARING, MARINES COMMIT THE BODY OF THEIR SERGEANT TO THE JUNGLE IN WHICH HE WAS KILLED

IN A PRIMITIVE ARMY FIELD HOSPITAL A NURSE WITH A FLASHLIGHT MOVES AMONG THE SLEEPING VICTIMS OF THE JAPANESE—AND THE JUNGLE

IN THE FIRST CENTRAL PACIFIC INVASION MARINES ON TARAWA ATTACK ACROSS COCONUT-LOG SEA WALL AGAINST VICIOUS JAPANESE GUNFIRE

Central Pacific

just grew. Early in the war the road to victory against Japan apparently lay along the Solomons-New Guinea axis through the southern Philippines, thence on to Singapore, Burma and China (which would furnish bases to bomb Japan out of the war). The seizure of the Marshall Islands and Truk in the Carolines was scheduled, but its purpose was to tighten the communications line to Australia and break into Japan's inner defense line. By the middle of 1943, however, it was obvious that Rabaul, which was holding up the New Guinea advance, was tougher than anybody had envisioned. The U.S. Joint Chiefs of Staff, to whom the Allies had delegated Pacific responsibility, gave top priority to a westward advance across the great ocean. As a preliminary Admiral Nimitz was instructed in July of 1943 to seize the Gilbert Islands, a string of coral atolls that lie across the equator some 2,200 miles southwest of Hawaii. For Operation Galvanic, Nimitz asked General MacArthur to return the 1st Marine Division, which had been in Australia since Guadalcanal. But MacArthur planned to use the 1st to capture Rabaul, and he refused. Nimitz then decided to bring up the 2nd Marine Division from New Zealand and to employ elements of the 27th Infantry Division, then in training on Oahu. The soldiers were assigned the capture of lightly defended Makin Island. The marines drew Tarawa, an atoll whose main island, named Betio, was only one mile square.

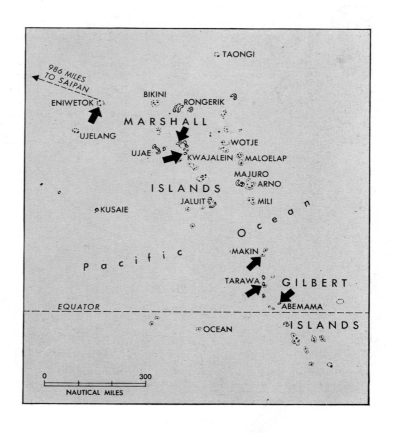

CROUCHING UNDER CROSSFIRE FROM THE MAZE OF JAP STRONGPOINTS ON TARAWA, MARINES CLIMBED THE SLOPES OF THIS SAND-BANKED BLOCKHOUSE AND,

TWO NAVY MEDICAL CORPSMEN IGNORE INTENSE JAPANESE FIRE TO CARRY A WOUNDED MARINE BACK TO THE AID STATION BELOW THE SEA WALL

Tarawa

had its D-day Nov. 20, 1943. Before the landing the remarkable total of 3,000 tons of bombs and naval gunfire—surely enough to kill every living thing—was poured upon the little island. But Tarawa's 4,836 defenders, dug in behind coconut-log pillboxes and concrete blockhouses (up to 96 inches thick), were undaunted. The first waves of marines wheeled through the water in new amphibian tractors. Subsequent waves learned the water over the reef was too shallow; their Higgins boats could not get in. The slow, half-mile trudge through the water began. Wading through murderous mortar and machine-gun fire, fortified only by a selfless devotion to duty and a sense of their own invincibility, the marines answered the call: "They need help bad on the beach." For 30 hours men were mowed down by the dozens, but more came on. Such was the battle discipline in the reinforcing waves that no man was seen to turn back from what appeared to be certain extinction. Once ashore, they piled over the sea wall with rifle, bayonet and flame thrower to weed out the determined defenders. After 76 hours it was over. The marines lost 990 killed, 2,296 wounded; but they dismissed forever the Japanese taunt that Americans were afraid to die.

FROM ITS TOP, FIRED AT ENEMY SOLDIERS ON OTHER SIDE

MARINE DEAD SPRAWLED ALONG THE INVASION BEACH NEAR A CRIPPLED AMERICAN TANK

JAP TANK WAS HIT NEAR SHELL-MARKED ENEMY COMMAND POST

JAPS COMMITTED HARA-KIRI BY FIRING RIFLES WITH THEIR BIG TOES

The Marshalls

had been Japanese since they were grabbed from Germany in World War I—a seizure later sanctioned by League of Nations mandate. As a consequence of Tarawa, Navy tacticians at Pearl Harbor were fearful, and also split: some wanted to start at Jaluit at the bottom of the chain and work up, but Nimitz voted with his chief planner Rear Admiral Forrest Sherman for plunging into the biggest and toughest of the atolls, Kwajalein. Assigned to the invasion were the Army's veteran 7th Infantry Division, to attack the southern end of the 60-mile-long atoll, and the new 4th Marine Division, to capture the twin islands of Roi and Namur in the north. The landing (Jan. 31, 1944) was preceded by a shelling from 50 warships and a bombing from the planes of 12 carriers plus aircraft based in the newly won Gilberts—total: 15,000 tons of hot steel. The new underwater demolition teams went in first to blow paths in the reefs and to clear beach obstacles. Artillery was set up on nearby small islands before the principal targets were assaulted. The Army introduced the wonderful amphibious truck, the DUKW (duck). Thus the lessons of indispensable Tarawa, written in the blood of 3,000 marines, saved other thousands. Although those of the 8,500 Japanese who survived the gunfire fought to the death, Kwajalein Atoll cost the lives of only 356 soldiers and marines. Such success caused Rear Admiral Richmond Kelly Turner, the operation's amphibious commander, to move on to Eniwetok, westernmost of the Marshalls, on Feb. 17—three months ahead of the Pacific timetable. Eniwetok's 3,400 defenders were killed at a cost of 247 Americans. From the new Marshalls bases heavy bombers were soon bombing the Marianas to the west and Truk to the south.

ON THE BEACHES OF NAMUR IN KWAJALEIN ATOLL, GREEN MARINES OF

UNMINDFUL OF ENEMY BODIES, SOLDIERS OF THE ARMY'S 7TH DIVISION PAUSED TO EAT C-RATIONS DURING THE FOUR-DAY FIGHT FOR KWAJALEIN

THE 4TH DIVISION ENCOUNTERED ENEMY FIRE FOR THE FIRST TIME BUT CLEARED THE ISLAND OF ITS OBSTINATE JAPANESE DEFENDERS IN ONLY TWO DAYS

AFTER ENIWETOK BATTLE A MARINE IS HELPED ABOARD HIS SHIP

ANOTHER EXHAUSTED MAN COMES BACK, FACE BLACK WITH DIRT

221

USING THE MASSIVE BUILDING TOOLS OF AMERICA, THE SEABEES MOVED MOUNTAINS OUT OF THE WAY OF THE U.S. ADVANCE ACROSS THE PACIFIC

ENGINEERS STAKE OUT FUTURE SEAPLANE RAMPS UNDERWATER

Seabees magically reshaped the coral-pocked face of the Pacific; their wand was the 20-ton bulldozer. Landing not far behind the infantry assault waves in almost every atoll or jungle operation, they blasted away reefs to make channels for the fleet, leveled hills and laid down landing strips in their place, lashed pontoons together to create artificial docks and brought to many a remote Pacific isle its first roads and hospitals. On more than one occasion they used their bulldozers to entomb nests of enemy snipers who were menacing Marine or Army mop-up squads. The naval construction battalions—official name for the Seabees (CBs)—had as their core many master craftsmen too old for the infantry, men with a zeal that matched their skill. Their advanced age led the marines (average age: 20) to crack, "Never hit a Seabee—he may be your grandfather." There were Seabees in all the war theaters, but the Pacific was their own great, big dish.

YOUNG SEABEES' MUSCLES CARRIED OUT THE OLDER MEN'S ORDERS

SEABEES USE AN AIR HOSE TO BORE OUT A HOLE FOR A DOCK TIMBER

A FEW DAYS AFTER ENIWETOK FELL SEABEES HAD CLEARED AN AIRSTRIP FOR U.S. BOMBERS, SOON WERE WIDENING IT (ABOVE) FOR MORE TO COME

SEABEE TRUCKS HAULED WHITE CORAL TO ENIWETOK AIRFIELD, BULLDOZERS GRADED IT AND ROLLERS TAMPED IT DOWN FOR THE RUNWAYS

SEABEES EMPLOYED THEIR FAVORITE WEAPON TO CLEAR AWAY NATIVE HUTS ON ULITHI. THEY BUILT NEW AND BETTER VILLAGE FOR NATIVES

IX

Invasion

D-day, 1944

VICTORY is a matter of massing an overwhelming weight of men, metal and high explosive against the enemy at the right place and the right time; from the middle of 1943 on, the U.S. began to deliver the tonnage where it was needed. The shipping situation had ceased to be critical. The ocean arteries of traffic were more secure east and west out of American ports into the distant theaters of war. The British Isles were stocked with sufficient raw materials not only to cover the needs of the civilian population but to allow British industry and transport to play their parts in preparing the expedition being mounted in England to blast a breach in the Westwall. Preceded by immense stocks of food and munitions, American troops had been pouring into England. When the decision was finally made to appoint General Eisenhower chief of Operation Overlord, he found himself in command of Allied forces which by June 1, 1944 were to total nearly three million men.

The preliminary work of charting the invasion had been under way for some time by an Anglo-American staff under a competent British officer, Lieut. General Frederick E. Morgan, who had been planning to land three divisions of British, American and Canadian troops. Eisenhower immediately suggested that the expedition be increased to five divisions. The plan was to land on the beaches of the Seine estuary under cover of intensive bombing from the air and shelling from the fleet; to storm the bluffs, and to nip off the port of Cherbourg on the Cotentin Peninsula. Once Cherbourg was cleared men and supplies could be poured into France for a rapid advance against the Wehrmacht.

IT was a plan of such danger and difficulty as to sober the most sanguine strategist. Troops untried under fire were being thrown against experienced Germans. The climate was an implacable enemy. The English Channel is one of the uneasiest bodies of water in the world. Only in early summer would there be hope of enough smooth weather to make the landings possible. The tide and the moon had to be right. The planners tried to foresee every eventuality. To guard against delay in the capture of a usable port, a series of complete floating harbors known in the code language of the time as "mulberries" and "gooseberries" were constructed in Britain. Cement caissons and metal pontoons were to be towed across the channel and sunk in line to form breakwaters to give the supply point a lee against the waves. Pipelines for fuel would be constructed, ready to drop on the channel bottom. Landing ships with bow ramps and a variety of amphibious vehicles were to be used. In the technical problems that arose the sober schooling of the British members of the team was admirably complemented by the buoyant improvisation of the Americans. It was General Eisenhower's job in heading up SHAEF (Supreme Headquarters, Allied Expeditionary Force) to set all this complicated machinery in motion and to keep it in motion against the snares and defenses of the German.

The moment for invasion was better chosen than anybody on our side knew at the time. The defenses of Europe were cracking from within. The Communist policy of cooperation with the United Nations, which had resulted from Roosevelt's friendly chats and his concessions to Stalin at Teheran, was welding together the discordant wings of the resistance movement so that for the first time the French were giving German communications serious trouble. Rifts were appearing in the German command itself. Appalled by the dogged imbecilities of Hitler's Russian strategy, civil and military officials had become involved in a conspiracy culminating in the attempted assassination of the Führer on July 20, 1944. In the immediate defense of the channel coast German military efficiency was hampered by the fact that Rommel and von Rundstedt had overlapping commands and that neither one of them could make important decisions without consulting Hitler. Hitler in defeat was more than ever his own general staff.

WHILE the British-American campaign of saturation bombing, even when it increased in intensity to the point where thousand-plane raids became a commonplace, was not proving as effective against German production as its proponents had hoped, it was wearing down the Luftwaffe. Like all dictatorships under the pressure of disaster, Hitler's government was degenerating into a writhing coil of intrigue and hatred. German industry continued capable of equipping great fighting forces but the will behind it was becoming confused. The Wehrmacht was still a dangerous foe, but the leadership was breaking. Men around Hitler centered all the hope that remained to them in two new weapons: V-1, a self-propelled flying bomb, and V-2, a long-range rocket with which they hoped to disrupt morale in England and boost morale at home.

If the military effectiveness of the destruction of the German cities was to remain a debatable question (the ethical questions it raises are greater and more terrible), there is no doubt at all about the success of the tactical bombing of German communications in preparation for D-day. The purpose was roughly to seal off the western promontory of France between the River Seine to the northeast and the River Loire to the south by destroying bridges and railroad yards and keeping important highway intersections under constant hammering from the air. The German commanders had to sit helpless in their headquarters and watch the destruction of the communications between their armies which the Luftwaffe no longer had the power to prevent.

Although the essential strategy of the Normandy landings had been laid down in the conferences of 1943 (Stalin had promised an offensive from the east a few days after the landings—a promise which he punctiliously carried out), the detail decisions were left to SHAEF, now established in Bushy Park just out of London. It was up to Eisenhower to make the decision, against substantial British advice, that, in spite of the great hazard of the operation, two American airborne divisions must be landed on the Cotentin Peninsula behind the westernmost invasion beaches. It was up to Eisenhower to make the final irrevocable decision that the landings, postponed from June 4 by a violent storm, would have to begin during the short space of clear skies and calm seas predicted for the morning of June 6. On the evening of June 5 he drove around the airfields at Newbury, headquarters of the 101st Airborne, to talk to the paratroopers who were waiting—with blackened faces—to take off on this desperate mission. The supreme commander watched the unarmed C-47s and their helpless glider tows go growling up the airstrips, plane after plane by the hundreds, as they took off for Normandy. Then he went back to advanced GHQ near Portsmouth to wait.   —JOHN DOS PASSOS

AT AN ENGLISH AIRFIELD AMERICAN BOMBER CREWMEN ARE BRIEFED ON TARGET OF THEIR NEXT MISSION OVER NAZI-HELD "FORTRESS EUROPE"

KEPT ALIVE AT HIGH ALTITUDES BY OXYGEN MASKS, RADIO OPERATOR AND ENGINEER OPERATE WAIST GUNS OF A B-17 AGAINST NAZI FIGHTERS

War in the Air

HEAVY WITH BOMBS FOR THE CONTINENT, AMERICAN FLYING FORTRESSES RISE FROM AN EIGHTH AIR FORCE FIELD IN A RURAL SECTION OF ENGLAND

THE airplane was the most romantic weapon universally used in World War II. The men who flew it, under all flags, were cocky, confident and passionately certain that airpower meant victory. In the first days of the European war the terror from the air hardly seemed exaggerated: Warsaw crumpled under Hitler's bombers and the Stukas blazed fiery trails for the Panzers. Many Americans were misled by the vision of a war in which a few thousand highly skilled young men would soar through the "wild blue yonder," drop their bombs unerringly from 5 miles and then leisurely return to base as the enemy struggled with fires, explosions and his own panicky desire to surrender. When the Nazi air blitz descended on London in the summer of 1940 the valiant British fighter pilots proved it wasn't that easy—even for Hitler's experienced and ruthless Luftwaffe.

While the rest of the warring nations were learning the possibilities (and the limitations) of airpower in actual combat, U.S. air strategists were experimenting with a prewar theory. This theory, which soon hardened into a fundamental concept, held that the most effective way to use long-range aircraft was for precision bombing in daylight. This sort of hazardous operation obviously would require a rugged aircraft. The Army Air Forces felt it had one in the B-17, the "Flying Fortress," with another one on the way—the B-24 "Liberator." Soon after Pearl Harbor the Air Forces got ready to test both its theory and its planes.

As rapidly as possible the Eighth Air Force was built up on that greatest of stationary aircraft carriers, England. The British, who had tried daylight raids and given them up as too costly, were skeptical (*p. 237*). But the Eighth persisted, and on Aug. 17, 1942, 12 B-17s flew the first mission, against Rouen, where Joan of Arc was burned at the stake. A little less than two months later the Eighth was ready to try a big one: 108 B-17s and B-24s attacked heavy industries at Lille. Contrary to the highly inflated reports at the time, these raids didn't do much damage; on the other hand, the American airmen were new at a game which the British and Germans had been practicing for about three years. They got better as they went along.

Before many months had passed the Fortresses were rising from new airstrips in many out-of-the-way corners of England (*above*). Early in the campaign the U.S. command began adjusting to a hard reality, which forced modifications in the original theory of daylight bombing. The fact was that unaccompanied long-range bombers could not successfully defend themselves from interceptor planes. When, on Oct. 14, 1943, the Germans knocked down 60 of 291 Fortresses over Schweinfurt, deep-penetration raids were called off. In 1944, with the arrival of the long-range P-51 fighter, they were resumed and the Eighth Air Force made up for lost time. Of all bombs dropped on Germany by the Allies in six years of war, 72% rained down on Hitler's Reich in the last ten months.

WAIST-GUNNER LOOKS ALONG HIS SIGHTS FOR NAZI PLANES IN THE EARLY MORNING SKY

NAVIGATOR LOOKS ACROSS HIS AERIAL MAPS AT THE BOMBER'S ENGINES AND A SISTER B-17

Main weapon of the Eighth Air Force bomber strategists was the B-17, which for three years sought out its distant targets through the bright, flak-filled skies of Europe. Flying in majestic, stepped formations (*left*), the B-17s were an awe-inspiring sight. First flown in 1935, the B-17 was improved until it could carry three tons of bombs for 1,100 miles at a speed of 220 mph. As German fighters made more and more kills, the Fortress sprouted more and more gun turrets on back, belly, nose, chin and tail until it boasted 13 .50-cal. machine guns. Even this heavy fire-power did not prove an adequate defense against the German interceptors, and fighter pilots accounted for most of the 30,700 German planes destroyed in the war. Americans got 20,000, British about half as many (against some 57,000 claimed).

FLARE bursts from returning bombers (*above*) meant wounded aboard. These planes were cleared to come in ahead of others so that immediate medical aid could be administered. The Flying Fortress proved to be a very tough plane, capable of withstanding tremendous punishment from German fighters and antiaircraft guns. The newspaper reader in the U.S. faced almost daily a photograph of a bomber sawed nearly in half or minus a huge section of wing, but still flying under its own power. The high casualty rate among bomber crews prompted the command to give airmen home leave after they had flown 25 missions. Similarly, to help maintain morale, the Air Forces distributed medals more than ten times as generously (per combat death) as any other service. Combat casualties totaled 63,881 men, of whom about 40% were killed. The U.S. lost 9,949 bombers and 8,420 fighters; had 8,000 more bombers damaged beyond repair, making the cost of dropping a ton of bombs on Germany about $28,000.

Pointblank

was code name given to the combined bomber offensive authorized at Casablanca to bring about "the progressive destruction and dislocation of the German military, industrial and economic system" and the collapse of Nazi morale. This decision for a 'round-the-clock offensive—Eighth Air Force by day, R.A.F. by night—settled the long, bitter argument between British and Americans over the efficacy of daylight raids. Air Marshal Sir Arthur Tedder and Major General Carl Spaatz (*below*) were designated to mastermind Operation Pointblank. Earlier the Eighth Air Force daylight raiders had concentrated on submarine construction yards and pens. When surface craft and air patrols ended the U-boat menace, bomber pilots were glad to turn to aircraft factories and oil refineries. There followed an all-out battle with the German air force in which the Allies were temporarily driven from the skies above much of Germany (they still had superiority over the Low Countries and in France). When the combined offensive began in June 1943, deep-penetration raids by daylight were still impossible, but late that year the Fifteenth Air Force, operating from Italian bases, began reaching across the Alps to strike aircraft plants in southern Germany. Early in 1944 the advent of the long-range fighter at what General H. H. Arnold called "just the saving moment" turned the tide. The far-flying P-51s not only protected the big bombers; they sought out the enemy. This consolidated Allied air superiority before D-day and almost nullified the ability of the once-vaunted Luftwaffe to prevent deep bombing raids. As the end neared the combined offensive began to pay off: German oil production dropped 90% in six months; transportation took a 75% loss in five months, and Ruhr steel was 80% knocked out in three months.

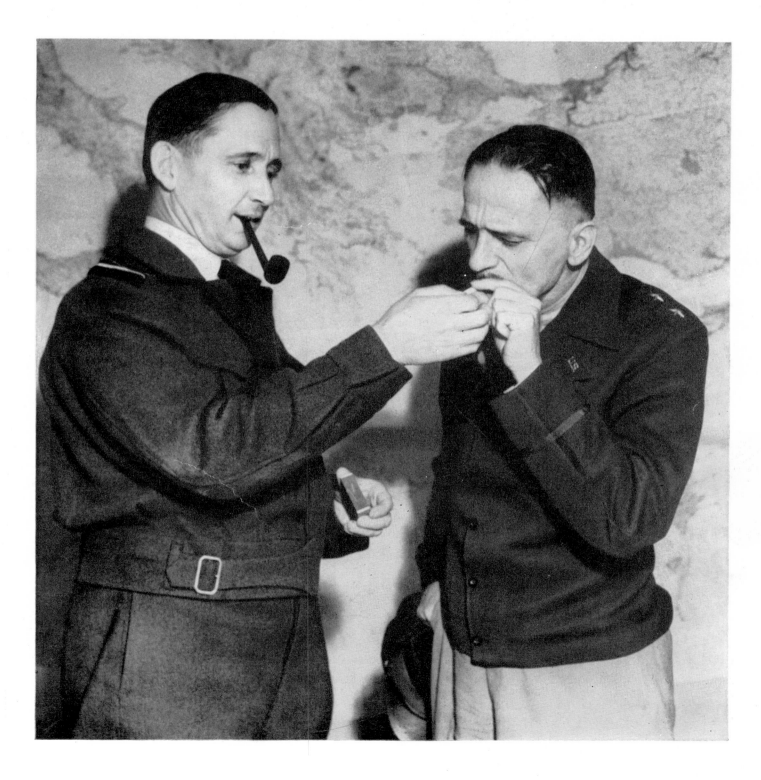

A GUN-CAMERA VIEW of Western Europe was provided by the Allies' tactical aircraft during the weeks just prior to D-day in Normandy. In that period all available planes were given tactical missions. This simply meant that they were assigned to clear the way for the soon-to-arrive ground forces, and then support the troops once the beachhead was established. No single outfit in this line of work compiled a more spectacular record than the Ninth (tactical) Air Force, commanded by Major General Hoyt S. Vandenberg. Between May 1 and June 6, 1944 the Ninth flew some 35,000 sorties, attacking from low levels enemy airfields, railroad yards, coastal gun positions, bridges and moving trains. Some of these targets appear in the pictures above, made by the pilots as they swooped

low to strafe or bomb. The fighters and bombers of the Eighth and Fifteenth (strategic) Air Forces joined in this massive attack, and the ultimate effort involved more than 7,000 Allied planes—just about everything that could fly. Although the tactical offensive proved generally effective—on some of the Normandy beaches troops got ashore without any serious opposition—there were the occasional tragedies which always are inevitable in the confusion of war. In some areas Frenchmen failed to heed leaflet warnings to evacuate prospective target zones, and a few days after D-day U.S. planes miscalculated and rained bombs on our own lines. This tragic error cost the lives of 88 men of the 30th Infantry Division and of Lieut. General Lesley McNair, the chief of U.S. ground forces.

"FLAK ALLEY" was a dead-end street for many Allied bombers. Planes like this B-24 Liberator flew through skies dotted with the grotesque black puffs of exploding ack-ack shells. The heaviest concentrations often caught the raiders when they were making their bomb runs—that moment when the automatic pilot guided the ship and evasive action was impossible. German antiaircraft probably was the best in the world, and it was accurate up to 25,000 feet, even through heavy overcast. Pilots could not get above it and still bomb effectively. Sometimes half the planes in a U.S. formation would suffer damage, and bombers which straggled behind the formation became easy prey for German fighters.

236

Attack by Night

THREE STIRLING BOMBERS OF THE R.A.F. FLY INTO THE DEEPENING DUSK TO DEPOSIT THEIR NIGHTLY TONNAGE OF INCENDIARIES ON GERMAN CITIES

T HE R.A.F., which was so brilliant in its victory over the Luftwaffe in the Battle of Britain, also first carried the war to Hitler's homeland. In 1940, standing alone against the Nazi menace, not knowing when, if ever, they would muster enough strength to invade the Continent, the British struck back with the only weapon at their command. The R.A.F. bravely tried daylight bombing against industrial targets. The experiment proved to be a costly failure. The British never forgot; the experience was the basis of all their disbelief of American hopes for daylight operations later in the war. Next the R.A.F. tried attacking strategic industries at night but, unable to find the targets, they abandoned that effort too. Then in 1942 the British turned to "area raids" on urban and industrial centers. In Operation Millennium, on May 30, 1943, the R.A.F. mounted its first 1,000-bomber mission—an attack on Cologne. Within an hour and a half the British unloaded 1,455 tons of bombs—two thirds

of them incendiaries—and 600 acres of the city were devastated. Two nights later the Ruhr city of Essen was given the same treatment. But it was not until a year later that the area raids reached their spectacular climax. In late July and early August of 1944 the R.A.F. pounded Hamburg mercilessly (*next page*). The shock effect was terrific. With one third of the city's homes destroyed, 60,000 or more people killed, little Joseph Goebbels told his diary —but not the German people—"A city of a million inhabitants has been destroyed in a manner unparalleled in history." Although Hamburg regained 80% of its preraid productive capacity within five months, there was little that Hitler could do about the deep scars on German morale. Much of the hope of victory lay buried in the rubble of Hamburg. These results were not obtained cheaply. The British lost 22,010 planes to enemy action, and in the course of the war had 79,281 airmen killed, wounded or captured—considerably more than the AAF, which was in action only half as long.

GUARDED BY GUNS ON ALSTER RIVER, HAMBURG LIES QUIET UNDER A MOONLIT SKY, THEN EXPLODES IN FIREWORKS AS SEARCHLIGHTS CATCH AN R.A.F. SCOUT PLANE

AN AERIAL MINE EXPLOSION LIGHTS UP HAMBURG, THEN FADES, LEAVING A DELICATE TRACERY OF FLAK AGAINST THE SMOKE OF ROARING FIRES ON THE SKYLINE

LOOMING OVER THE SUBURBS OF BERLIN, FORTIFIED FLAK TOWERS ARE SILHOUETTED BY FIRES AS A LARGE AERIAL MINE EXPLODES AND SEARCHLIGHTS CRISSCROSS

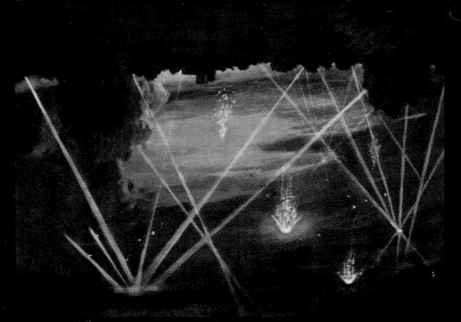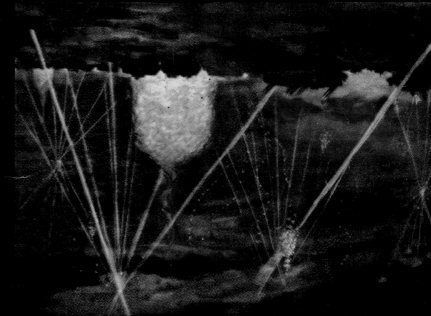

EXPLODING MINE BECOMES A MIGHTY BULGE OF FIRE ON THE BERLIN HORIZON AND FROM THE POTSDAM GARDENS (RIGHT) WHOLE SKY SEEMS TO HAVE TURNED RED

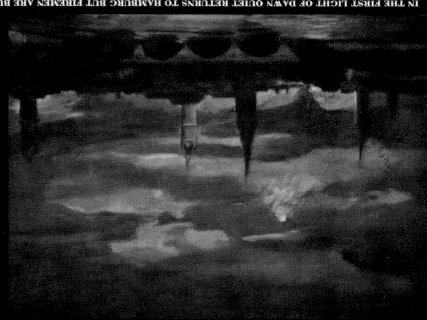

IN THE FIRST LIGHT OF DAWN QUIET RETURNS TO HAMBURG BUT FIREMEN ARE BUSY (RIGHT) POURING WATER FROM STREET AND ROOFTOP ON A FLAMING WAREHOUSE

R.A.F. SIGNAL FLARES (WHICH GERMANS CALLED "CHRISTMAS TREES") CAST A GLOW ON CHURCH TOWERS AND MASSIVE CONCRETE ANTIAIRCRAFT EMPLACEMENTS

THE Germans fought back against the night-raiding British as best they could, with searchlights, antiaircraft and interceptors (*above*), but the bombers finally prevailed. Thirty-one German cities had 500 acres or more destroyed: Berlin 6,437 (ten times as much as London), Hamburg 6,200, Dusseldorf 2,003, Cologne 1,994. One quarter of the tonnage of bombs dropped on Germany (1,461,864 tons by the U.S., 1,235,609 by the R.A.F.) fell on the cities. About 305,000 German civilians were killed, 780,000 wounded and 7,500,000 made homeless. These raids were primarily intended to destroy the morale of German civilians in the big centers. How well they succeeded remains a controversial question. The U.S. strategic-bombing survey, set up by President Roosevelt in 1944 to determine what actually had been

accomplished, calculates that morale *was* affected—three fourths of all Germans thought the war was lost by 1944, but how much bombing contributed cannot be measured. Unbombed cities had 51% willing to surrender; bombed cities, only 58%. The daylight precision raids, with their numbing effect on German industry, undoubtedly contributed to this defeatism. Although Eighth Air Force claims usually exceeded performance (in the 1942 raid on Lille the Eighth claimed 57 German planes, actually got only two), by 1944 performance was good enough, as the production collapse indicates. Both the AAF and the R.A.F. learned from each other: in the last months the British began flying daylight missions, and against Japan a year later the U.S. strategic air forces switched to area attacks to burn out hidden, cottage industries.

Men and matériel

were gathered in such unprecedented quantities that wags insisted England would sink but for the barrage balloons. In 1943 the U-boats in the Atlantic sank only three million tons while 19 million tons were abuilding, and the great preparation for D-day began, of which a 15,000-man *Queen Mary* load of troops (*below*) was only a fractional part. In July 1943, with D-day still nearly a year away, 753,000 tons of supplies poured through British ports; by May 1944 this volume reached 1,950,000 tons. Covered storage space occupied 20 million square feet; uncovered, 44 million. Jammed into the United Kingdom were 2,876,000 troops: 39 combat divisions (20 U.S.,

14 British, three Canadian, one Polish, one French). The stream of American combat divisions had begun to flow in the fall of 1943. It continued until D-day at the rate of two divisions per month (some were routed through the assault training center at Woolacombe). In the U.S. 40 more divisions got ready to sail as called, and 10 Allied divisions (seven French, three American) got ready to move from the Mediterranean into the south of France. For the air attacks 163 'dromes were built in England. Fifty thousand military vehicles were assembled; 170 miles of new railroad were laid down to shift the supplies, and 1,000 locomotives and 20,000 railroad cars were sent over for transfer to the Continent. For the U.S. Army alone 124,000 hospital beds were sent to England.

IN ENGLAND THE U.S. MASSED WEAPONS FOR INVASION. HERE, ROWS OF 105-MM. HOWITZERS ARE SURROUNDED BY HOODED ANTIAIRCRAFT GUNS

ALONG A COUNTRY ROAD TREES SHELTERED AN AMMUNITION DUMP FROM NAZI AIR RECONNAISSANCE. EACH STEEL BAY HELD 32 TONS OF SHELLS

AWAITING D-DAY IN AN ENGLISH MOTOR PARK, A DOUBLE LINE OF U.S. TRUCKS STRETCHED, FENDER TO FENDER, AS FAR AS THE EYE COULD SEE

BEFORE DISPERSAL, CENTRAL DEPOT WAS PILED WITH PREFABRICATED MATERIALS FOR BARRACKS IN FRANCE. AT LEFT ARE NISSEN HUT SECTIONS

243

IN 1944 THE END OF AMERICA'S GREAT AUTOMOTIVE ASSEMBLY LINE WAS IN BRITAIN, WHERE THE U.S. CONCENTRATED THE LARGEST NUMBER OF MILITARY

VEHICLES IN HISTORY FOR THE INVASION. AT LEFT ARE SHERMAN TANKS; COVERING THE PLAIN ARE HALF-TRACKS, PRIME MOVERS OF BOTH MEN AND GUNS

TANK CARS BUILT IN THE U.S. WERE ASSEMBLED IN BRITAIN. IN FRANCE THEY HAULED FUEL WHICH CROSSED CHANNEL IN UNDERWATER PIPES

AS AMERICAN AIR FORCES "BEEFED UP" FOR D-DAY, FIGHTERS AND ATTACK BOMBERS WERE SENT TO BRITAIN IN SECTIONS FOR FINAL ASSEMBLY

Supreme command

of Overlord was given to the country supplying the most troops. First choice was General George C. Marshall, but at the last moment Roosevelt told him, "I feel I could not sleep at night with you out of the country," and picked Eisenhower, who took over in London on Jan. 14, 1944. Sea and air commanders, Admiral Bertram Ramsay and Air Marshal Trafford Leigh-Mallory, were British, as was Eisenhower's deputy, Air Marshal Tedder. In initial operations Field Marshal Montgomery commanded the ground forces, but three months after the landing the two army groups, his and Lieut. General Bradley's, each reported directly to Eisenhower (*above, left to right:* Bradley, Ramsay, Eisenhower, Montgomery, Tedder, Leigh-Mallory and the supreme commander's chief of staff, Major General Walter Bedell Smith). Inevitably, differences arose. Strategic airmen wanted to keep their long-range bombers independent of Eisenhower, but he got his way—and all the planes. Underlying some of the differences was the American policy of giving generals freedom of action, as against the British system which forced even top commanders to clear nearly every move with London headquarters, which had to clear, frequently, with the ubiquitous Prime Minister. Eisenhower's mission as handed down by the Combined Chiefs of Staff was broad and simply worded: "Enter the continent of Europe and . . . undertake operations aimed at the heart of Germany and the destruction of her armed forces." The mission worked out this way: land in Normandy, pursue the enemy on a broad front gaining necessary ports, destroy his forces west of the Rhine, envelop the Ruhr and clean out the remainder of Germany. First and worst in this program was the cross-channel operation, and Eisenhower and Montgomery insisted that the assault include at least five divisions landing from the sea, immediately followed by two more, with three airborne divisions dropped behind the beach. The invasion area was to be carved into a strategic island by a massive air assault on locomotive depots, airfields, coastal batteries, radar stations and bridges over the Seine, Somme and Loire.

Landing craft

had to be assembled which could carry simultaneously 20,111 vehicles and 176,475 men. Powerfully motored, shallow-draft boats and ships which could put tanks and trucks ashore were unknown until just before the war; amphibious assault on heavily defended shores was considered insane, anyway. Such craft were foreign to the world's boat yards; priorities were too low. Finally in late 1943 Production Chief Donald Nelson declared that LSTs and LCTs were "the most important single instrument of war [in] the European theater." Irked by the thorny problem, General Marshall declared, "Prior to the present war I never heard of any landing craft except a rubber boat. Now I think of little else." After two annoying years Churchill observed (to Assistant Secretary of War John McCloy) in April 1944, "The destinies of two great empires . . . seemed to be tied up by some God-damned things called LSTs, whose engines themselves had to be tickled on by . . . LST engine experts of which there was a great shortage." Eventually Operation Overlord had enough bottoms, but no more than enough: 9,000 ships and landing craft protected by 702 warships and 25 minesweeper flotillas.

AT THE DOCKSIDE CHAPLAIN BLESSED THE MEN BOARDING INVASION SHIPS

DECKS WERE JAMMED WITH ARMY TRUCKS AND SOLDIERS IN COMBAT GEAR

AT AN ENGLISH PORT A MOTORIZED ARTILLERY DETACHMENT BOUND FOR

NORMANDY ROLLED OVER THE RAMPS INTO THE CAVERNOUS HULLS OF LSTs. THE INVASION FLEET INCLUDED 233 OF THESE 2,200-TON OCEAN-GOING VESSELS

Airborne

planners embarked three divisions in a total of 1,384 transports and 867 gliders. The 6th British was to drop near Caen and protect the left flank while securing the bridges over the Orne. On the right the U.S. 82nd and 101st planned to land about 6 miles beyond Utah beach, near Ste.-Mère-Eglise and Carentan. Five months of planning had to be partially revised one week before D-day when it was learned that Hitler had personally ordered his 91st Division into the target zone of the 82nd. The area had been covered by machine guns and mortars and booby-trapped with "Rommel asparagus," poles strung with wires which tripped Teller mines. The 82nd's drop zone was shifted a number of miles to the east.

U.S. PARATROOPS WITH THEIR FACES CAMOUFLAGED WAITED FOR TAKE-OFF

ON EVE OF D-DAY PARATROOP UNITS MARCHED OUT TO BOARD THEIR C-47

POISED ON RUNWAYS, DOUBLE COLUMN OF TROOP-CARRYING BRITISH GLIDERS WERE FLANKED BY HALIFAX BOMBERS THAT WERE TO TOW THEM TO NORMANDY.

TRANSPORT PLANES. AIRBORNE SOLDIERS LED THE INVASION, DROPPING INTO BATTLE AN HOUR BEFORE THE AERIAL BOMBARDMENT OF NORMANDY STARTED

ALL OF THEM BORE SPECIAL STRIPE MARKINGS OF OPERATION OVERLORD

TROOPS PLUNGED INTO BATTLE AS SOON AS THE GLIDERS LANDED IN FRANCE

PARACHUTE SILK SHROUDED EIGHT SOLDIERS KILLED IN A GLIDER CRACK-UP

FROM THE AIR, enemy coast defenses and beach obstacles were attacked by 2,219 bombers and fighter bombers which dropped 7,616 tons in support of the assault. These B-26s are pulling up after a bombing run. The Allies' air superiority was overwhelming; only 160 German planes were seen on D-day. To complete German confusion about the landing points, coastal batteries from Holland to Spain were bombed in the last few days.

FROM THE SEA, battleship shells supported landing as LCTs headed for Normandy coast. Naval gunfire silenced most shore batteries, though all big U.S. ships were hit except one. Firing on the five beaches were six battleships, two monitors, 22 cruisers and 63 destroyers; LCGs (landing craft, guns) provided floating batteries, and LCRs (landing craft, rockets) had a total firepower equivalent to a salvo from 80 light cruisers.

FROM DEEP INLAND, the Germans brought up railroad guns to oppose the invaders. However Allied control of the air limited the use of these weapons, which had to be concealed by day from the fighter bombers.

FROM THE COAST, the Germans fired back with a few guns which, like the one at the top, had survived naval and air battering. After the battle this Nazi coastal pillbox (*below*) was a honeycomb of U.S. shell pits.

LOADED WITH IMPERIAL TROOPS, THE LANDING VESSELS OF THE CANADIAN NAVY HEADED TOWARD A HORIZON ALMOST SOLID WITH INVASION SHIPPING

PONTOON "RHINO" FERRIES LIGHTERED TRUCKS AND DERRICKS FROM SHIPS TO BEACHES

READY FOR BATTLE, U.S. INFANTRYMEN PACKED THE DECKS

Curtain rose as assault troops, en route to the Normandy beaches, heard Eisenhower's order of the day: "You are about to embark upon the great crusade . . . good luck! And let us all beseech the blessing of Almighty God upon this great and noble undertaking." Ahead of the transports and landing craft plowed more than 200 minesweepers, rooting out and exploding enemy mines. Only the U.S.S. *Osprey* was sunk by mines; German submarines, including the new snorkel, came out but drew back without sinking a single ship. LCCs (landing craft, control) worked their way into position 3,000 yards off the French beaches, ready to direct the boats toward shore when they came from the transport area, 10 to 14 miles behind. Battleships, cruisers and other naval gun platforms already were firing on and over the beaches. The last prelanding air strikes began at H-hour minus 30 and ended at H minus 5, just before the first troops got ashore. Meanwhile, Field Marshal Rommel, commander of Army Group B which defended the area, was home in Obersalzburg on a visit. The weather seemed to preclude a landing, and SS spies in the French resistance who had warned of such a thing were assumed to be misinformed.

AMERICAN TROOPS WERE TRANSPORTED TO NORMANDY BY LCIs, EACH VESSEL TOWING A BARRAGE BALLOON AS IT MOVED IN THE ORDERLY FORMATION

OF LCIs DURING THE ROUGH CHANNEL CROSSING. OF SIX ALLIED DIVISIONS THAT LANDED ON D-DAY, THREE WERE U.S., TWO WERE BRITISH, ONE CANADIAN

255

THE INVASION BEGINS as soldiers jump from the ramp of an LCT and start wading through the surf toward a beach called Omaha. Troops landing in this sector (designated "Easy Red") met only moderate opposition, but some were slain by German machine-gun bullets and mortar shells. The assault was made by the 1st Division, veterans of North Africa and Sicily, and the 29th National Guard Division, in combat for the first time. One battalion of the 1st suffered 30% casualties in half an hour and was awarded 740 Bronze Stars. By the end of D-day the two divisions had cleared the Omaha beaches, having

had 3,000 casualties. On Utah beach the 4th Division had it better, losing only 197 men (60 in the water). Left of Omaha one Canadian and two British divisions landed smoothly and advanced almost to Caen, despite a counterattack by the 21st Panzer Division; near Caen, British airborne troops captured bridges over the Orne on schedule. U.S. airborne divisions were less fortunate, coming down in the darkness over a wide area and enduring heavy casualties (1,500 each in the 101st and 82nd). Their dreadful misfortune was to run into antiairborne exercises the Germans happened to be holding that morning.

AFTER STORMING BEACHHEADS WEST OF CAEN ON D-DAY, BRITISH INFANTRYMEN KEPT CLOSE TO THE SAND, WHILE WAITING TO ADVANCE INLAND

AMPHIBIOUS ENGINEERS obtain shelter from the intense German fire behind steel hedgehogs which formed part of the perilous line of obstacles Field Marshal Rommel had erected in surf in front of Omaha beach.

THIS WOUNDED SOLDIER, luckier than some, was pulled from the surf. Many lost in D-day's moderately high seas were overburdened with equipment which proved to be too heavy for amphibious operations.

A DEAD AMERICAN lies at the barricades of Western Europe. He was a member of one of several special Army-Navy demolition teams which went ahead of the assault waves at Omaha and suffered 41% casualties.

A LIVE GERMAN digs himself out of the sand after being buried by the near miss of a heavy shell. Omaha was defended at 12 strongpoints containing 60 artillery pieces and numerous machine guns in 35 pillboxes.

ON JUNE 9, THREE DAYS AFTER THE LANDING AT UTAH BEACH, THESE GERMANS SURRENDERED TO U.S. TROOPS FIGHTING TOWARD CHERBOURG

ALLIED CONVOYS MASSED OFFSHORE WHILE ALONG OMAHA BEACH LSTs DISCHARGED TONS OF EQUIPMENT NEEDED TO CONSOLIDATE THE LANDING

AFTER LANDING ITS LOAD OF TANKS ON THE BEACH, AN LCT SHUTTLES BACK TO THE ATTACK TRANSPORTS WITH A CARGO OF AMERICAN WOUNDED

Beachhead in Normandy

DESTROYER MOVED IN THROUGH SHOAL WATER TO ANSWER GERMAN BATTERIES SHELLING THE WELTER OF LANDING BOATS OFF OMAHA BEACH

SHELLS STRADDLE AN LCI STRANDED AMONG BARRIER STAKES BY THE TIDE

T HE invasion of Europe was one of the most difficult operations ever attempted. Fortunately for the Allies the top German generals were divided on how to stop it. Von Rundstedt, as Hitler's commander in chief in the west, believed the Allies would land in the Somme-Calais area. His idea was to trap Eisenhower's men ashore, then blow them off Europe with a counterattack. But Rommel, commander in France under von Rundstedt, insisted that the assaulting troops be stopped in the water. With Hitler, Rommel felt that Normandy would be the target, and early in 1944 he began to build up coastal defenses there. Until then the "Atlantic wall" was only a myth. Finally German leaders compromised: infantry was placed forward, armor held back. Rommel's guns and Rommel's men, firing from bluffs 100 to 200 feet high, made a bloody shambles of one beachhead. This was Omaha, and some of its terror, frustration and heroism are reflected in the paintings on this page by Navy Artist Dwight Shepler.

ON Omaha beach Rommel tried to do what he had originally proposed: hurl the invaders into the sea. He very nearly succeeded. The aid stations filled up, and on D-day afternoon Lieut. Mitchell Jamieson made sketches for the powerful picture below, in which men are dying for lack of boats to evacuate them. All that day, from the heights above the beach, the Germans could look down the throats of the Americans. Rommel's 12 strongpoints on the bluffs were to have been knocked out by no less than 480 B-24s carrying 1,300 tons of bombs. Weather forced all bombers to drop their loads as far as 3 miles inland, which helped the assault waves not at all. Naval gunfire suffered from poor planning and execution. The scheduled gunfire (always more effective than bombs on enemy beaches) was considerably less on Omaha than that which had proved inadequate at Tarawa in the Pacific. The 7th Infantry Division had landed at Kwajalein two months after Tarawa and four months before Omaha. It was calculated that Omaha's defenses were three times as strong as Kwajalein's and its defenders were four times as many. Yet only one third as much ammunition was ordered for Omaha; the British pilots trying to spot targets from swift fighter planes were inexperienced; and, as usual, the foot soldier paid. Five of the 16 demolition teams blew gaps in the beach defenses, but only one managed to install the markers necessary to guide the infantry. Of eight infantry companies in the first wave, only one landed intact. During the day only 43 of 96 tanks reached the beach, and six of 16 bulldozers. Shot up or sunk were 26 artillery pieces, 50 landing craft and 2,300 of 2,400 tons of supplies. Communication was lost when radios went into the water. The American infantrymen were pinned down, hanging on "by their eyelashes," said Montgomery; "looking like so many heavily laden bundles on the flat pebbly stretch between the sea and the first cover," said Correspondent Ernest Hemingway. Late that afternoon the gunfire plan was revamped, and destroyers moved inshore and began to knock out pillboxes ahead of the advancing infantry.

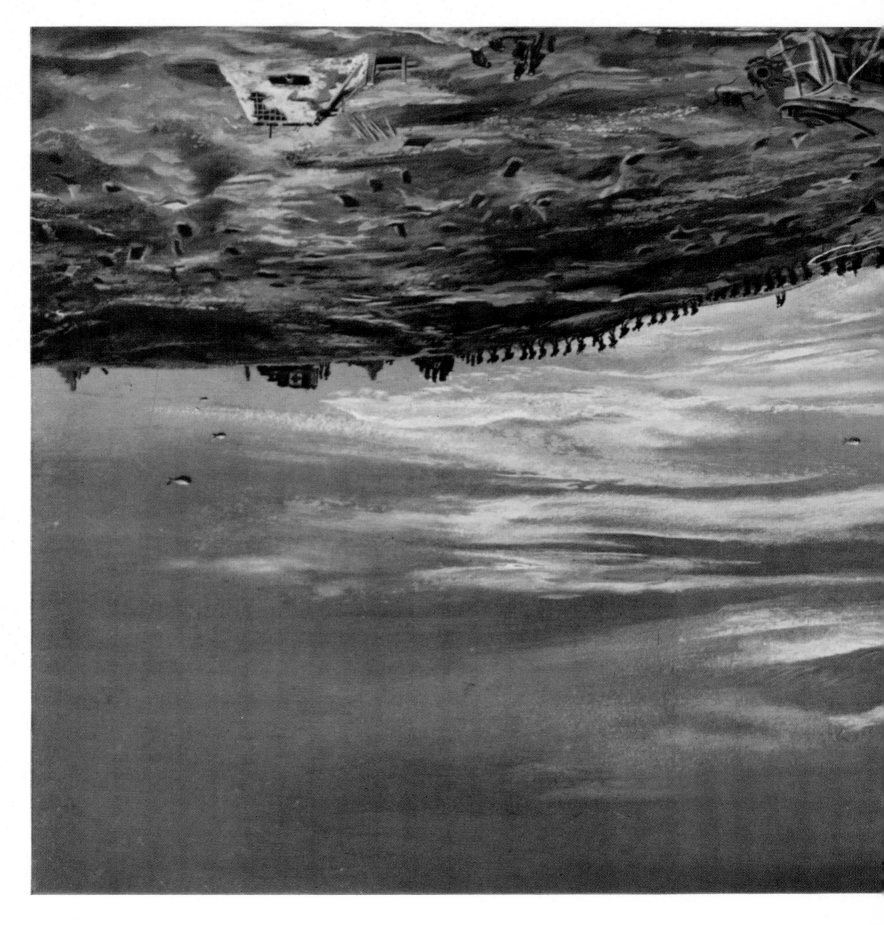

A week after D-day Aaron Bohrod painted this haunting picture of troops moving cautiously across the desolation that had been Omaha beach. What the Americans met at Omaha was not 1,000 troops "of doubtful morale" but seasoned soldiers of the 352nd Infantry Division, which had escaped detection by G-2. What the Allies gained was a never-to-be-lost grip on the Continent. Hitler's intuition had proved superior to Rundstedt's intelligence, had told him the landings would come in Normandy. But it also whispered, "Wait before counterattacking; this is only a diversion." That was fatal.

SILENT GERMAN PRISONERS DUG GRAVES FOR THE D-DAY DEAD IN A BURIAL GROUND ON A HILLTOP ABOVE OMAHA BEACH

A GERMAN PAINTED THIS SOMBER VIEW OF THE ALLIED INVASION FLEET, SEEN ACROSS A BELT OF UNDERWATER BOAT-TRAPS EXPOSED BY THE TIDE

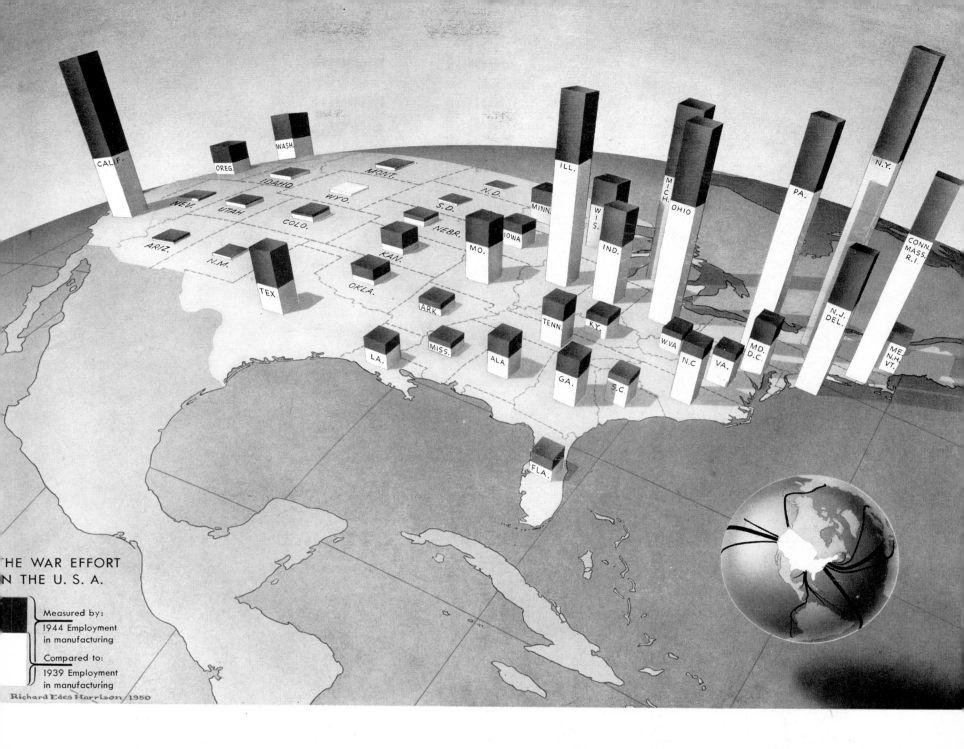

THE WAR EFFORT
IN THE U. S. A.

Measured by:
1944 Employment
in manufacturing

Compared to:
1939 Employment
in manufacturing

Richard Edes Harrison 1950

X
The Home Front

U.S.A.: 1941-1945

WORLD WAR II restored to the American people an essential unity of purpose which they had lacked for years. Employes and management alike were willing to throw everything they had into an effort to make production hum to win the war. This challenge, in spite of occasional conflicts over profits and wages, filled the country with a sense of well-being. Production was something Americans understood.

The problems to be solved before the productive potential could be realized were of dazzling complexity. Industries using steel, of which the automobile industry was largest and best equipped, had to be converted to the production of military vehicles still in the blueprint stage, of guns, of airplanes and of a staggering variety of new devices which engineers often had to redesign and standardize for the purposes of the assembly line. Shipyards had to be expanded to replace ships sunk and to meet demands for new tonnage. An industry had to be improvised to make synthetic rubber to take the place of the natural rubber lost by Japan's conquest of the East Indies. Electric power had to be found to turn the wheels of myriad new plants that made explosives, refined aluminum or picked magnesium out of sea water. The use of raw materials in scarce supply had to be curtailed without doing the civilian economy too much damage. The farmers had to be induced to raise more wheat and corn and hogs and steers. In virtually every field wartime needs carried the day over conflicts of interest. The result was a permanent increase in the country's productivity. More corn grew on less acres; the building of airplanes was turned into a mass-production industry; the time it took to build a freighter was continually shortened.

THESE results were not attained without painful heaving and hauling. Each essential product bid for priority in manpower and materials against every other product; for example, in order to produce all the synthetic rubber we needed we had to hold back other important materials. Each war industry was plagued with bottlenecks. To introduce harmony into this maze of energies and potentialities, commission after commission was rigged in Washington until their initials had run through the alphabet several times over. The extraordinary thing about the proliferating government apparatus which made Washington the control center of industry was not that plans and programs often became mired but that so many of them succeeded and that the Administration was successful in exhorting the diverse human elements manning the machinery of production into working as a team.

None of this achievement would have been possible if we had not had a population tolerably skilled in the use of machine tools and used to the give and take of organized effort. Instead of the completed economy the economists talked about, American society proved to be still remarkably fluid. As each new plant opened men and women lined up at the personnel offices to learn new skills. Housewives took up welding. High-school kids learned to run lathes. Old people remembered half-forgotten trades. The population was on the move. Families from the Ozarks and the Alleghenies managed to patch up jalopies and move to the new shipyards on the Gulf Coast or to new steel plants in California. Trailer camps became a feature of the roadside landscape. War production set off a migration comparable to the westward movement after the Civil War. When it was over the population of the West had once more grown dramatically. After the depression and the lack of confidence of the '30s, the demands of a war economy stirred up the American people like a concrete mixer. High wages and profits, the enthusiasm of effort and strain, the knowledge of new industries sprouting beyond every horizon gave the average American the feeling that his work was needed and that he was part of a civilization that was still building.

At the top of this pyramid of energies sat the President. Franklin Delano Roosevelt, the first man to be four times elected President of the U.S., had the resilience and the flexibility of the people he represented. He had their gift of improvisation. He had their optimism. By an immense buoyancy of will he had conquered the miseries of the life of a paralytic and made them as if they had never been. His character was many-sided, impressionable, unpredictable. He was the Hudson River *patroon*, the Groton boy, the Gold-Coaster from Harvard, the New York machine politician. He loved political maneuver and ships and sailing and postage stamps and his country's history and the jovial prestidigitator's ease with which he could manage men. He loved to drive in an open car, even campaigning in the rain, so that the people could see him. He had a taste for people and something of the politician's superiority toward them: they were so easy to handle. If a project went wrong he would call the fellow into his study for a friendly chat and possibly create another agency. His voice over the radio enchanted the electorate. His wording was as sure in its way as Churchill's. Sitting in the oval study at the White House with the great blue globe in the embrasure of the window behind him, with his cigaret in the long holder cocked at an angle, he tried to keep in his control all the pieces on the intricate gaming boards of war and policy.

As the prospects of the war changed from stalemate to victory, the problems that accumulated on the President's desk became more difficult. The question of what sort of a society would rise from the wreckage of Europe became paramount. Roosevelt simply took it for granted that it would be based on the freedoms which were the commonplaces of Anglo-American propaganda. When the President set out for his last conference with Churchill and Stalin at Yalta in the devastated Crimea, Eisenhower's armies were preparing to cross the Rhine and MacArthur was in Luzon. The conference was a complete success, so the newspapers told us. Stalin promised to send representatives to San Francisco to organize the United Nations that would assure peace for the world's suffering peoples. In return for rights to the Manchurian railways and Port Arthur and Dairen he promised help in the war against Japan. He showed certain reservations about what sort of government he would allow the Poles to choose for themselves, and regarding the four freedoms he was distinctly noncommittal. Roosevelt and his advisers went home to Washington. The details, they told each other, could be ironed out at San Francisco. But the President was very, very tired. He had never spared himself but now he needed a rest. He went down to Warm Springs, his old resting place, and there on April 12, 1945 he complained of a terrific headache, lost consciousness and died. —JOHN DOS PASSOS

267

THE FIRST STEADILY MOVING BOMBER ASSEMBLY LINE TURNED OUT THE B-24

THESE MEN PLANNED WILLOW RUN, WORLD'S BIGGEST BOMBER PLANT

AN OVERHEAD CONVEYOR SPEEDED MASS PRODUCTION OF 500-POUND BOMBS

WORKING AT NIGHT WITH PREFABRICATED SECTIONS (RIGHT), SHIPYARD

SHERMAN TANKS GOT TRACKS AND TURRETS ALONG ASSEMBLY LINE

At home

the power was generated which exposed as idiocy all the cunning of the dictators. Hitler and Tojo never had a chance, provided the American industrial machine were properly harnessed to war, and provided the U.S. and her allies employed the machine's produce with sufficient will and skill. The harnessing was slow at first, but eventually it poured forth 296,429 airplanes, 86,333 tanks, 319,000 artillery pieces, 64,546 landing craft, 11,900 warships and cargo vessels and 42 billion bullets (1,400 for each enemy in uniform). The pipedream of the '30s, the $100 billion economy, became the $200 billion economy. Production of steel rose 70%; aluminum and magnesium, 429% and 3,358% respectively. The earth itself yielded raw materials 60% faster than ever before. In 1939 production for war was a 2% drip of total national production; by 1943 it amounted to a 40% torrent. Munitions alone employed 225,000 workers (more than half of them women) in 58 plants making shells, bombs and explosives—plants owned by the government and operated by companies which in peacetime produced roofing, Kodaks, Quaker Oats and Coca-Cola.

IN PORTLAND, ORE. FULFILLED ITS DRAMATIC PROMISE BY LAUNCHING THESE THREE LIBERTY SHIPS AND DELIVERING THREE OTHERS ON THE SAME DAY

IN 1941 A GUARD WATCHED OVER FIRST BIG U.S. RAILWAY GUN BUILT SINCE 1918 ON TEST RUN TO ARMY'S PROVING GROUND AT ABERDEEN, MD.

LIFEBOATS CAME FROM PREWAR STOVE FACTORY IN INDIANA

The machines

didn't run themselves, though the astonishing assembly line sometimes appeared to be automatic. Techniques improved: in merchant-shipbuilding the jobs that required 100 man hours in 1941 were cut to 45 man hours; the traditionally handmade airplane yielded after much tribulation to mass production. The number of war workers dropped a million as the services began scraping the bottom of the barrel of effective fighting manpower, but production still climbed. It was a time for bold thinking and intensive organization. But all depended on human beings, and the people settled down to the task of winning the war so their beloved men could come back from over the seas. The armed services claimed 11 million men, yet the civilian labor force remained constant at 55 millions. It included women who had never before worked outside their homes, old men who still possessed a skill and many who never had one, and adolescents awaiting the military's call. People worked harder. The average work week in manufacturing went from 37.7 hours a week to 45.2. Absenteeism was remarkably low, though the new workers were less robust than the men they replaced. Civilians grumbled about the shortage of gasoline, shoes, meat, sugar, whisky and coffee; they admired cartoons depicting insolent hotel clerks and elusive salesmen. But in spite of "hardships" the standard of living reached a historic high.

270

HEAVY SOUTHERN PACIFIC FREIGHT TRAIN HAULS ARMY TRUCKS THROUGH THE MOUNTAINS OF THE WEST. MAN ON SECOND FLATCAR IS A GUARD

271

The Joint Chiefs of Staff Ran America's War

THE U.S. was exceptionally fortunate in its military leaders. They held incalculable power; a word from them could mean life or death to 10,000 men tomorrow or six months hence. With their British counterparts the U.S. Joint Chiefs of Staff made the military decisions just below the highest level (Roosevelt and Churchill). A decision of the Joint Chiefs—with whom Roosevelt's Admiral William D. Leahy sat as chairman—had to be unanimous or it was referred to the President, in whom the ultimate American power has always resided. After 1942's disputes over antisubmarine warfare and Pacific strategy, the accord among Army, Navy and AAF leaders was superb.

George Marshall's honesty, patience and modesty served to endear him to congressmen, the public and military men alike. When the war was over President Truman called the embarrassed general "the greatest military man this country ever produced." Admiral King, the stern, gaunt "sundowner," had a warm side too, but he carefully concealed it from everyone in a blue uniform. General Henry H. Arnold, the genial flier who was the first of the Joint Chiefs to die (January 1950), concentrated on building up the Army

Air Forces which eventually embraced more than 72,000 planes and 2,300,000 men. In their Washington map room (*above*) and elsewhere these three men left records revealing their human fallibility as well as their achievements. Some of Marshall's judgments seem in retrospect absurd: his belief that Europe could be invaded in 1942 by green troops, his insistence on keeping "Vinegar Joe" Stilwell in a job for which he was unsuited. King was the gadfly who demanded that the Pacific be remembered ("Ernie King's beloved ocean," growled Churchill). At Casablanca, King pushed the Pacific's supply allotment from 15% to 30%. Almost alone the admiral foresaw the necessity of stopping the Japanese at Guadalcanal. But he was so immersed in his own service he saw the Marianas as naval bases, not airfields to bomb Japan. "Hap" Arnold was swept away by the "bomber boys" and was caught at war's beginning with fighter planes inferior to enemy models. He told the world in February 1943 Berlin would fall that year. In spite of such miscalculations, and as Admiral King protested when Roosevelt proposed detaching Marshall to command Overlord, the Joint Chiefs of Staff were "a winning combination."

COMMANDER OF GREATEST ARMY IN U.S. HISTORY, GENERAL GEORGE C. MARSHALL LED 11,600,000 SOLDIERS TO WORLDWIDE VICTORY

ADMIRAL ERNEST J. KING BUILT UP U.S. NAVY TO 14,390,000 TONS AND EXTENDED ITS SWAY ACROSS 6,000 MILES OF THE PACIFIC OCEAN

UNDER GENERAL HENRY H. ARNOLD AMERICA'S WARTIME AIR FORCE ROSE TO VIRTUAL EQUALITY WITH THE SENIOR MILITARY SERVICES

GENERAL DWIGHT D. EISENHOWER WAS THE COMMANDER IN EUROPE

ADMIRAL CHESTER W. NIMITZ COMMANDED THE PACIFIC OCEAN AREAS

GENERAL DOUGLAS MACARTHUR LED ALLIES IN SOUTHWEST PACIFIC

LORD LOUIS MOUNTBATTEN DIRECTED THE FORCES IN SOUTHEAST ASIA

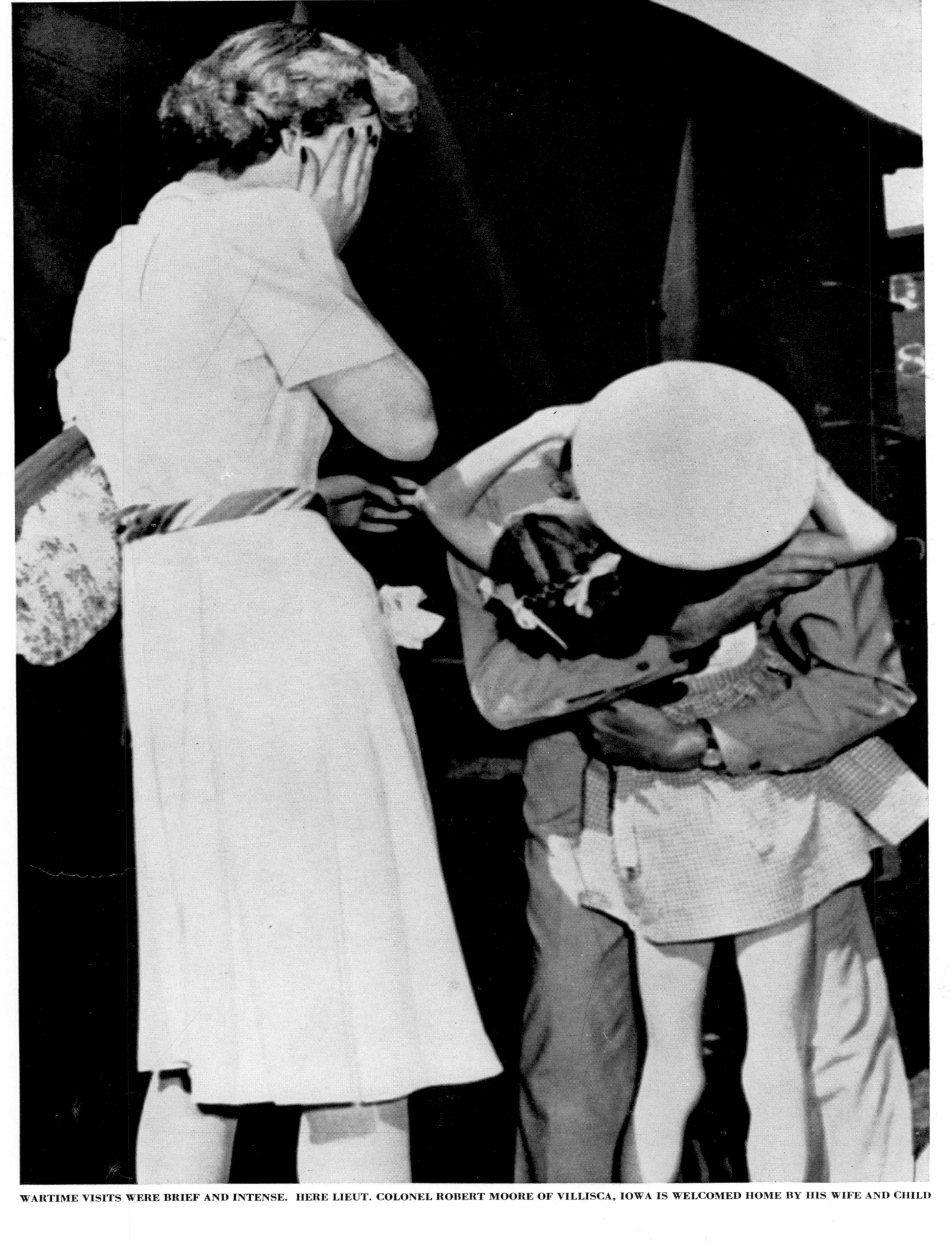

WARTIME VISITS WERE BRIEF AND INTENSE. HERE LIEUT. COLONEL ROBERT MOORE OF VILLISCA, IOWA IS WELCOMED HOME BY HIS WIFE AND CHILD

EMERGENCY TRAVEL coincided with the prosperous public's desire to see America, and congested scenes like this (Chicago's Union Station) were commonplace. The military had taken half the Pullmans and a sixth of the coaches. Chances of getting on a plane without a priority were slim; an A card virtually immobilized the family car, with about three gallons of gasoline a week. So it was sit on a suitcase in the aisle or stay home.

EMERGENCY HOUSING projects sprouted in many cities where war plants had attracted new workers. This development was built hurriedly by the government near San Diego. In some areas whole new cities sprang up. The three Pacific Coast states acquired 1,273,564 new civilians and the country as a whole had a nonmilitary population shift of 15 million. The gain in and around frantic Washington, D.C., was half a million.

WAR BOND RALLY at Indianapolis was led by Actress Carole Lombard, who sold more than $2 millions' worth that day. This was a month after Pearl Harbor, and posters overhead are relics of World War I. Early next evening Miss Lombard's plane crashed in Nevada, killing 21, including her. From May 1941 to December 1945 U.S. Treasury sold $54,404,617,-000 in War Bonds, helped to avert inflation by draining off excess cash.

Death came to the 32nd President of the United States on April 12, 1945, in Warm Springs, Ga., at 3:35 p.m. central war time. In burning Berlin it was past suppertime for Adolf Hitler, who had only three more weeks to live in his dungeon retreat. In Honolulu, by now a rear area, the morning surfboarders glided over the crested waves. It was April 13 on Okinawa; the troops were eating 10-in-1 rations before the H-hour jump-off (more than a hundred of them would die during the day). All over the world people of all colors, getting the news at all hours, would say, "He was a great man; we may not see his like again." When the President's body was carried from his Warm Springs cottage en route to the White House (*below*), a U.S. Navy musician (*left*) wept as he played *Nearer My God to Thee*.

TIME and SPACE

A Flow-Map of German Defeat

Richard Edes Harrison 1950

XI
Victory in Europe

Europe: 1944-45

THE day President Roosevelt died the Russians were shooting their way into the suburbs of Vienna. Ever since they had freed Moscow from the threat of German encirclement the Soviet armies had been methodically hammering the Wehrmacht. Their summer offensives of 1944 had started immediately after the Normandy landings with thrusts into Finland and, later, toward Estonia and Latvia. Next, on the central front, they broke through in such force that by mid-August they had reached the outskirts of Warsaw. In the south they pushed through Moldavia and Bessarabia so fast that the Romanian government switched sides. So did Bulgaria. The Romanian surrender gave the Russians the Ploesti oil fields, the overlordship of the Balkans, and opened to them the ancient invasion route of the Huns and the Turks up the Danube valley into Central Europe. The grand strategy was developing. By occupying Vienna and Berlin they would secure control of Central Europe, thus establishing a broad area of defense against attack from the West, and laying the foundation for further extensions of Soviet power. By 1944 the Russians had the most effective tanks in the field, plenty of artillery, and they outnumbered the Germans two to one. Hitler's generals staged counterattack after counterattack, but when they did manage to break through they found no Russian supply to disrupt. A Soviet soldier lived off the land, receiving occasionally a cartload of the black bread that was his staple food. The infantry depended on its own legs and deployed over the fields, each man pulling up vegetables and throwing what he found into a sack on his back. By midwinter the Red armies were ready to cross the frozen Vistula. Leaving behind them in Warsaw a government carefully rigged for the Poles, the Soviet armies crowded into East Prussia and launched a mighty thrust aimed at Berlin. By April 25, 1945, on a broken bridge across the Elbe, the men of the Soviet outposts were shaking hands with Americans advancing from the west.

IN August 1944 Patton's Third Army smashed out of Normandy at Avranches and swung in a curve like a thrown lasso down through Brittany and eastward round Paris. The eminently successful August landings on the French Riviera had aided in the rout of the Wehrmacht from France. After fierce fighting in the Low Countries, Antwerp had with difficulty been opened as a supply port. Against the Antwerp wharves so needed for the unloading of material for the Allied armies advancing toward the Rhine, the Germans made effective use of their new weapons, the self-propelled flying bomb (V-1) and long-range rocket (V-2), which had come into production too late to hinder the cross-channel invasion but not too late to inflict losses and misery on the war-worn Londoners. Difficulties of supply slowed up pursuit of the Wehrmacht by victorious armies advancing on a broad front against the entire German line. Fighting on their own frontier, the Germans were able to pull themselves together during the winter slowdown. They defeated a British airborne attempt to take Arnhem and, aided by foul weather, broke through the American line in the Ardennes. For a few days it looked as if the old luck would return to the Wehrmacht, but the Americans put up a dogged defense and when the weather cleared the Allies made short work of the enemy. At the end of March 1945 British, French and American armies had begun to cross the Rhine. They boxed off the Ruhr and in April, against disintegrating defense, stormed across the ruined heart of Germany.

GERMAN opposition was weakened greatly because the Luftwaffe had virtually ceased to exist. Many German planes were destroyed by Allied bombing, and once the British and American air forces had started systematic bombing of synthetic-oil plants a creeping paralysis had overcome what was left of Göring's air arm. Lack of fuel kept planes on the ground. And in a war dependent on mobility the Germans found their Panzer divisions and tanks all but immobilized. As the Nazi regime fell the disciplined German life became completely disorganized. The question was: who among the German leaders had enough authority left to capitulate?

In Italy the German generals took the matter into their own hands. For weary months British and Americans, isolated from the main theaters of war, had been forcing their way up the narrow Italian peninsula against an enemy who contested every spur of the Apennines and every pebbly river crossing. Now, disheartened by news from home, the Germans began to give ground. Mussolini's puppet dominion in the Gran Sasso mountains as a pensioner of Hitler collapsed, and the fallen dictator was caught by partisans as he tried to escape into Switzerland. They killed him at the little town of Dongo and trussed him up by his heels in a Milan square.

Hitler himself was spending these last doomed days of April in a deep bunker under the ruins of the Reich Chancellery in Berlin. With him was Eva Braun, Goebbels and his family and a little frightened household of cooks and secretaries and valets, which reportedly included one of Hitler's doubles. The bunker was admirably constructed of reinforced concrete, but as the Russians moved their artillery forward it was more and more cut off by shellfire from the rest of Berlin. Hitler sat at his desk busy with papers, issuing orders to armies that had ceased to exist to die in defense of lines long since in the hands of the Allies. He himself, he told his household, would die in Berlin. In the early morning of April 29, the day after Mussolini met his end, Hitler was married to Eva Braun. They opened champagne and, in a wedding breakfast with Goebbels and his wife, drank toasts. Hitler dictated his will. Everything he had was to go to the party or the state, except his collection of pictures which he wanted to leave to his home town of Linz. He also dictated his political testament, expelling Himmler and Göring as traitors and blaming the war and the ruin of Europe on the British and especially the Jews he had worked so hard to exterminate. He appointed Grand Admiral Karl Doenitz as his successor. He ordered his dog to be killed. A crazy curtain of hysteria had dropped over Hitler's last moments. Most of the reports agree that he and Eva killed themselves and that Goebbels ordered his wife to go into their bedroom and kill their children as they slept, that she took poison and that he shot himself. Hitler's death was announced May 1. Berlin capitulated to the Russians next day. As he had often threatened, Hitler brought the whole European structure down with him as he fell. The ruin of Germany left Soviet Russia the paramount power on the great Eurasian continent. —JOHN DOS PASSOS.

AMERICANS BLAST a pillbox with satchel charges during final attack on Cherbourg, June 26. This big port, captured by Major General J. Lawton Collins' VII Corps, could not be made fully operational until mid-August, after the Navy had cleared the harbor and its approaches of mines. The Allies' only other port was an artificial one built on the British beaches; severe gales destroyed similar facilities on U.S. beaches.

CANADIANS FIRE their 5.5-inch guns to lay down barrage near Caen, facing eastern end of 50-mile beachhead, as troop convoy moves along road. Germans fiercely defended area, fearing breakout by the British.

BRITISH SEARCH for enemy remnants in the rubble of Caen, which was finally captured by the Allies on July 9. Seven thousand tons of bombs were dropped on Caen by 2,200 planes, killing more than 5,000 civilians.

Breakout at St. Lô

ON JULY 25 FRENCHMEN IN A SHATTERED TOWN ON THE NORMAN COAST WATCHED HEAVY BOMBERS FLY INLAND TO START THE ATTACK ON ST. LÔ

BY the end of June 1944 there were nearly a million Allied soldiers and more than 170,000 vehicles in Normandy. The "lodgment phase" was ended. Montgomery laid down the plan for the next phase: hold as many German divisions as possible on the left (British) flank, and swing the right (American) flank southward and eastward in a wide sweep toward Paris. Preparations for the offensive consumed much time and brought sharp criticism from those segments of press and public which had assumed that the war in Europe was nearly over once the landing had succeeded. The battle for the jump-off positions was also expensive, particularly in the fighting inland over the Normandy hedgerows—60,000 Allied casualties in the first three weeks, including 9,000 killed. The Germans had difficulties too. The Allied air offensive made reinforcement hazardous; troops were delayed time after time by blown bridges, and artillery had to be sent south, by way of Paris, in order to reach the front. Fear of a second amphibious operation in the Pas de Calais region stopped Hitler from reinforcing Normandy more heavily.

Late in July the Americans achieved the positions they had hoped to hold on June 11. On July 25 the area west of St. Lô was saturated by an intensive air attack which paralyzed the Germans facing Bradley's First Army—70% of the Panzer Lehr

Division's personnel were killed, wounded or stunned, and most of its tanks and artillery were knocked out. Through the Panzer Lehr hole the 2nd and 3rd Armored and 1st Infantry Divisions poured. By July 27 a clear breakthrough had been achieved; next day Coutances was captured, and on the sixth day Avranches. Lieut. General Patton's new Third Army entered the picture Aug. 1 from the Normandy beaches. His VIII Corps drove to the west along the Brittany highways toward Brest, while his XV, XII and XX Corps passed through the First Army's lines and fanned out south and west. Hitler, thoroughly alarmed, ordered a counterattack (over von Kluge's protest). On Aug. 7 elements of six Panzer divisions struck at Mortain. For four days the battle raged, with Allied fighter-bombers—mostly R.A.F. rocket-firing Typhoons—furnishing outstanding support to the U.S. infantry. By Aug. 13 the cream of the German Panzers in the west was gone. Hitler had handed France to Eisenhower. Hitler had, however, won a sort of victory at home. After many false starts Hitler's generals finally devised a "foolproof" plan to kill their Führer on July 20. But he walked to the other end of the room when the time bomb went off. The whole conspiracy stood revealed; 700 German officers, including Rommel and von Kluge, were killed or committed suicide. Hitler was free to pursue his—and Germany's—*Götterdämmerung*.

A COLUMN OF SHERMAN TANKS SUPPORTED BY INFANTRYMEN OF THE U.S. FIRST ARMY PUSHED SWIFTLY THROUGH THE TOWN OF ST. LO, DESTROYED DURING THE

2,500-PLANE BOMBING ATTACK WHICH PRECEDED THE BATTLE. AT RIGHT: ONE DECAPITATED TOWER RISES FROM THE RUINS OF THE 14TH CENTURY CATHEDRAL

U.S. ARMOR (BACKGROUND) LUMBERED OVER THE BOMB-CRATERED BREAKTHROUGH AREA PAST SMASHED NAZI TANKS AND THEIR DEAD CREWMEN

A JEEP CARRIED A FULL LOAD OF WOUNDED BACK ACROSS THE BATTLEFIELD PAST A GERMAN MINE-FIELD MARKER

SMOKE POURS from German positions blasted by 1,200 Allied aircraft on the Caen-Falaise road. The British drove south from Caen as Americans swung north to Argentan, pocketing the German Seventh Army.

CHARRED BODIES of the crew of a German Tiger tank are part of the bag in the fearsome "killing grounds" of the Falaise pocket. In this famous Allied victory about 100,000 Germans were killed or captured.

A SECOND LANDING, in south of France, took place Aug. 15. Three U.S. divisions of the Sixth Army Group under Lieut. General Jacob Devers spearheaded between Cannes and Toulon, followed by seven French divisions. Allies reached the Normandy forces Sept. 11. Eisenhower had wanted another port; Churchill wanted to invade the Balkans instead. Most historians side with Churchill, call southern France unnecessary.

SOLDIERS OF RESISTANCE sniped at Germans with captured rifles, used arms and grenades dropped by parachute. During most of occupation Allies landed planes on secret F.F.I. airfields.

LIBERATION OF PARIS came when F.F.I.—French Forces of the Interior—rose up on Aug. 19, 1944. Here F.F.I. men fire a machine gun at Germans in Montmartre. Eisenhower had planned to by-pass Paris but had to support revolt.

A WOMAN PATRIOT, wearing a German helmet and captured pistol, joined other Parisians in shooting at Nazis from behind sandbags as Allies, racing down from Normandy, neared city.

YOUNG FRENCHMEN TORE UP THE PLACE ST. MICHEL TO STRENGTHEN A BARRICADE OF COBBLESTONES PILED UP BEHIND AN OVERTURNED TRUCK

RESISTANCE FIGHTER (LEFT) TOOK PRECIOUS AMMUNITION FROM THE CORPSE OF A GERMAN SOLDIER SHOT NEAR ST. LAZARE RAILROAD STATION

A GERMAN ALLY, in the improbable person of an aged Japanese sniper, was captured in Paris. Unlike Japanese sharpshooters on Pacific islands, he surrendered rather than fight to the death.

A YOUNG GERMAN was captured near Hotel de Ville (city hall). Though Paris revolt complicated Allied plans, Eisenhower said resistance movement was of "inestimable value" in campaign.

GENERAL DE GAULLE paraded in Paris despite sniping by Nazis and Vichyites. First to enter the city was Major General Jacques Leclerc's French division, but De Gaulle asked for (and got) two U.S. divisions to maintain his position.

291

INVASION OF HOLLAND was attempted by air on Sept. 17, 23 days after Paris was liberated. Eisenhower used his airborne forces to spearhead a dash for the north German plains before winter set in. Here waves of U.S. paratroops drop near Grave as livestock graze beside gliders that had landed earlier. The British 1st Airborne Division was dropped at Arnhem; the American 82nd and 101st near Nijmegen and Eindhoven.

FIGHTING NEAR ARNHEM, British shells streak across a field outlined by burning haystacks. The British Guards Armored Division and XXX Corps raced down the corridor to Arnhem through the American lines to support their 1st Airborne. But the Germans closed in and the weather prevented reinforcements by plane. The 1st Airborne had to be withdrawn across the Waal after losing 7,000 men in a valiant effort to hold.

"THE PORT OF ANTWERP is essential," said Bradley, now commanding the Twelfth Army Group (Hodges' First Army, Patton's Third). The Allies had outrun their supplies, which now had to come 300 miles from Normandy. Antwerp fell Sept. 4, but the estuary had to be cleared. Before port was open Nov. 26, Canadians and British suffered 27,633 casualties killing Germans on South Beveland and Walcheren Islands.

A V-2 ROCKET struck an Antwerp intersection, killing many civilians. The missiles were 47 feet long, weighed 3,000 pounds and were usually launched from Holland. They were erratic but many hit their targets.

GUIDED MISSILES—the first of about 10,000—were launched against Antwerp in mid-October. The V-1 bomb, and later the V-2 rocket, had been used against England, beginning in June, killing 8,403, injuring 22,718.

A BOY'S BODY burned alongside truck hit by a V-2. Despite attacks that disrupted communications and supply, and killed 2,862 civilians and injured 7,778 others, Antwerp proved to be a valuable supply port.

ON THE NORTHERN FLANK OF THE GERMAN BULGE U.S. SOLDIERS LAUNCHED A COUNTERATTACK IN THE ZERO WEATHER OF EARLY JANUARY 1945

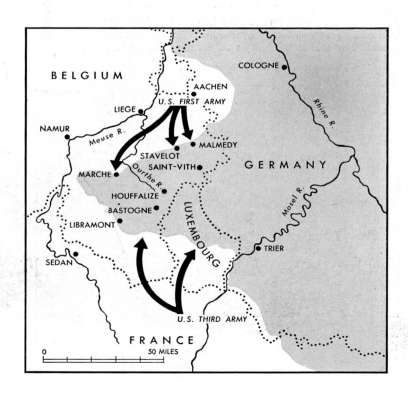

The Bulge was what Americans called a 50-mile wedge the Germans drove into their lines in December of 1944. Just when the U.S. First Army had been lulled into a false sense of security, Hitler struck through the fog-clouded Ardennes with most of his remaining armored reserves, gambling on capturing sufficient gasoline to gain Liége and Antwerp. He ordered three of von Rundstedt's armies—the Seventh, and the Fifth and Sixth Panzers (ten tank divisions, 14 infantry)—to attack on Dec. 16 over a 75-mile front which was held by only five U.S. divisions. Two great gaps were torn in the lines. Some new divisions were scattered, but the 2nd Infantry fought back heroically, as did the 7th Armored, which hung on grimly at St. Vith to split the German advance. The First Army turned south to block the way to Liége. Montgomery sent troops to prevent a Meuse crossing, and Patton struck hard against the southern flank. On Dec. 23 the weather cleared and the Air Forces began wrecking German tanks and trucks inside the Bulge. Early in January von Rundstedt withdrew, having lost more than 600 tanks and suffered some 90,000 casualties.

FOXHOLES IN SNOW of the Ardennes are dug by U.S. infantrymen after death of a comrade from German artillery fire. Total Allied casualties in winter weather, which hindered men and planes, were 77,000.

GROUNDED FOR BATTLE, men of the 82nd Airborne Division advance behind tank after helping bolster northern flank of Bulge. Like other Americans in the north, they were under Montgomery's command.

A HEINOUS CRIME was the murder of U.S. prisoners near Malmédy on second day. Later their bodies were tagged for identification and in 1946 the Nazi killers were put on trial for the "Malmédy massacre."

IN FAMOUS BASTOGNE, where Major General Anthony C. McAuliffe answered a German demand for surrender of 101st Airborne with word "Nuts!", a weary infantryman rests after surviving Battle of Bulge.

ON THE EDGE OF THE EXPANDING BULGE ATTACKING GERMANS SKULKED THROUGH THE FIELDS BESIDE A ROAD JAMMED WITH U.S. VEHICLES

AFTER SCOUTING THE ROAD LEADER BECKONED HIS COMRADES INTO THE OPEN, WHERE THEY LOPED ALONG PAST A BURNING U.S. HALF-TRACK

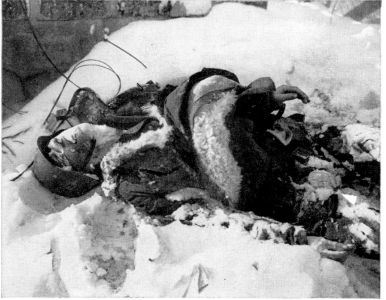

GERMAN LOOTERS ENJOYED U.S. CIGARETS ONLY A SHORT TIME; ONE DIED IN THE SNOW WITH A BOX OF AMERICAN MATCHES UNDER HIS LEFT HAND

Fight to the Rhine

WINTER SNOW AND MIST HID THE GERMANS IN NORTHERN ARDENNES FOREST AS U.S. ARMIES STARTED SQUEEZING THEM BACK OUT OF THE BULGE

HITLER'S defeat in the Bulge battle was overwhelming. In addition to the ground losses, his gamble with his dwindling air resources proved disastrous, and he was now open as never before to great and devastating Allied air attacks. General Kurt Manteuffel, one of his closer confidants, has stated the position clearly: "After the Ardennes failure, Hitler started a 'corporal's' war. There were no big plans—only a multitude of piecemeal fights." This small war was vicious and protracted as the Allied attack toward the Rhine began; the German will to fight was still strong, especially among elite units like the SS and parachute divisions. But the Allies could not fail unless they began fighting among themselves—which they almost did. Montgomery, who had always favored a thrust in the north (his area) rather than an attack on a broad front, held a press conference and implied that in the Bulge the Americans had to call him in to save their skins. For a time the U.S. and British press boiled over with the Bradley *vs.* Montgomery debate, but it was quickly forgotten as the Allies fought their way into Germany.

ONE U.S. GUN CARRIAGE HALTS AS ANOTHER SLIDES OFF THE ICY ROAD

297

AT REMAGEN ON MARCH 7, U.S. PATROLS SEIZED THE LUDENDORFF BRIDGE ACROSS THE RHINE. FIVE DIVISIONS GOT ACROSS BEFORE BRIDGE COLLAPSED AND BY

THE battle of the Rhineland began almost as soon as the Bulge was no more. On Jan. 20, 1945 Lieut. General Jacob L. Devers started the preliminaries with his Sixth Army Group. His objective was to eliminate the Germans in the Colmar pocket west of the Rhine between the Swiss border and the Saar. Colmar surrendered on Feb. 3. Five days later the Canadian army jumped off in the north, attacking southeastward between the Maas and the Rhine, but ran into floods as well as savage opposition from German parachutists. With the Canadians, Lieut. General William H. Simpson's U.S. Ninth Army (part of Montgomery's group) cleared the area west of the Rhine in the north. The First Army, now returned to Bradley's group, drove toward Cologne and Remagen while the Third struck toward Coblenz. Along a 400-mile front the enemy was pushed through his own country up against his own beloved river. The question of getting across remained.

MARCH 24 THEY HAD A 25-MILE GRIP ON GERMANY'S VITALS

FOR 20 centuries control of the Rhine, one of Europe's greatest natural barriers, had been a vital factor in the politics of the Continent. No invading troops had crossed it since Napoleon in 1805. The Germans had, of course, arranged to blow up the bridges which spanned the river, and the Allies had brought along their own crossing equipment: 2,500 boats, 6,000 pontoon floats, 100,000 tons of bridging material, 315,000 feet of wire rope and 8,000 feet of chain. The U.S. Navy showed up with fleets of LCMs and LCVPs, about 1,000 sailors and a handful of Seabees. But the first crossing of the Rhine this March of 1945 belonged to a group of soldiers who, in Eisenhower's words, seized "one of those rare and fleeting opportunities which occasionally present themselves in war." The 9th Armored Division was leading the III Corps of Hodges' First Army in the race toward the 1,200-foot Ludendorff Bridge at Remagen, with Brig. General William M. Hoge's combat command out in front. The defense on the other side was weak and bewildered, unable to stem the American torrent that was soon sweeping across. Hitler relieved von Rundstedt and brought Kesselring up from Italy.

RUPTURED PILLBOX GUARDED SIEGFRIED LINE'S "DRAGON-TOOTH" TANK TRAPS AT AACHEN

BITTER FIGHTING LEFT LONG LINE OF CRIPPLED AMERICAN TANKS IN THE HURTGEN FOREST

THE DYING GERMAN AIR FORCE LEFT ITS PLUMAGE IN THE SNOW, LOSING SOME 1,600 PLANES DURING THE BATTLE OF THE BULGE

PUSHING THE GERMANS BACK FROM BELGIUM, MEN OF THE U.S. FIRST ARMY WARMED UP ALONG THE WINTER ROAD TO THE RHINE

CROSSING THE RHINE SOUTH OF MAINZ, ASSAULT TROOPS OF U.S. THIRD ARMY LAY LOW AS THEIR AMPHIBIOUS TRUCK NEARED THE EAST BANK

Rhine crossing

exposed the heart of the enemy homeland to Allied assault. To exploit the Remagen bridgehead (*map*), General Eisenhower hurried the III, V and VII Corps across the historic river. The operation required considerable engineering wizardry, especially after the collapse of the Ludendorff span on March 17. The first big Treadway bridge—metal tracks on pontoons capable of supporting tanks and other vehicles—was put down in ten hours and 11 minutes. Grateful Major General Collins bought champagne for his hairy-eared engineers. The Germans, defending the Rhine line from Switzerland to the North Sea with 70 undermanned divisions, could meet the Remagen threat only by weakening their defense elsewhere. On March 22 General Patton rushed up to the Rhine at Oppenheim. The enemy had destroyed all bridges, so Major General Stafford Irwin's 5th Division was rowed across in small boats. Thirty-six hours later General Montgomery's Twenty-first Group made a more deliberate thrust along a four-division front in the north. Monty telegraphed his punch but German defenses were weak. The 30th and 79th U.S. Divisions suffered only 31 casualties. By April 1 seven Allied armies had crossed the river: the U.S. Ninth, First, Seventh and Third; British Second, Canadian First and French First. Winston Churchill followed the British troops across and, with his feet planted firmly on German soil, predicted an early and decisive victory.

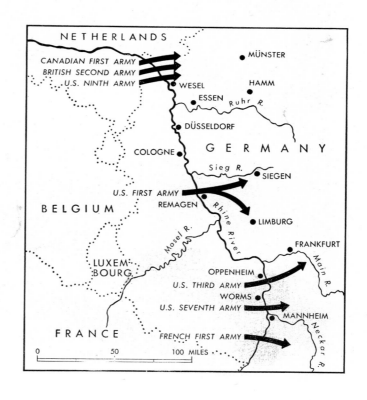

TO SPAN THE RHINE assault craft and bridging materials were assembled in big supply depots. Most elaborate build-up was in Montgomery's northern sector, where the principal thrust was made. A few LCMs and LCVPs were brought to the front via the Continent's inland waterways, but most of the landing craft were transported overland (on specially constructed trailers) despite their size: up to 45 feet long, 14 feet wide.

ENGINEERS UNLOADED BRIDGE BEAMS NEAR A BROKEN RHINE SPAN

LIFT SHOVEL DUG GRAVEL FROM RAILROAD BED FOR BRIDGEHEADS

NINTH ARMY TRUCK CRANE LAID A STEEL TREAD ON FIRST PONTOON

LAUNCHES SHOVED THE LAST LINK INTO PLACE FOR BINDING ROPES

BRITISH ENGINEERS BUILT A HIGHWAY BRIDGE FROM BOTH BANKS

EN ROUTE TO THE RHINE, MAAS RIVER WAS SPANNED WITH PILINGS

MOTOR CONVOY CROSSED FINISHED PONTOON BRIDGE AT REMAGEN

AT REES THE BRITISH LAID DOWN A PERMANENT RAILWAY BRIDGE

THIS PONTOON BRIDGE, thrown across the Rhine at Worms by some of the 75,000 Army engineers, was named for the commanding general of the U.S. Seventh Army, who had come to Europe from the Pacific. In the background are the ruins of the original bridge, which was destroyed by the Germans in a futile effort to keep the Allies on the western side of the river. "Courtesy" signs were posted by most proud engineering units.

BRITISH AND AMERICAN AIRBORNE TROOPS MADE LANDINGS BETWEEN EMMERICH AND WESEL, EXPANDING THE BRIDGEHEAD NORTH OF THE RUHR

SOME WERE CAUGHT in the trees but cut themselves loose. Others, not so lucky, made easy targets. Operation Varsity used a total of 1,572 planes and 1,326 gliders, protected by an air umbrella of 3,042 fighters.

SOME WERE HURT, but this paratrooper being carried to aid station was one of the relatively few casualties. Only 4% of the gliders were destroyed; 55 transport planes were lost, mostly to antiaircraft fire.

AIRBORNE TROOPS start forming for the attack after clearing the landing area and capturing the first of 3,500 prisoners taken during the first day. In what General Eisenhower called Europe's most successful airborne operation Montgomery pulled two surprises—he launched the amphibious assault before the airdrop and he spotted the drop within an area which his own artillery could support. Germans were deceived on both counts.

The Ruhr

with its great industries was the major objective of the assault across the Rhine. The whole area was bombed for more than a month in an effort to isolate it as Normandy was isolated prior to D-day. On Feb. 21, 1945 the Air Forces launched Operation Clarion to block off transportation from the Ruhr, thus depriving the Wehrmacht of vital munitions; 9,000 aircraft from bases in Britain, France, Belgium and Holland took part. Targets were now so close to the advance bases of fighters and bombers that planes often flew two sorties a day. Bridges, communications centers, dikes and railroad yards were hit, and 5,000-ton high-explosive packages fell on Essen and Dortmund-Ems in the heart of the Ruhr. During four days (March 21–24) the Allied Air Forces flew 42,000 missions over Germany—more than in all of 1942. The Luftwaffe apparently was doomed; some days the Allies had 80 aircraft flying for each German plane. But German scientists might still pull a whopping rabbit out of Hitler's hat, so airfields where jets were based got particular attention, as did snorkel submarine pens and U-boat plants.

CANNON-ARMED ME-410 MAKES CLOSE PASS AT AN AMERICAN BOMBER

AIR ATTACKS FIRED HAMBURG SHIPYARDS WHICH SPAWNED U-BOATS

EIGHT OF HAMBURG'S OIL REFINERIES WERE LEFT BURNING BY ONE OF THE

EIGHTH AIR FORCE'S REPEATED DEMOLITION RAIDS ON GERMAN INDUSTRY

RAIDS FELLED BRIDGES, GUTTED MEDIEVAL BUILDINGS IN BREMEN

IN THE RUHR, BOCHUM'S PLANTS AND RAIL SIDINGS WERE SMASHED

BOMB CRATERS GAVE NORTHERN RHINE CITY OF WESEL A LUNAR LOOK

IN FLOODED HOLLAND Canadian troops utilized Buffaloes (armored amphibian vehicles) to advance after the Germans blasted the dikes in an effort to halt the attack. These drastic flooding tactics finally forced

Eisenhower to call off the attack lest Holland be ruined. He agreed to halt the advance if Artur Seyss-Inquart, Nazi high commissioner, persuaded the Germans to stop flooding and allow relief supplies to be brought in.

IN THE FIELD Canadian and British troops used mortars to slug it out with Nazis of the First Parachute Army. The Canadians' mission was to clear the coastal belt and protect the left flank of the Ruhr attack.

HOUSE-TO-HOUSE fighting became intense at Arnhem before Germans were driven out. City and its vital bridge across the lower Rhine finally were liberated on April 15, 1945, seven months after the initial assault.

Ruhr trap

was the largest pocket envelopment in history, a modern, inflated version of the Battle of Cannae (216 B.C.), when Hannibal gobbled up the Romans. West of the Rhine the Germans lost 350,000 prisoners in March alone. Not only was the Rhine line breached; Allied airpower had now deprived the Wehrmacht of mobility and air support and equipment. Faced with possible loss of Germany's vital industries, Field Marshal Walther Model, commanding Army Group B, could only mass men in the Ruhr. But by the time Montgomery had crossed the Rhine at Wesel, Bradley had thrown an army into the Remagen bridgehead. March 26, 1945 Lieut. General Courtney Hodges' First Army attacked eastward when the Germans were expecting to be struck from the Sieg River in the south. Quickly linking his troops with Patton's forces at Giessen, Hodges turned north, meeting Lieut. General William Simpson's Ninth Army at Lippstadt on April 1, and completing the encirclement of the Ruhr. With some armored elements driving east to prevent the enemy from regrouping, other parts of Bradley's forces remained to clean up the Ruhr. By April 14 the pocket was split in two; four days later all had ended. Even the most optimistic Allied officers were staggered at this haul of 325,000 prisoners. After collapse of the Ruhr Colonel General Alfred Jodl, the German chief of staff, had no over-all operations plan. A German front in Western Europe no longer existed.

GERMAN TANKS attempted to hold Ruhr cities by covering the vital street intersections. Here a Mark V burns after being hit three times by 90-mm. shells. Hitler said fight on, though situation was hopeless.

ALLIED INFANTRY fought their way across the rubble of ruined factories in the industrial heart of Germany; in many towns German civilians were found fighting alongside Nazi soldiers. With the trap springing shut,

General Bradley ordered the destruction or capture of German forces in the enormous Ruhr pocket by a frontal assault. He used three corps totaling 17 divisions, leaving a fourth corps to hold the line of the Rhine.

DEFEATED AND DISARMED, THESE GERMAN PRISONERS WERE PART OF A MASS OF 82,000 POCKETED EAST OF THE RIVER RHINE NEAR GUMMERSBACH

Prisoners captured in the Ruhr included 30 general officers and troops from 21 divisions, three armies and two army groups. There was little in front of Berlin, 275 miles to the east, to stop Eisenhower's armies. In the final drive toward the capital armored divisions, supplied by air, advanced as much as 100 miles a day. But Eisenhower did not drive on to Berlin, as Churchill urged. He informed Stalin that he would stop on the Elbe—55 miles west of Berlin—and await Soviet forces (which were within 30 miles of the city on the east). Some critics have called Eisenhower's halt the war's greatest blunder, but he figured that Berlin was militarily worthless, and zones of occupation had already been set, anyway. Besides, he was anxious 1) to drive north and stop a German retreat into Denmark and 2) rush south to disrupt a "national redoubt" which Hitler had once planned in the Bavarian Alps as the last citadel of Nazism. Eisenhower's seven armies (four American, one each of British, Canadians and French) quickly accomplished these purposes. In overrunning Germany they uncovered the results of Nazism's hideous inhumanity—gas chambers, scheduled starvation, human vivisection: every conceivable atrocity for millions of people Hitler didn't like. The names of these concentration camps—Dachau, Buchenwald, Belsen—will live as long as the memory of World War II itself.

JOURNEY'S END FOR THIS GERMAN WAS INSIDE A WIRE STOCKADE

THE BODIES OF 3,000 SLAVE LABORERS WERE LAID OUT IN A STREET AT NORDHAUSEN WHERE THEY HAD BEEN STARVED AND BEATEN TO DEATH

AT BELSEN THE SS GUARDS WERE FORCED TO BURY THEIR VICTIMS

A FREED AMERICAN PRISONER WAS GAUNT WITH NEAR-STARVATION

311

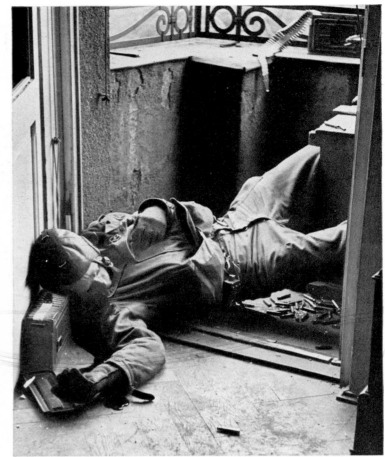

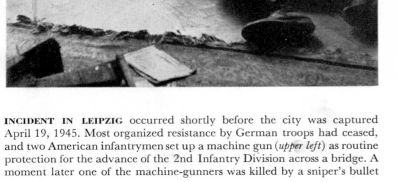

INCIDENT IN LEIPZIG occurred shortly before the city was captured April 19, 1945. Most organized resistance by German troops had ceased, and two American infantrymen set up a machine gun (*upper left*) as routine protection for the advance of the 2nd Infantry Division across a bridge. A moment later one of the machine-gunners was killed by a sniper's bullet (*upper right*). A friend moved forward to help him, found it too late and took over the gun (*below, left* and *right*). Other members of the platoon took to the streets to search out the sniper and surrounded several German soldiers in a streetcar, who hastily surrendered. Such opposition continued to plague the Western Allies after the collapse of the Ruhr.

Retreat from Russia

TWO GERMANS MANNING AN ISOLATED GUN POSITION WATCHED THE WINTER WASTES OF RUSSIA FOR THE FIRST SIGN OF THE ADVANCING RED ARMY

TO the Germans, who had anticipated an inevitable victory over Russia in 1941 and at least a stalemate in 1942 and 1943 while the Reich's Western enemies were brought to their senses, the last year and a half of war boiled with chaos that seemed inexplicable. These somber paintings by German artists reflect the plight of Hitler's soldiers in retreat and defeat. The close of the Russian offensive in 1943 found the Germans being pushed back along the entire 2,000-mile front. That was only the beginning. In December 1943 the two behemoths were squared off against each other for a war that strained the imagination. There were 207 German divisions; the Finns, Hungarians and Romanians added 49 more (according to Soviet figures), and the Spanish "Blue Division" which Francisco Franco contributed to Hitler made a 50th. Against these 257 divisions the Russians could muster more than 400—better equipped and better trained than ever before. During 1944 ten great battles were fought; the Russians won them all. At the year's beginning the Germans still occupied 180,000 square miles of ·Russian territory; before the cold dawn of 1945 no Germans except war prisoners remained on Soviet soil, and Russians were already in East Prussia. During the year Germany and her satellites lost 136 divisions. In some sectors the Russian armies advanced nearly 700 miles, from the Dnieper River to the Carpathian Mountains. The greatest defeat was in the Ukraine, which had been conquered so easily in 1941 when millions of Ukrainians seemed happy to escape the Soviet yoke. But when Marshal Georgi Zhukov staged his March 1944 offensive the surviving Ukrainians seemed just as happy to get from under the Nazi heel. Zhukov destroyed 70 German divisions in a great offensive near Kamenets Podolsk, while his running mate Marshal Ivan Konev captured 500 tanks and 12,000 vehicles. By April they were approaching the border of Czechoslovakia. General Fedor Tolbukhin and Marshal Alexander Vasilevsky overwhelmed German and Romanian defenders in the Crimea, killing or capturing 11,500 Germans as the Black Sea fleet and Soviet air force sank 198 supply and troop ships (again according to Soviet figures). In the north Marshal Leonid Govorov pierced the Mannerheim line and Finland later in the year switched sides. Romania and Bulgaria dropped out. Before the end of 1944 the Germans were fighting almost alone in the East, and in the squeeze Hitler was turning desperately to his mad Ardennes offensive.

EARLY in 1945 Adolf Hitler's world began to disintegrate, not only in the Ardennes but also on the other vast front. The Russian thrust against East Prussia, where German airmen vainly flew from puny emergency air-strips (*above*), ended in victory 15 days after it began. In the south the push against Vienna was preceded by Marshal Tolbukhin's attack on Budapest, which fell Feb. 13. Marshal Rodion Malinovsky took Vienna April 13. Hitler's Colonel General Guderian, father of the blitzkrieg, now in command in the east, concentrated most of his 120 divisions (including 30 Panzers) to defend Berlin, but Zhukov and Konev bowled him over with 22,000 guns. On May 1 Stalin declared the Germans in the last three months of the war had lost a million killed, 800,000 prisoners, 12,000 tanks and 23,000 artillery pieces. The Russian army had in four years become a mighty factor in world politics.

WITH THE BLEAK DAWN A NAZI COLUMN RESUMED ITS RETREAT THROUGH EAST PRUSSIA

A SMALL GERMAN PATROL SORTIED THROUGH THE WOODS AGAINST ADVANCING RUSSIANS

ENTRENCHED IN THE SACRED PRUSSIAN SOIL OF THE FATHERLAND, WORN NAZI VETERANS WAITED FOR THE NEXT MASSIVE BLOW BY THE RED ARMY

AT REICH CHANCELLERY IN BERLIN, HITLER SENT GERMAN BOYS OFF TO DO A MAN'S HOPELESS JOB IN THE GAPING RANKS OF THE WEHRMACHT

Hitler encountered his fate on April 30, 1945, his Third Reich having lasted 988 years less than the millennium he predicted for it. Already the Russians were in the ruins of Berlin. At Eisenhower's orders the Western Allies had been waiting for 12 days on the Elbe. Now there was but one role left for Hitler to play. His stage was the narrow confines of the *Führerbunker*, more than 50 feet beneath the Reich Chancellery. He was almost alone. The strident voice that once had harangued Nazism's mobs mumbled marriage vows as Eva Braun, for more than 10 years Hitler's mistress, became his wife. At his Bavarian retreat Göring decided he should now become Führer under terms of a 1941 decree, and he proposed to take over "by 10 o'clock tonight" (April 23). "A crass ultimatum," screamed Hitler and ordered Göring's arrest. At first timidly, then boldly, Heinrich Himmler tried to conduct peace negotiations through Count Folke Bernadotte of Sweden. But in his last will and testament, signed April 29, Hitler had designated Grand Admiral Karl Doenitz the new Führer. Then, according to reliable reports, he surrendered to a deep melancholia. At 3:30 p.m. on the 30th a single pistol shot was heard within the bunker, above the muffled boom of Russian shells outside. Hitler's body was found on a blood-soaked sofa, a bullet through the head. Lifeless beside him was Eva Braun, poisoned. The bodies were carried to the garden by SS men and soaked with gasoline. If there were any remains, they have defied searchers' efforts to find them, and in the imagination of the faithful Adolf Hitler still turns up periodically in one or another remote corner of the earth.

OBVIOUSLY SHAKEN, HITLER INSPECTED THE RUIN OF GERMANY

317

Fall of Berlin

came at 1 p.m. on May 2, 1945—just 48 hours after Hitler's suicide and 12 days after the beginning of the attack by some two million soldiers of the armies of Marshals Georgi Zhukov and Ivan Konev. Hitler had issued orders to "drown the Russians in a sea of blood and hold Berlin at all costs," and thousands of civilians rushed to help the soldiers at the hastily erected barricades. The onrushing waves of Red infantrymen were buttressed by some 4,000 tanks, 2,000 guns and mortars and nearly 5,000 planes. Berlin's fanatical defenders fell back to fight from house to house and, finally, in subways and sewers. By their suicidal stand the Nazi extremists brought vastly greater devastation to what had been the world's fourth largest city, in which the R.A.F. and AAF bombers had laid waste 6,000 acres by round-the-clock raids. The final cataclysm might have been avoided, but on May Day a sniper shot a Red Army major who was accompanying a German peace emissary under a white flag. In retaliation the Russians loosed a 24-hour artillery barrage. It was General Kurt Weidling himself, commander of the remnants of the half million Nazi defenders, who scrambled out of the ruins to surrender, this time irrevocably. The Red banner was unfurled over the gutted Reichstag building. It was almost 42 months since the Russians had begun fighting off the apparently unbeatable Nazi legions at the gates of Moscow.

A RUSSIAN HOWITZER BLASTED THE STUBBORN NAZIS IN THE HEART OF BERLIN

VICTORIOUS RUSSIANS RODE THEIR TANK-DESTROYERS PAST A SILENCED TANK (RIGHT) WITH WHICH NAZIS HAD DEFENDED THIS BERLIN SQUARE

DURING 12 DAYS OF SAVAGE STREET FIGHTING IN BERLIN, RED ARTILLERY COMPLETED THE DESOLATION LEFT BY FOUR YEARS OF ALLIED BOMBING

RED ARMY SOLDIERS LEFT HUNDREDS OF AUTOGRAPHS ON BERLIN'S BOMB-GUTTED REICHSTAG, WHICH GORING FIRST VANDALIZED BY FIRE IN 1933

Surrender of an absolutely beaten Germany was signed at 2:41 a.m. on May 7, 1945 at General Eisenhower's headquarters in the technical college at Rheims, France. Fighting in Europe ended the next midnight. The final collapse had begun in the West on April 29: a million demoralized men gave up in Italy, 400,000 in Bavaria, another million in the Hamburg area. On May 4 word reached Eisenhower from Flensburg, where Grand Admiral Doenitz had set up the government authorized in Hitler's last testament, that Admiral Hans Georg Friedeburg, the new head of the German navy, was on the way to Allied headquarters to negotiate surrender. At first the Germans insisted on surrendering only to the Western Allies. But General Eisenhower sent word that nothing less than unconditional surrender to all the Allies, including the Russian, would be accepted. Finally, at a long wooden table in the bare, map-plastered war room of Allied headquarters, the unconditional documents were signed. Then Doenitz' representative, Colonel General Jodl, was taken into Eisenhower's office and charged with responsibility for carrying out the terms. At Russian headquarters in Berlin 45 hours later the ceremonies were repeated.

SURROUNDED BY MAPS RECORDING THE FALL OF THE REICH, THE ALLIED HIGH COMMAND RECEIVES GERMANY'S UNCONDITIONAL SURRENDER

GENERAL JODL, WEHRMACHT CHIEF OF STAFF, SIGNS FOR GERMANY

WALTER BEDELL SMITH SIGNS IN BEHALF OF GENERAL EISENHOWER

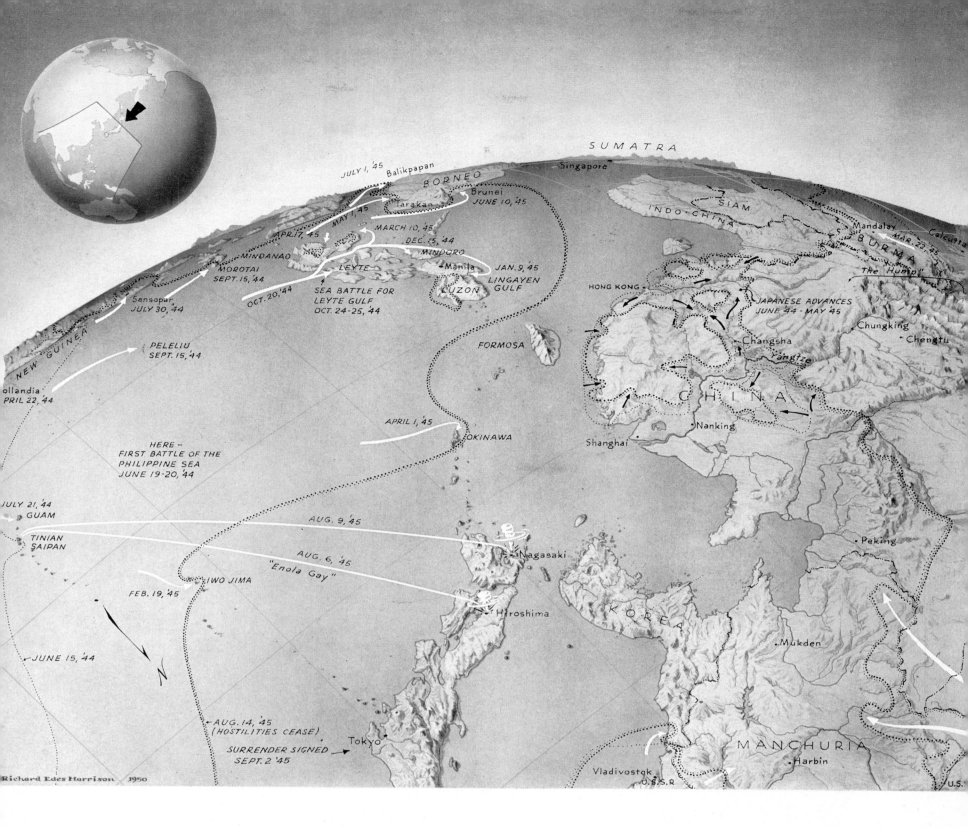

XII

Victory in the Pacific

Pacific: 1944–45

THE last year of the war against Japan finds no anchor in plausibility, nor any reliable modern precedent except the suicide charge which the Balinese men and women, armed with spears, made against Dutch rifles and artillery in 1906. Nine days after the Normandy landings, and 5,000 miles west of San Francisco, American troops started blasting the Japanese out of their caves on the craggy island of Saipan in the Marianas. In the course of this operation a part of the Japanese imperial fleet came out and Mitscher's pilots swept its flight decks almost clean of planes. The loss of this strategic island and the failure of the fleet so shook Tokyo (only 1,270 miles away) that Tojo's cabinet fell out of office. It should have been evident to all, as Admiral Kawai said it was to him, that "the Marianas Islands formed the very front line of the mainland of Japan." The B-29s were plainly due; Japan's best pilots were all gone down in flames. With the conquest of Saipan, decisions on the final course of Pacific strategy were needed, and Roosevelt went to Honolulu from Washington and MacArthur from Brisbane to discuss them. There was disagreement. The Navy was willing to land MacArthur in the southern Philippines, now that the Central and Southwest Pacific were converging, but figured it wasn't necessary to take him back to Manila. Instead the admirals favored seizing Formosa, then going on to the China coast to cut off the Japanese homeland from all southern resources. MacArthur, publicly and fervently committed to returning to Luzon, turned from the conference believing he had lost his case, but at the last minute the President beckoned him and said, in effect, "All right, we'll go back to Manila."

IT remained for "Bull" Halsey, boss of the rampaging Third Fleet, to swing the strategy again, at a time when the 1st Marine Divison was securing the Philippines' flank in the battle of Peleliu. The Joint Chiefs of Staff, who were in session at Quebec, quickly obtained the endorsement of both Pacific commands for Halsey's proposal to jump to Leyte in the central Philippines in October 1944 instead of invading Mindanao in December. This put the burden of covering the landing on Halsey's carrier forces, since MacArthur's own fighter planes could not cover all the way from newly seized Morotai. But Halsey would try anything. In mid-October, as the great Allied invasion force approached Leyte, Japan's Admiral Toyoda threw the switch for his long-planned showdown with the U.S. Navy. He had little hope of winning, but he gambled anyway. With the Leyte beachhead only four days old, Halsey's Third Fleet and Admiral Thomas C. Kinkaid's Seventh Fleet met the imperial navy in a desperate battle. Mistakes were made by both sides in this engagement—the greatest naval battle ever fought—but fortunately the most serious errors were committed by the Japanese. When it was over (and its crucial stage lasted only a few hours) the Battle for Leyte Gulf had reduced the Japanese navy to an insignificant factor in future operations.

Months before the victory of Leyte Gulf (in fact, as soon as Saipan fell), many high officers in Japan realized that the Japanese cause was lost. There were some cautious movements toward peace even then, but the Japanese people were uninformed and the army warlords recognized only two choices: victory or death. With the stupendous American victory in the Philippines (MacArthur was back in Luzon by January 1945), suicide had become an official Japanese tactic. The nightmare days of the Kamikazes were at hand, and U.S. forces were confronted by the terrifying spectacle of Japanese pilots seeking godhood at the Yasukuni shrine by crashing their planes into American ships, immolating themselves in the name of the god-emperor. By this time in the war U.S. pilots had achieved a superiority so decisive that rubbing out Japanese pilots was nearly as easy as potting toy balloons with a shotgun. The supposedly vulnerable carriers had no hesitation about standing off the Philippines or Formosa for days at a time. The Kamikazes changed all that; pilots who could get through the fighter screen and antiaircraft fire found they could hit with their bombs if they rode down with them. At a sacrifice of no life except his own, the suicide pilot might take 200 or 300 Americans with him. Altogether 650 suicide missions were flown against ships around the Philippines and 174 were successful. At Okinawa defenses were better, but the number of suicide attempts was greater: 279 ships were hit in 1,900 tries. For a time a few thousand incredibly brave aerial guerrillas threatened to stultify the efforts of the entire, mighty U.S. armada. But the fleet had come to stay, and stay it did. Among some 13,000 U.S. sailors killed in the last year of the war, Kamikazes accounted for nearly three fourths.

OTHERWISE the fight moved remorselessly toward its end. In January 1945 Halsey was able to take his task force into the South China Sea itself, and in one day sank 46 ships off the Indochina coast (he claimed only 41). While MacArthur's forces mopped up the Philippines, the Marines captured Iwo Jima to give the B-29s based in the Marianas both fighter cover and a midway emergency field for damaged bombers. With long-range fighters to support them, the B-29s—defying enemy antiaircraft fire—came down below 10,000 feet and began area fire-bombing. Half the built-up section of Tokyo was incinerated; in some other cities even more was wiped out. As a preliminary to the actual invasion of Japan, Marine and Army forces landed in Okinawa—380 miles south of Japan proper—and conquered that island group in three grueling months.

In July, while the Potsdam Conference was in session, the first atomic explosion occurred in New Mexico. The conference drafted an ultimatum calling on the Japanese to surrender. When an unsatisfactory answer came from Tokyo, President Truman, mindful of the terrible cost in American lives on Iwo Jima and Okinawa, authorized the Air Forces to drop two atomic bombs on Japanese cities. On Aug. 6 Hiroshima was obliterated. On Aug. 8 Stalin, acting on a decision (and timetable) approved at Yalta, declared war on the Japanese, and the next day, while a second bomb was destroying a large part of Nagasaki, Soviet troops crossed the Manchurian border and proceeded to achieve the Kremlin's aims of far-eastern expansion where the czar's government had been thwarted in 1905. On Sept. 2 a capitulation signed on the battleship *Missouri* in Tokyo Bay ended the hostilities begun at Pearl Harbor and put the Japanese emperor and his government under the orders of General MacArthur. The Pacific phase of the second of the world wars of the bloody 20th Century had ended, but its ending brought no peace.   —JOHN DOS PASSOS

OFF THE NEW GUINEA COAST two PT boats (patrol, torpedo) set out on a night mission. The PTs, sometimes called "Petes," were used for both combat and rescue work. They shot up many barges and damaged some larger ships, such as the old cruiser *Abukuma*, which was thereupon sunk by Army Air Forces bombers. The 77-foot boats usually carried two officers, nine men, four torpedoes, five machine guns and, later, rockets.

DAYLIGHT HIDE-OUTS for PTs frequently were jungle creeks. At night their white wakes (at 45 mph) lent credence to their motto (from John Paul Jones): "Give me a fast ship, for I intend to go in harm's way."

JAPANESE PRISONER is hauled aboard in Surigao Strait after his ship had been sunk. The PTs led the attack on the southern Japanese force in the Battle for Leyte Gulf and later searched the area for survivors.

Ship to Shore

IN THIS PAINTING BY TOM LEA, A WAR-DAUBED ASSAULT MARINE STARES INTO THE SMOKE BARRAGE CLOAKING PELELIU'S BLAZING BEACHES

EVER since primitive man paddled across a lake intent upon slaying his enemy, the amphibious assault has been one of the most hazardous of all military operations. The advantage lies with the solidly grounded defender if he can bring his stones (or bombs or artillery shells) to bear upon his assailant who must approach the shore slowly and infirmly. The assailant must not only get ashore, he must assure himself of steady reinforcements and supplies—Churchill's Gallipoli campaign of 1915 failed because reinforcements were insufficient. The long and costly Gallipoli frustration (nine months, 120,000 British casualties) had a profound effect on military thinking of the next quarter century. Adolph Hitler's plan for bringing the British to account never seriously contemplated a landing on England's shores. Conversely, the Allies built up bases and adopted a plan for their own great crossing of the English Channel. But this took four years. Between wars Gallipoli burned the memory of others besides Hitler. The U.S. Army had no instruction manuals for amphibious warfare until 1940. The U.S. Navy was preoccupied with the idea of sweeping the enemy fleet from the seas. Amphibious warfare was entrusted to a branch of the Navy—the U.S. Marine Corps. During the '30s the marines developed the rudimentary amphibious techniques and tactics for World War II, plus some of the equipment (the amphibian tractor they evolved from a vehicle used for rescue work in the Florida Everglades).

Beginning in 1941 Major General Holland M. ("Howlin' Mad") Smith's Atlantic Fleet marines trained Army personnel in hit-the-beach techniques, including the divisions which later led the assaults in North Africa, Sicily, Normandy and southern France. But it was in the island-dotted Pacific that amphibious warfare reached its full fruition. Altogether 163 amphibious landings were made in that ocean, 68 of them opposed. None failed, for the reason that the U.S. rarely undertook an operation until it could bring overwhelming weight to bear against the Japanese. The pattern as finally evolved represented the most notable contribution the U.S. made to the science of war. First, air superiority was established by knocking out all enemy aviation within several hundred miles—by carrier planes or (for shorter leaps forward) by land-based aircraft. Naval gunfire pounded beach targets for several hours or several days before the amtracs and boats began unloading (the more naval gunfire the fewer casualties was the rule). As the small craft moved through the long, last, guts-gripping mile, guns, rockets and planes opened up with all the firepower they could deliver. Once a beachhead had been cleared the LSTs, LCIs and other ramped vehicles snuggled up with supplies; when a deep-water channel had been cleared and pontoon piers built, the bigger cargo ships could move in to discharge their carefully combat-loaded goods of war. In Pacific invasions one factor was constant: the enemy waiting on the beach would fight to the death.

325

Ulithi atoll became the Pacific fleet's big forward base after its seizure (unopposed) in September 1944. Even with the battle fleet away in action, the lagoon was heavily populated with auxiliary vessels (*left*). And at other times, such as the assemblage before the invasion of Okinawa, more than 1,000 ships might be seen within this circle of reef-linked islands. Ulithi was the rendezvous point, 360 miles southwest of Guam, for fighting ships and supply ships, and it was here the former got bombs, beans and bullets. After weeks at sea 15,000 sailors at a time went ashore on Mogmog Island for a feel of the land and a can of beer.

AMTRACS CIRCLED OFF PELELIU BEFORE LANDING 1ST MARINE DIVISION, WHICH TOOK 6,265 CASUALTIES IN 28-DAY BATTLE

NAVY ARTIST JON WHITCOMB PAINTED AN AMPHIBIAN TANK LEADING A LINE OF LANDING VEHICLES ASHORE ON PELELIU

SOFTENING UP SAIPAN FOR INVASION, U.S. CARRIER BOMBERS CAUGHT THE ENEMY'S BIG FLYING BOATS ON THEIR TANAPAG HARBOR RAMPS (LEFT)

Saipan marked the breaching of Japan's inner defense line and the fall of the capital of her South Seas empire. This loss caused Fleet Admiral Osami Nagano, the emperor's naval adviser, to cry, "This is terrible! Hell is on us!" The bewildered premier, General Tojo, was dismissed. The day of flat atolls was over. Saipan's 29,662 well-armed defenders were dug into mountainside caves—digging them out was a job for the infantry. The 2nd and 4th Marine Divisions landed on June 15, 1944 in the face of heavy mortar and artillery fire, which caused 2,500 casualties. Next night elements of the Army's 27th Division began landing. Meanwhile a Japanese naval task force was hurrying toward Saipan, and submarines sank two 30,000-ton carriers and Vice Admiral Marc Mitscher's pilots sank another and destroyed more than 300 planes in the Philippine Sea battle. Ashore, fighting continued hot. When Saipan had been crossed the three U.S. divisions swung north and began the uphill battle for 1,554-foot-high Tapotchau and other hills of the 15-mile-long island. Because the National Guardsmen could not keep up with his hell-for-leather marines, Lieut. General Smith relieved the 27th's Major General Ralph Smith, setting off a controversy which overshadowed the good news of Saipan's fall on July 9. Saipan cost 4,442 dead, 12,724 wounded. In July, Holland Smith's forces moved into nearby Tinian and Guam to complete capture of the trio of Marianas bases for the B-29s.

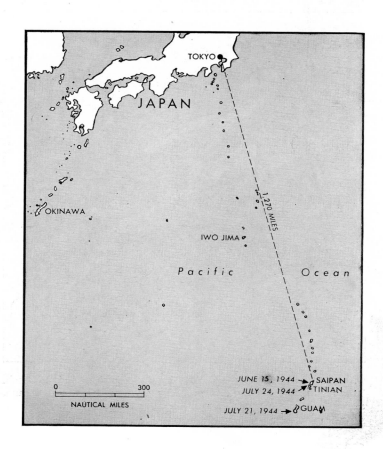

THE FIRST WAVE OF MARINES CROUCHED ALONG THE SAIPAN BEACH WHERE 700 AMTRACS (LEFT) LANDED 8,000 MEN IN THE FIRST 20 MINUTES

TWO MARINES are shot by Japanese snipers as they hit the Saipan beach. This remarkable photograph, made by a Coast Guard cameraman, shows these members of an assault battalion at instant of their falling.

A RIFLEMAN pauses beside a dead Japanese during mop-up following war's biggest banzai attack. More than 2,000 fanatical enemy soldiers fell upon U.S. lines, killed 500 infantrymen before being annihilated.

SAIPAN CIVILIANS surrender to U.S. soldiers after coming out of caves where they had hidden during shelling. Island's civilian population (3,282 native Chamorros, 20,280 Japanese) suffered many casualties.

JAPANESE WOMAN gets helping hand from soldier. Late in the battle about 1,000 terrified civilians, crazed by propaganda stories of American "brutality," committed suicide by drowning or with grenades.

BULLDOZER SCOOPED OUT A MASS GRAVE FOR SOME OF THE 2,000 JAPANESE WHO DIED FOR THE EMPEROR IN A FINAL BANZAI CHARGE ON JULY 7

TWENTY LSTs PUSHED INTO THE EDGE OF LEYTE'S TACLOBAN AIRSTRIP AND UNLOADED ACROSS THE EARTH RAMPS BUILT UP WITH BULLDOZERS

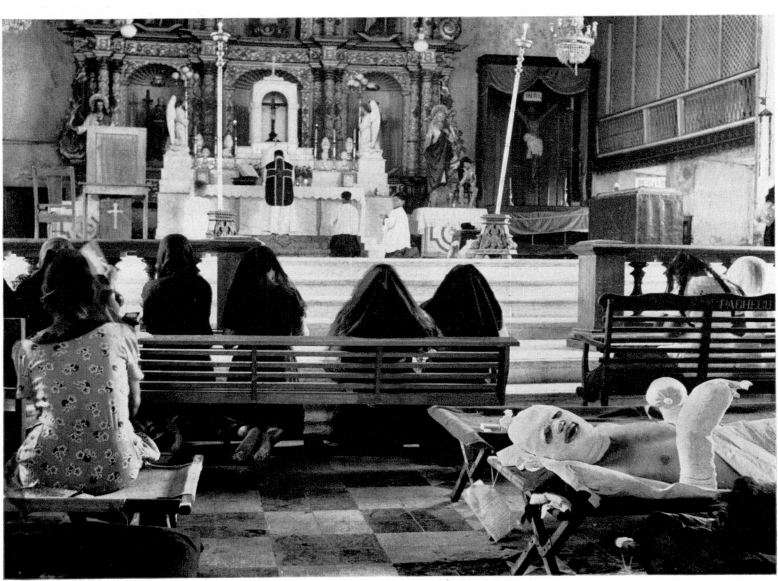

IN A CATHEDRAL ON LEYTE WHICH THE ARMY WAS USING AS A HOSPITAL, FILIPINOS WORSHIPED QUIETLY NEXT TO A BADLY BURNED AMERICAN

IN MINDORO INVASION EIGHT WEEKS AFTER LEYTE U.S. SHIPS WERE SET AFLAME BY CRASH-DIVING PILOTS OF JAPAN'S KAMIKAZE (SUICIDE) CORPS

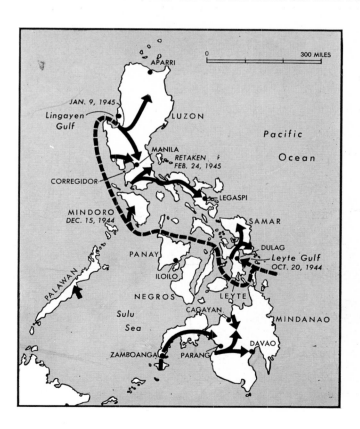

The return

to the Philippines had to await a two-year jungle-hopping campaign up the New Guinea coast—from Buna to the Huon Gulf to Saidor, Aitape, Hollandia, Wakde, Biak, Noemfoor and Sansapor. The Southwest Pacific war was limited by the range of its fighter planes (only at Hollandia did it have support from carriers), and it suffered from being tail-end-Charlie on the supply line. Admiral Halsey's Third Fleet fliers began to unlock the Philippines on Sept. 9, 1944; in the next two weeks they sank 69 ships and destroyed 893 planes in far-ranging strikes from southern Mindanao to Manila. Halsey suggested that the southern Philippines be leap-frogged: to go 300 miles farther north to Leyte in the center and do it immediately instead of waiting until December. Nimitz agreed and Lieut. General Richard Sutherland, speaking for General MacArthur (who was on a radio-silent cruiser off Morotai), also concurred. On Oct. 20 Lieut. General Walter Krueger's Sixth Army landed on Leyte without serious opposition, Major General Franklin Sibert's X Corps on the right and Major General John Hodge's XXIV Corps (loaned by Nimitz) on the left. But before the jungles were won two months later, 2,888 GIs had paid for Leyte with their lives. The Japanese, who had lost 56,263, would lose 27,000 more in the mop-up. The victorious Americans went on to Samar, Mindoro, Luzon and Mindanao (*map*).

333

Leyte Gulf landings precipitated the greatest naval action of all time and the last of the four decisive battles in the war against Japan (the others: Midway, Guadalcanal and Saipan). Admiral Soemu Toyoda, Japan's third commander in chief of the combined fleet, had no more of those finely trained carrier pilots. But he still had nine battleships (including the mighty *Yamato* and *Musashi*, never before committed), 23 cruisers (14 heavy, nine light) and 63 destroyers. With the Leyte landings he invoked Sho Operation No. 1, the fleet's defense of the Philippines. His strength he divided into four forces (*map*), the principal one commanded by Vice Admiral Takeo Kurita consisting of five battleships, 12 cruisers, 15 destroyers. The northern force (ironically named the main body) was Vice Admiral Jisaburo Ozawa's—a decoy to lure Admiral Halsey north while Kurita broke through center to the Leyte beachhead. Halsey took the bait, believing his carrier pilots had already mangled Kurita (they had in fact sunk the *Musashi* with torpedoes and bombs). The Japanese southern force was ravaged by Vice Admiral Thomas C. Kinkaid's Seventh (Southwest Pacific) Fleet, but Kurita bored through the unguarded center to the entrance of Leyte Gulf and opened fire on the flimsy escort carriers (which fought like adolescent tigers). Almost within sight of the "soft" transports, Kurita inexplicably took fright and fled back through San Bernardino Strait. The adventure cost Toyoda four carriers, three battleships, ten cruisers (6 heavy, 4 light), nine destroyers and all reasonable hope of delaying his country's defeat much longer. Only the oriental madness called Kamikaze was left to Japan.

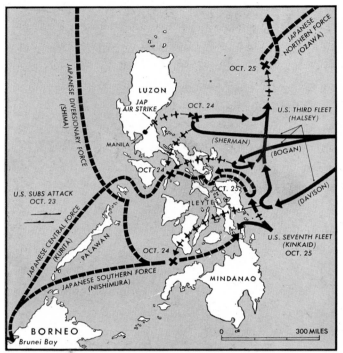

U.S. FLEETS MET ALL THREE PRONGS OF THE JAPANESE ATTACK

HER DECK BUCKLED BY EXPLOSIONS, JAP CARRIER "ZUIHO" COULD NOT ESCAPE

UNDER FIRE OFF SAMAR, ESCORT CARRIER CREWMEN WATCHED TENSELY AS JAP BATTLESHIP SALVO SPLASHED TO THE LEFT OF A SISTER CARRIER

U.S. CARRIER PLANE CAST A SHADOW OF DOOM OVER THE "MUSASHI" (LEFT), ONE OF WORLD'S TWO BIGGEST BATTLESHIPS, AS A TORPEDO HIT HER

IN MANILA BAY THE FAR EAST AIR FORCE HAMMERED CORREGIDOR BEFORE A COMBINED PARATROOP AND SEABORNE LANDING TOOK THE "ROCK"

The liberation of the Philippines became a certainty after the invasion of Luzon. An armada of 800 ships headed through the Sulu Sea on Jan. 3, 1945; next day the Japanese began spending the hoarded remnants of their air strength. On Jan. 6 the Kamikazes plowed into 16 ships, damaging ten seriously. But the toll taken by Halsey's carrier pilots and Kenney's Leyte- and Mindoro-based Far East Air Force also mounted (the Japanese lost 9,000 planes in the Philippines). Krueger's Sixth Army troops—Major General Innis Swift's I Corps on the left, Major General Oscar Griswold's XIV on the right—went ashore Jan. 9 at Lingayan Gulf to find that General Tomoyuki Yamashita had left these beaches virtually undefended. On Jan. 27 the 1st Cavalry Division landed and got its orders from MacArthur: "Go to Manila. Go around the Nips, bounce off the Nips, but go to Manila. Free the internees at Santo Tomas." Then began the 1st's 100-mile, 66-hour race for Manila, with no protection except sharpshooting Marine dive bombers. The 11th Airborne Division landed south of Manila and slugged its way toward the city. The 3,400 American internees were rescued before their captors could kill them, but 16,000 Japanese marines defended Manila house by house and it had to be blown to bits by artillery.

A JAPANESE OFFICER in a B-25 points out his division's command post on Mindanao so Americans can bomb it. If a Japanese surrendered he was counted dead back home, so he was quite likely to change sides.

FIGHTING INSIDE MANILA, INFANTRY CROSSED THE PASIG RIVER ON FEB. 7 TO ATTACK THE LAST-DITCH DEFENDERS IN THE OLD WALLED CITY

NATURE OF THE ENEMY was revealed in Japanese treatment of military prisoners. All were emaciated, like sailor and marine in the center (more than 30% died, against 1% in Germany). Japanese made the shocking photograph (*left*) of the beheading of a captured Australian pilot in New Guinea. Liberated prisoners (*right*) were greeted by MacArthur, who estimated that his troops killed or captured 300,000 Japanese in Philippines.

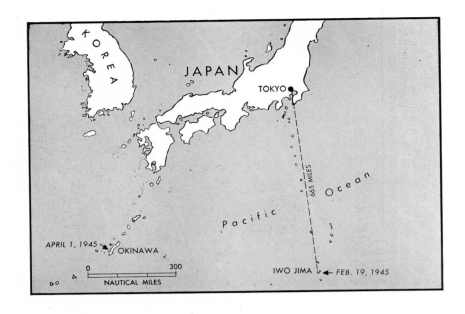

Iwo Jima

was, of all the many Pacific islands, perhaps the only one whose capture was unavoidably necessary. If the B-29 bombing of Japan were to succeed, the 8-mile-square island had to be obtained as a base for long-range fighters and a haven for crippled Superforts. Labyrinthine Iwo was known to be the Pacific's toughest nut, and the final staff briefing at Saipan was in the nature of a salute to men who were about to die. Only a frontal assault could be made, said Navy Secretary James Forrestal (who went along), which left "very little choice except to take it by force of arms, by character and courage." Selected for the task were the 3rd, 4th and 5th Marine Divisions. D-day was Feb. 19, 1945. The first waves got ashore all right, but the 22,817 dug-in defenders soon opened up with artillery and mortars (including the 320-mm. variety). The battle lasted 26 days, cost 5,563 dead, 17,343 wounded. Casualties, including replacements, exceeded 100% in several infantry battalions and reached at least 50% in all others.

AT 9 A.M. THE FIRST WAVE OF AMTRACS STREAMED INTO IWO JIMA. AN HOUR LATER BIG JAPANESE GUNS ON MT. SURIBACHI (LEFT) PINNED THE MARINES TO

"HOWLIN' MAD" SMITH LED IWO INVASION

ON D-DAY AFTERNOON THE RESERVES FINALLY GOT THROUGH ENEMY FIRE TO THE VOLCANIC SHORE

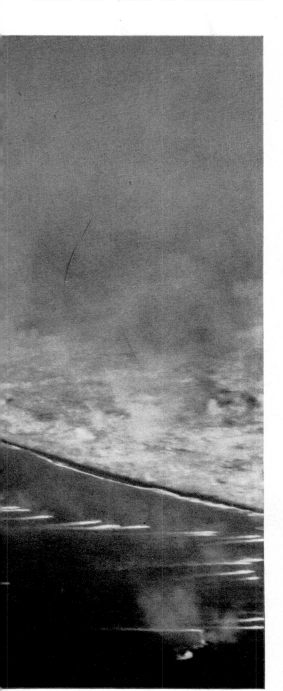

THE BEACH AND CUT OFF ALL REINFORCEMENT

MASSED OFF EAST BEACH, SHIPS FED NEEDED SUPPLIES INTO THE BLOODY 26-DAY FIGHT FOR IWO JIMA

BATTLE SUPPLIES had to be unloaded in rough weather that hampered operations for four days after D-day and slowed evacuation of the wounded from Iwo's black, volcanic ash. Died-of-wounds rate was the war's highest: 8%.

A FEW PRISONERS were taken (the 1% usual in Central Pacific battles), but most of Lieut. General Tadamichi Kuribayashi's husky defenders fought from their tunnels until killed, making Iwo truly "a beachhead in Hell."

B-24 TAKES OFF from Motoyama Field No. 1 beside crippled B-29, one of the 2,400 which made emergency landings (saving some 26,000 fliers). Grateful airmen named planes for each of the Marine divisions in the Iwo campaign.

DEMOLITION TEAM DUCKED AS MARINE AT RIGHT DETONATED A CHARGE

WOUNDED PILOT BROUGHT HIS BURNING PLANE HOME TO THE CARRIER

LANDING FIGHTER BROKE THE TRIP-LINES AND HURTLED OVER THE SIDE

SLAND FORMED BY THE 850-FOOT FLIGHT DECK OF THE "ESSEX"-CLASS CARRIER "RANDOLPH." AT HER STERN ROWS OF COMBAT PLANES WAIT WITH FOLDED WINGS

343

GUNS OF CARRIER "WASP" SENT DIVE BOMBER DOWN IN JAPANESE WATERS   KAMIKAZE EXPLODED ON THE DECK OF THE CARRIER "INTREPID" OFF LUZON

THE BURNING CARRIER "FRANKLIN" WALLOWED 60 MILES OFF THE COAST OF JAPAN AFTER TAKING TWO BOMBS ON HER PLANE-CROWDED DECKS. HER CREW

A PHILIPPINE-BASED KAMIKAZE PILOT MADE A FUNERAL PYRE FOR HIMSELF AMID PLANES PARKED ON THE STERN OF LIGHT CARRIER "BELLEAU WOOD"

LOST 772 MEN, BUT BROUGHT THE SHIP HOME UNDER HER OWN STEAM

HALSEY WAS BOSS OF THE THIRD FLEET

SPRUANCE COMMANDED FIFTH FLEET

Kamikaze was the name (meaning "divine wind") that the Japanese navy gave its suicide pilots; the army fliers, who joined later in self-immolation against U.S. ships, had an analogous term, *Tokko Tai*. Organized suicide was not attempted until the Philippine invasion was under way. According to the Japanese story Vice Admiral Masabumi Arima made the first Kamikaze attack on a carrier of Halsey's fleet off the Philippines Oct. 15, 1944, but he must have missed: no U.S. ships were hit between the 14th and 18th. Nonetheless he lighted "the fuse of the ardent wishes" among his fanatically courageous pilots and they soon began crashing regularly on U.S. flight decks, to the bewilderment of the two dissimilar admirals (*above*) who alternated as fleet commanders: flamboyant "Bull" Halsey of the Third, shy Ray Spruance of the Fifth (they used the same ships; only the fleet numbers changed). Censorship prohibited mention of Kamikazes for six months, lest Tokyo learn how effective they had been. Then Halsey trumpeted they were only "1% effective." Postwar records show that the Kamikaze rate was astoundingly effective: 474 hits on U.S. ships for the 2,550 planes expended (18.6%). Fortunately the Japanese had not started their suicide tactics until the U.S. was rich with ships.

345

Okinawa was the Pacific's epic amphibious operation: 183,000 troops and 747,000 tons of cargo were loaded into 430 assault transports and landing ships at 11 different ports from Seattle to Ulithi to Leyte. During the three hours preceding the landing on April Fool's Day 1945 (it was also Easter), the ships and gunboats fired 44,825 rounds of 5- to 16-inch shells, 33,000 rockets and 22,500 mortar shells. Altogether Okinawa involved 1,381 ships. The landing was shockingly easy, despite predictions that it would out-Iwo Iwo. Lieut. General Simon Bolivar Buckner's Tenth Army landed four divisions abreast: Major General Roy Geiger's III Amphibious Corps on the left, Major General Hodge's XXIV (up from Leyte) on the right. While the 6th Marine Division was cleaning out the northern two thirds of the island, the 7th, 27th, 77th and 96th Infantry Divisions and 1st Marine Division in the south were running into deeply entrenched defenders before Shuri Castle, the seat of the ancient Okinawan kings. Meanwhile Kamikazes struck at ships offshore—355 suicide pilots in a 36-hour period beginning April 6. Nearly all were shot down, but six ships were sunk, 22 others damaged. Toyoda's mighty *Yamato* steamed toward Okinawa in a bold follow-up, but "Pete" Mitscher's Task Force 58 was waiting. *Yamato* rolled over and sank two hours after five bombs and ten torpedoes pierced her. Still the Kamikazes came—1,900 of them among the 4,155 planes Japan lost in combat at Okinawa, 2,655 more were lost operationally. Before it was over the Navy had taken higher casualties than in any similar period in its history (4,907 killed, 4,824 wounded); 36 ships were sunk, 368 damaged. Tenth Army casualties (in seven divisions) shot up to 39,420, of which 7,604 were dead. Over a 53-day period the American advance averaged a scant 133 yards a day. Okinawa was secured on June 21, three days after a piece of rock deflected by an artillery shell pierced General Buckner's heart. Japanese dead amounted to about 100,000, with possibly 20,000 others sealed in caves. The way to Japan was now open.

FIVE DAYS BEFORE THE INVASION OF OKINAWA ROCKET-FIRING LSMs SENT THEIR FIERY VOLLEYS INTO THE NEARBY ISLAND OF TOKASHIKI SHIMA

U.S.S. "TENNESSEE" WAS ONE OF THE TEN OLD BATTLESHIPS THAT BOMBARDED OKINAWA ON APRIL 1 AS THE TROOP-LOADED AMTRACS PLOWED IN

AHEAD OF THE GROUND FORCES, LOW-FLYING MARINE CORSAIR FIRED ITS WING LOAD OF EIGHT 5-INCH ROCKETS INTO JAP POSITIONS IN THE HILLS

LANDING ON OKINAWA, TROOPS MET NO ENEMY FIRE. SPLASHES (RIGHT) WERE FROM FLYING DEBRIS AS MEN BLASTED HOLE THROUGH SEA WALL

INLAND, THE JAPANESE WERE DEEPLY DUG IN. NEAR NAHA MARINES SET OFF EXPLOSIVES IN A CAVE AND WAITED FOR ANY SURVIVORS TO COME OUT

FLAME-THROWING TANKS CREMATED THE JAPS IN THEIR HILLSIDE CAVES DURING THE SLOW, HARD FIGHT FOR THE SOUTHERN END OF THE ISLAND

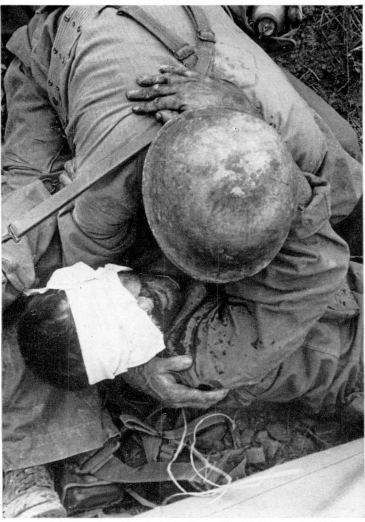

A FRONT-LINE MEDIC LIFTS A BLINDED SOLDIER ONTO A STRETCHER

SOLDIER HAS A HEAD WOUND BANDAGED. NOTE HIS PIERCED HELMET

349

B-29 BASE AT GUAM was one of three in Marianas and the headquarters of Major General Curtis LeMay's XXI Bomber Command, which comprised about 1,000 Superfortresses at its peak. Total of 33,041 sorties were flown from the Marianas and China bases, 90% of them in the last five months of the war, after Iwo Jima had been captured. Altogether 485 B-29s were lost, 2,707 damaged. Number of AAF fliers killed: 3,041.

B-29S OVER YOKOHAMA, which was 44% destroyed (Tokyo 51%, Osaka 26%), drop cargoes of incendiaries. The number of Japanese killed by B-29 raids was more than 300,000. During night of March 9–10 LeMay brought planes down to 7,000 feet, dropped bombs on Tokyo that burned up 97,000 persons—more than were killed by either atomic bomb. In these attacks 180 square miles in 66 Japanese cities were consumed by flames.

CITY IN FLAMES became a usual sight. This picture was made during fire-bomb raid on Nagoya, Japan's third largest city. Nagoya was hit often until it was 31% destroyed under weight of 10,145 tons of bombs.

SHIP IN FLAMES was the work of Halsey's fast carrier pilots. In July of 1945 they sank the huge battleships *Hyuga* (*above*), *Ise* and *Haruna*, as well as two carriers and five cruisers, leaving Japan with no navy at all.

351

F. D. Roosevelt
President of the United States
White House
Washington, D.C.

Nassau Point
Peconic, Long Island
August 2nd, 1939

Sir:

Some recent work by E. Fermi and L. Szilard, which has been communicated to me in manuscript, leads me to expect that the element uranium may be turned into a new and important source of energy in the immediate future. Certain aspects of the situation which has arisen seem to call for watchfulness and, if necessary, quick action on the part of the Administration. I believe therefore that it is my duty to bring to your attention the following facts and recommendation.

In the course of the last four months it has been made probable through the work of Joliot in France as well as Fermi and Szilard in America - that it may become possible to set up a nuclear chain reaction in a large mass of uranium, by which vast amount...

A Man from Missouri Makes a Decision

WHEN President Roosevelt received Albert Einstein's letter (*above*) events were set in motion which culminated six years later in a decision by Harry S. Truman—the most awesome decision ever required of a single mortal. In 1939 Roosevelt set up an advisory committee on uranium, with $6,000 to spend. A month before Pearl Harbor joint British-American research indicated that a bomb of "superlatively destructive power" was possible with uranium fission. By May 1943 the research phase was ended and the huge plants built by Army Engineers at Oak Ridge, Tenn., Hanford, Wash. and Los Alamos, N. Mex. began to run the cost of the Manhattan Project to $2 billion. The atomic age dawned at 5:30 a.m., July 16, 1945 in the New Mexico desert. The success of an explosion 20,000 times as powerful as TNT was messaged to President Truman at Potsdam. When he was informed, Stalin showed a "lack of interest," and it seemed "he had not grasped the importance of the discovery," thought Secretary of State James Byrnes (who had no way of knowing that Stalin's U.S. spies had kept him well posted). Should history's deadliest force be set loose to obliterate human life? The losses at Iwo Jima and Okinawa weighed heavily on U.S. leaders. The Kamikazes indicated that Japanese fanaticism knew no bounds. U.S. casualties in the Pacific were already 300,000, and estimates of the cost of invading Japan were set at nearly a million more. War Secretary Stimson noted that the soldiers being deployed from Europe to the Pacific were "weary in a way that no one merely reading reports could readily understand." Premier Suzuki scorned Truman's surrender ultimatum as "unworthy of public notice." At 1:45 a.m., Aug. 6 the B-29 *Enola Gay* took off from Tinian Island; at 8:15 it dropped an atomic bomb on the city of Hiroshima which killed 78,150 Japanese. On Aug. 9 the only other atomic bomb then in existence fell on Nagasaki, killing 23,753 more. Japan surrendered (*p. 357*). At Bikini in 1946 a more powerful bomb was exploded (*opposite*). In five seconds its dreadful cloud was two miles wide (*pp. 354, 355*). Though the Second World War was over, people everywhere trembled in the hot, white glare of the new age.

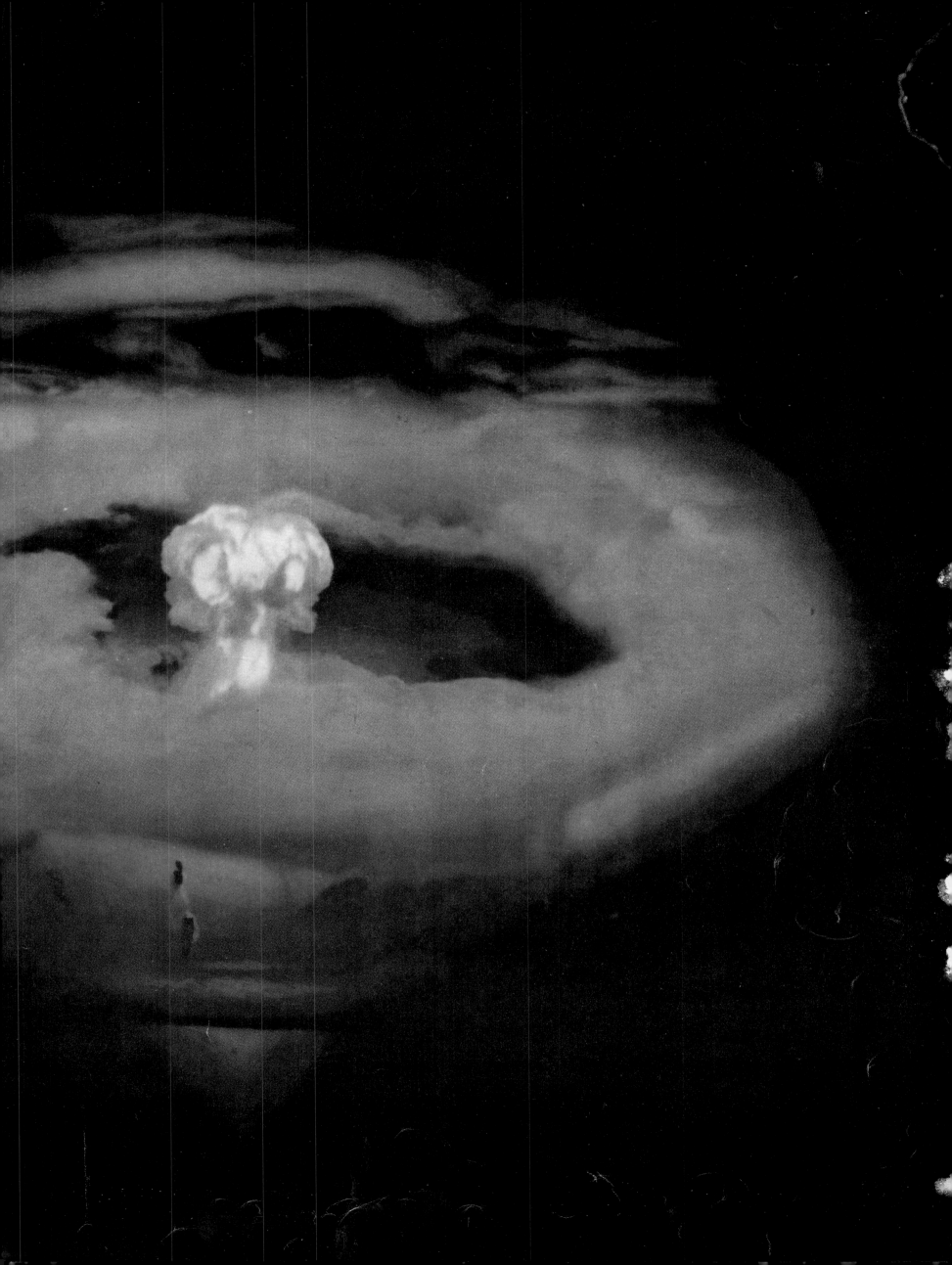

THE Second World War ended on Sept. 2, 1945 aboard the battleship *Missouri* in Tokyo Bay. The formal ceremonies climaxed a fortnight of curious (some thought ominous) tension that followed the three thunderclaps of early August: the atomic attacks on Hiroshima and Nagasaki, and the Soviet Union's Aug. 8 invasion of Manchuria. On Aug. 10 the Japanese had bowed to the Potsdam ultimatum, provided the emperor could be retained. The U.S. agreed, and on Aug. 15 the Japanese accepted this slightly conditioned "unconditional surrender." No one was sure they meant it. Admiral Halsey instructed Vice Admiral John S. McCain's Task Force 38 pilots to shoot down "all snoopers . . . in a friendly sort of way," and the U.S. went on

with its original plans for the invasion of Japan. (On Nov. 1 the Sixth Army was to land on Kyushu; in the spring of 1946 two more armies, the Eighth and Tenth, were to land on the Tokyo plain. It was learned later that the Japanese had guessed the invasion targets and had mobilized 5,000 suicide planes.) None of the late-August precautions proved necessary. The occupation started without incident, and on Sept. 2 the last Japanese foreign minister, Mamoru Shigemitsu, signed the surrender documents. As General of the Army Douglas MacArthur, the Allied supreme commander, boomed out: "These proceedings are closed!" 400 B-29s soared above the bay and 1,500 carrier planes roared across the *Missouri*, mast-high, in a dramatic salute to the final victory.

357

Epilogue

WHEN the Japanese capitulated in Tokyo Bay 11 million Americans in uniform heaved a sigh of relief and were ready to go home. Not more than a third of them had ever heard a shot fired in anger; the rest, men and women, had been spread round the globe in a thousand bases engaged in the manifold enterprises of staging and supply. Most of them, except for a tiny minority of professional officers brought up to conform to the military code, had found the rigid stratification of rank in the Army and Navy irksome and archaic. As a result the war's end saw many changes in the traditional distinctions between officers and enlisted men: the latter were permitted to sit on courts-martial for the first time, and many social barriers within the services were let down. During the war, which involved teamwork between the services on a scale never dreamed of before in any conflict in our history, there was also planted the idea of unifying the services, which became a reality two years later. The experience, too, of working under desperate urgency in close cooperation with the military of other nations laid the groundwork for a permanent design for mutual assistance among the Western democracies. But as the brass in the Pentagon laid away its plans for the final amphibious landing on the Japanese islands that was to have been the last great episode of the war, redeployment turned into a stampede toward the separation center.

THE war was over, and America had fought it in its characteristic way. It was a war of giant equipment, broad mechanization, mass movements of incredible volumes of matériel. It was a war also of strange symbols, with the cigaret ultimately achieving the distinction of a medium of exchange. And it was a war conspicuously lacking in brass bands, in epic songs or slogans. To the GIs the Germans were "Krauts" and Japanese were "yellow bastards," and the best reason for killing them was to keep them from killing you. Thus, while the war had been a triumph of technical organization, "war aims"—itself one of the great phrases of the war—were never formalized. In the initial stages of the invasion of Europe "liberation," the releasing of captive peoples from the Nazi yoke, had been a high and definite purpose, but the term later became a catchword for anything from looting to sheer destruction. "Unconditional surrender" was the immediate thing we were fighting for, and the United Nations, which was already under construction at San Francisco while America's armies were meeting the Russians on the Elbe, became the idealistic repository of the political effects of the war. Hopes ran high that the U.N. would successfully consolidate the victory and translate its meaning into political terms that would insure peace.

For ourselves, we had proved our national competence in the rigging of mass production, in the mastery of the problems of global logistics, in the invention of the rudimentary but adequate portable civilization we created wherever we set up a base on islands overgrown with jungle or the muskeg under the Arctic Circle or in the driving dust of North Africa. Through great advances in medicine and public health slimy pestholes like Guadalcanal could be turned into convalescent areas a few months after they ceased to be fighting fronts. We had made many inventions in the art of war and by harnessing our industrial knowledge to the discoveries of the physicists we had managed to hand the world the terrible enigma of atomic energy.

YET the emotional revulsion against war and all its works, which had played such an important part in the nation's state of mind after World War I, showed itself very little after World War II. This was partly because better measures were undertaken to prepare for the civilian soldier's homecoming. Men and women of the Armed Services, for all their greater numbers, fitted more easily into civilian life than their fathers had after the previous war. They came back into a still-expanding economy. The GI Bill of Rights helped even the opportunities for an education for veterans who had been inducted during the years they might have been training for their peacetime careers. Most GIs came home to resume seriously their civilian lives, and there was no mass attempt to take over political control of the country. No unified force of exservicemen appeared in politics.

The U.S. emerged from the war with a deepened sense of responsibility. As soon as the fighting stopped we kept from starvation many of the world's conquered populations, some of which were later to be lashed by propaganda to hate us and everything we stood for. We made a start in engineering a revival of Europe. But we were still considerably less successful politically than technologically. We didn't know too well how to explain to the Germans exactly what we meant by democracy, but we were able to plan and continue the airlift during the blockade of Berlin. In the years following the collapse of the Axis powers we learned too that we must assume world responsibilities or perish off the earth, and that if we went down, the concept of freedom on which civilization in the West was built would go down with us. We learned that for a people as for a man the road to greatness is very hard.

Appendixes

I. A Note on Casualty Statistics

INSISTENCE on knowing the price paid for wars has been a characteristic postwar reaction in democracies. During the 19th Century this insistence accounted for the evolution of casualty statistics, nowhere further evolved than in the U.S., which issued fairly reliable figures even in wartime. For a variety of reasons, this is not true of many other belligerents.

Five years after World War II the casualties of a number of the belligerents remained unknown because, in some instances, their statistical agencies were smashed by defeat. Intentional misrepresentations were frequent—for morale purposes during the war and for political purposes afterward. As late as 1950 some governments preferred not to issue World War II figures because they might have proved too painful to their own people or too humiliating in comparison with similar figures of ex-enemies or ex-coalition partners. For example, after World War II it was claimed that Germany lost far more men, if prisoners of war were included, to the Western Allies than to Russia. This would help explain the failure of the Soviet government to publish anything like final and complete data on its own casualties, which might appear too high when matched with those inflicted on the Germans.

Conversely, after the war some of the belligerents, notably the U.S. and Great Britain, gave complete statistics that they obviously could not reveal in wartime. Postwar findings in many cases have corrected wartime claims. During the war (and later) General George Kenney insisted that his fliers sank 22 out of 22 ships in the Bismarck Sea, March 1–3, 1943, destroyed 55 planes and 15,000 men. Records now show that in the Bismarck Sea battle, great victory though it was, the Japanese lost 12 out of 16 ships, 20 to 30 planes and less than 4,000 men. As Churchill remarked of a similar adjustment in British statistics: "In the upshot we got two to one . . . instead of three to one. . . . But this was enough." American casualty statistics, already quite reliable as far as they were published while the war was on, extended into amazing detail after hostilities ended. The U.S. Navy even reported how many of its men committed suicide between Pearl Harbor and Jan. 1, 1947—in the Navy proper no less than 60 officers and 184 enlisted men on ships and overseas, and 114 officers and 289 enlisted men "Stateside," plus 42 suicides overseas and 51 in the home areas in the Marines.

Early estimates adopted by General of the Army George C. Marshall give military casualties (battle deaths plus the missing unlikely to return) of the eight leading military powers as follows:

Allies

United States	295,904
British Commonwealth	452,570
U.S.S.R.	7,500,000
France	200,000
China (since 1937)	2,200,000
Total	**10,648,474**

Axis

Germany	2,850,000
Italy	300,000
Japan	1,506,000
Total	**4,656,000**

To this tentative total of more than 15 million, hundreds of thousands more from the smaller belligerents (such as the Netherlands, Greece, Poland and Hungary, with their army and state governments largely wiped out) would have to be added. There is some reason to think that both the Russian and German data are too low, the best German estimate arriving at a figure of 2,150,000 military deaths and about one million persons missing who must be considered dead.

World War II was *dur aux grands* (hard on the great ones)—much more than many a preceding one—taking the lives of numerous commanders. It was also hard on the noncombatants. In Belgium civilian casualties outnumbered those of the armed forces. In Germany it is estimated that civilian casualties were one to four, compared with the military casualties; they occurred largely during the last two years of the war and for several months were higher than those of the Wehrmacht. Japanese civilian deaths from bombing are tentatively estimated at one to five, compared with military deaths. The data on the atom-bombed cities of Hiroshima and Nagasaki promise to remain tentative, but a seemingly reliable 1949 estimate for Hiroshima was 78,150 dead, and for Nagasaki 23,753. However the general unreliability of all war statistics is further evidenced by the fact that the mayor of Hiroshima reported that 247,000 had been killed by the atomic bomb, and a study of the Nagasaki bombing made by a research committee in Japan gave a figure of 73,884 deaths—both figures more than three times the other estimates.

—ALFRED VAGTS

II. A Note on the Cost of World War II*

LIKE reports of war casualties, estimates of war costs depend on what government is furnishing the figures and for what purposes statistics have been prepared. Each nation reporting on the amount of World War II damage would naturally tend to exaggerate abroad her losses for the purpose of securing reparations and outside reconstruction aid, at the same time minimizing destruction at home in order to encourage her people to greater efforts in rebuilding. One guess-estimate, however, on the total value of all things destroyed in all theaters of the war runs as high as two and a quarter trillion dollars.

Another heavy item in the costs of war is the direct military expenditures of all the participating nations, which are roughly reckoned in World War II at a little over a trillion dollars. But no one, in the respective governments or out, can pin down what it cost these nations to prepare for World War II or what continuing expenses (interest on the public debt, veterans' services, etc.) they will have to meet in the years to come as a result of that war.

To the very rough estimate of three and a quarter trillion dollars for World War II's direct costs and destruction, statisticians also add another three-quarter trillion dollars to cover "indirect costs." These costs include the looting of one nation's manpower, raw materials and manufactures by another; the waste caused by reckless wartime use of natural resources and losses incurred through the disruption of trade and finance. The total direct and indirect cost-estimates for World War II: $4,000,000,000,000.

Thus World War II has been called the Four Trillion Dollar War which took the lives of 40 million civilians and men in uniform. For comparative U.S. expenditures and battle deaths for all major wars in American history, see below.

*Estimates based on an article by C. Hartley Grattan, *Harper's*, April 1949.

BATTLE DEATHS AND DIRECT EXPENDITURES OF THE U.S.

IN ALL MAJOR WARS (ESTIMATED)

Wars	Battle Deaths	Expenditures
American Revolution	4,435	(*No dependable estimate available*)
War of 1812	2,187	$133,700,000
Mexican War	1,733	166,000,000
Civil War (the Union)	112,246	4,006,000,000
Civil War (the Confederacy)	74,524	2,099,768,707
Spanish-American War	361	568,700,000
World War I	52,429	25,729,000,000
World War II	256,330	350,000,000,000
Totals	504,245	382,703,168,707

A Selective Glossary of World War II Personalities

ALEXANDER, FIELD MARSHAL SIR HAROLD
Commander in chief British forces Middle East; Eisenhower's deputy in North Africa; later commander in chief Allied armies in Italy.

ARNOLD, GENERAL OF THE ARMY HENRY H.
Commanding general U.S. Army Air Forces; died 1950.

BARBEY, VICE ADMIRAL DANIEL E.
Commanding Seventh Amphibious Force in Southwest Pacific area.

BARUCH, BERNARD
U.S. Elder Statesman and adviser on war production and postwar policies.

BEAVERBROOK, LORD, W. MAXWELL AITKEN
British Minister for Aircraft Production; later Minister of Supply and Lord Privy Seal.

BENEŠ, DR. EDUARD
President of Czechoslovakia and head of Czech government in exile; died 1948.

BIDDLE, ANTHONY J. DREXEL JR.
U.S. Ambassador to Poland; later to the governments in exile.

BLAMEY, GENERAL SIR THOMAS A.
Commanding Australian Imperial Forces Middle East; later Allied Land Forces Southwest Pacific area.

BOCK, FIELD MARSHAL FEDOR VON
Army commander Poland, Low Countries, France, Russia; killed in action 1945.

BRADLEY, GENERAL OMAR NELSON
Commanding U.S. II Corps in Tunisia; later Twelfth Army Group in Western Europe.

BRERETON, LIEUT. GENERAL LEWIS H.
Commanding U.S. Middle East Air Force and First Allied Airborne Army on Western front.

BUCKNER, LIEUT. GENERAL SIMON B. JR.
Commanding U.S. forces in Alaska; later Tenth Army; killed at Okinawa 1945.

BULLITT, WILLIAM CHRISTIAN
U.S. Ambassador at Fall of France.

BUSH, VANNEVAR
Director U.S. Office of Scientific Research and Development.

BYRNES, JAMES FRANCIS
Director U.S. Economic Stabilization Board to 1943; director of War Mobilization to 1945; Secretary of State in 1945.

CATES, MAJOR GENERAL CLIFTON B.
Commanding 4th Marine Division at Iwo Jima.

CHAMBERLAIN, NEVILLE
British Prime Minister, succeeded by Churchill May 10, 1940; died Nov. 9, 1940.

CHENNAULT, MAJOR GENERAL CLAIRE
Organized Flying Tigers; later commanding U.S. Fourteenth Air Force against Japan.

CHIANG KAI-SHEK
President of Chinese republic; generalissimo and supreme commander of China theater.

CHURCHILL, WINSTON
British Prime Minister 1940–45.

CLARK, GENERAL MARK WAYNE
Secret advance envoy to North Africa in Allied invasion; later commanding U.S. Fifth Army and Fifteenth Army Group in Italian campaign.

COLLINS, LIEUT. GENERAL J. LAWTON
Commanding U.S. VII Corps in Europe.

CONINGHAM, AIR VICE MARSHAL SIR ARTHUR
Formed First Tactical Air Force North Africa 1943; later commander in chief Second Tactical Air Force; died 1948.

CRERAR, LIEUT. GENERAL H.D.G.
Chief of Canadian general staff; later commanding First Canadian Army on the Western front.

CUNNINGHAM, ADMIRAL SIR ANDREW
Allied naval commander Mediterranean 1943–46.

DALADIER, ÉDOUARD
Premier of war cabinet before Fall of France; imprisoned during war by the Germans.

DARLAN, ADMIRAL JEAN
Vichy French Vice Premier, negotiated armistice with Allies in North Africa; later governor of North Africa; assassinated 1942.

DE GAULLE, GENERAL CHARLES
President French Committee of National Liberation; supreme commander Free French armed forces.

DEMPSEY, LIEUT. GENERAL SIR MILES C.
Commanding British Second Army on Western front; later Fourteenth Army in Far East.

DEVERS, GENERAL JACOB LOUCKS
Deputy supreme Allied commander Mediterranean theater; later commanding U.S. Sixth Army Group on Western front.

DOENITZ, GRAND ADMIRAL KARL
Commander in chief German U-boat force; later of the navy; surrendered German armed forces to Allies; sentenced to ten years' imprisonment as war criminal.

DONOVAN, MAJOR GENERAL WILLIAM J.
Director Office of Strategic Services.

DOOLITTLE, LIEUT. GENERAL JAMES
Bombed Tokyo from *Hornet;* later commanding Twelfth Air Force in North Africa and the Eighth and Fifteenth (strategic) Air Forces.

DOWDING, AIR CHIEF MARSHAL SIR HUGH
Commander in chief R.A.F. Fighter Command in Battle of Britain.

EAKER, LIEUT. GENERAL IRA C.
Commanding Eighth Air Force in England; later commander in chief Mediterranean Allied Air Forces.

EDEN, ANTHONY
British Foreign Minister 1940–45.

EICHELBERGER, LIEUT. GENERAL ROBERT L.
Commanding U.S. I Corps; later the Eighth Army in Southwest Pacific.

EISENHOWER, GENERAL OF THE ARMY DWIGHT D.
Commanding ETO, commander in chief North African invasion; later supreme commander Allied Expeditionary Forces.

FERMI, ENRICO
Atomic-bomb physicist.

FORRESTAL, JAMES V.
U.S. Secretary of the Navy 1944–45; died 1949.

FRASER, ADMIRAL SIR BRUCE AUSTIN
Commander in chief home fleet; later commander in chief British Pacific fleet.

FREYBERG, LIEUT. GENERAL SIR BERNARD
Commander in chief Allied forces in Crete and commanding New Zealand forces throughout war.

FRIEDEBURG, ADMIRAL HANS-GEORG
Surrendered all forces in northwest Germany; two weeks later committed suicide 1945.

GAMELIN, GENERAL MAURICE GUSTAVE
Allied commander in chief at opening of German offensive; replaced by Weygand.

GEIGER, LIEUT. GENERAL ROY
Commanding all U.S. aviation units at Guadalcanal; III Amphibious Corps; later Tenth Army on Okinawa; died 1947.

GEROW, LIEUT. GENERAL LEONARD T.
Commanding U.S. V Corps in Europe; later Fifteenth Army.

GIRAUD, GENERAL HENRI HONORÉ
Captured by Germans in 1940, escaped to become commander in chief French forces in North Africa and Joint President with De Gaulle, Committee of National Liberation; died 1949.

GOEBBELS, PAUL JOSEPH
German Minister of National Enlightenment and Propaganda; committed suicide 1945.

GÖRING, FIELD MARSHAL HERMANN
German Minister of Aviation and air force commander in chief; sentenced to death but committed suicide in prison 1946.

GRAZIANI, MARSHAL RODOLFO
Commanding Italian forces, North Africa; surrendered Ligurian army 1945; sentenced by Italians to brief prison term for treason.

GROVES, MAJOR GENERAL LESLIE RICHARD
Officer in charge U.S. atomic-bomb project.

GUDERIAN, COLONEL GENERAL HEINZ
German Panzer expert; commander in chief mechanized units in Poland; replaced Jodl as chief of staff of army; later commander in chief German armies Eastern front.

HALIFAX, EARL OF, EDWARD WOOD
British Ambassador to Washington 1940–46.

HALSEY, ADMIRAL WILLIAM F.
Commanding U.S. task forces in Marshalls and Gilberts; later South Pacific Force and U.S. Third Fleet.

HARRIMAN, WILLIAM AVERELL
Special representative of President to London and Moscow; later Ambassador to Russia.

HARRIS, AIR CHIEF MARSHAL SIR ARTHUR T.
Commander R.A.F. Bomber Command

HERRIOT, ÉDOUARD
President Chamber of Deputies at Fall of France; interned by Germans; liberated 1945 by Russians.

HESS, WALTER RICHARD RUDOLF
German deputy Führer interned in Britain after solo "peace mission" flight; sentenced to life imprisonment 1946.

HIMMLER, HEINRICH
Gestapo chief; later commander in chief German home army; committed suicide after capture by British 1945.

HIROHITO
Emperor of Japan.

HITLER, ADOLF
German dictator; probable suicide 1945.

HOBBY, COLONEL OVETA CULP
Director U.S. Women's Army Corps (WAC).

HODGES, GENERAL COURTNEY H.
Commanding First Army on Western front.

HOMMA, GENERAL MASAHARU
Commanding Japanese army forces in attack on Philippines; convicted for ordering Bataan Death March; executed 1946.

HOPKINS, HARRY L.
Special adviser and assistant to the President; chairman Munitions Assignment Board; died 1946.

HULL, CORDELL
U.S. Secretary of State to 1944.

JODL, COLONEL GENERAL ALFRED
Chief of staff of German High Command; signer of unconditional surrender May 7, 1945; executed as war criminal 1946.

JUIN, GENERAL ALPHONSE PIERRE
Commander in chief French forces in North Africa; later commander French forces in Tunisia and Italy.

KEITEL, FIELD MARSHAL WILHELM
Chief of High Command of German armed forces; executed as war criminal 1946.

KENNEY, GENERAL GEORGE C.
Commanding Allied Air Forces in Southwest Pacific; later Far East Air Forces.

KESSELRING, FIELD MARSHAL ALBERT
Commanding German forces in Sicily and southern Italy; sentenced to life imprisonment as war criminal 1947.

KIMMEL, ADMIRAL HUSBAND EDWARD
Commander in chief U.S. Pacific Fleet at Pearl Harbor; retired and held responsible for "errors of judgment" in not preparing for Japanese attack.

KING, FLEET ADMIRAL ERNEST JOSEPH
Commander in chief U.S. Fleet and chief of naval operations.

KING, WILLIAM LYON MACKENZIE
Canadian Prime Minister; died 1950.

KINKAID, ADMIRAL THOMAS C.
Commanding U.S. North Pacific force in Aleutian campaign; later U.S. Seventh Fleet and Allied Naval Forces Southwest Pacific.

KLUGE, FIELD MARSHAL GUNTHER VON
Invaded France, Russia; later commander in chief Western front; implicated in plot against Hitler; committed suicide 1944.

KNOX, FRANK
U.S. Secretary of Navy; died 1944.

KNUDSEN, LIEUT. GENERAL WILLIAM S.
Director General U.S. Office of Production Management; later directing production for War Department; died 1948.

KONEV, MARSHAL IVAN
Shared in defense of Moscow and, with Zhukov, in fall of Berlin.

KRUEGER, GENERAL WALTER
Commander U.S. Sixth Army in Southwest Pacific.

KRUG, JULIUS
Chairman, U.S. War Production Board, succeeding Nelson.

KURIBAYASHI, LIEUT. GENERAL TADAMICHI
Commanding Japanese troops at Iwo Jima; presumably killed during attack.

KURITA, VICE ADMIRAL TAKEO
Commanding Japanese carrier support group at Guadalcanal; later commander in chief Second Fleet at Battle for Leyte Gulf.

KURUSU, SABURO
Special Japanese "peace envoy" to Washington on eve of planned attack on Pearl Harbor.

LAND, VICE ADMIRAL EMORY SCOTT
U.S. War Shipping Administrator.

LAVAL, PIERRE
Vichy French Foreign Minister; convicted of treason and executed 1945.

LEAHY, FLEET ADMIRAL WILLIAM D.
U.S. Ambassador to Vichy France; later chief of staff to President.

LECLERC, MAJOR GENERAL JACQUES
Led Free French forces across Libyan desert to join British Eighth Army in Tripoli; later commanding French 2nd Armored Division in liberation of France; killed in air crash 1947.

LEHMAN, HERBERT H.
Director General, UNRRA.

LEIGH-MALLORY, AIR CHIEF MARSHAL SIR TRAFFORD
Air commander in chief Allied Expeditionary Air Force in Normandy invasion; killed in air crash 1944.

LEOPOLD III
King of the Belgians; surrendered unconditionally to the Germans; liberated by U.S. troops May 1945.

MAC ARTHUR, GENERAL OF THE ARMY DOUGLAS
Commander in chief U.S. and Filipino forces during invasion of Philippines; later supreme commander Allied forces in Southwest Pacific.

MANNERHEIM, FIELD MARSHAL BARON CARL
Finnish commander in chief, later President.

MARSHALL, GENERAL OF THE ARMY GEORGE
U.S. Army chief of staff.

MC AFEE, CAPTAIN MILDRED
Director U.S. Women's Reserve of the Navy (WAVES).

MC NAIR, LIEUT. GENERAL LESLEY J.
Chief of U.S. Army Ground Forces; killed accidentally by U.S. bombs during Normandy campaign 1944.

MC NARNEY, GENERAL JOSEPH T.
U.S. deputy chief of staff, later deputy supreme commander Mediterranean theater.

MIHAILOVICH, GENERAL DRAJA
Leader of Chetnik forces in Yugoslavia; later found "guilty of treason and war crimes" by Tito's government; executed 1946.

MITSCHER, VICE ADMIRAL MARC ANDREW
Commander, air, Solomons; later Task Force 58, Pacific Fleet; died 1947.

MONTGOMERY, FIELD MARSHAL SIR BERNARD LAW
Commander British Eighth Army in North Africa, Sicily and Italy; later commander in chief ground forces SHAEF; also Twenty-first Army Group.

MOUNTBATTEN, ADMIRAL LORD LOUIS
Supreme Allied commander in Southeast Asia.

MURPHY, ROBERT D.
Special U.S. emissary to North Africa in preparation for Allied landings; later chief civil affairs officer, AFHQ.

MUSSOLINI, BENITO
Italian dictator; killed by Italian partisans April 28, 1945.

NAGUMO, VICE ADMIRAL CHUICHI
Commander Japanese attack force at Pearl Harbor: probable suicide at Saipan 1944.

NELSON, DONALD MARR
Chairman U.S. War Production Board to 1944.

NIMITZ, FLEET ADMIRAL CHESTER WILLIAM
Commander in chief U.S. Pacific Fleet.

NOMURA, ADMIRAL KICHISABURO
Japanese Ambassador to U.S. at time of Pearl Harbor.

OPPENHEIMER, J. ROBERT
U.S. atomic-bomb physicist.

PATCH, LIEUT. GENERAL ALEXANDER M.
Commanding U.S. Army forces in South Pacific; later Seventh Army in invasion of southern France; died 1945.

PATTON, GENERAL GEORGE S. JR.
Commanding U.S. Seventh Army in Sicily; later Third Army on Western front; died 1945.

PÉTAIN, MARSHAL HENRI PHILIPPE
Head of State, Vichy France; later sentenced to life imprisonment.

POUND, ADMIRAL OF THE FLEET SIR ALFRED
First Sea Lord and chief of the British naval staff; died 1943.

QUISLING, VIDKUN
Norwegian pro-Nazi traitor; executed for treason at Oslo 1945.

RADFORD, REAR ADMIRAL ARTHUR W.
Commanding U.S. carrier task groups in the Central and Western Pacific.

RAEDER, GRAND ADMIRAL DR. ERICH
Commander in chief German navy, succeeded by Doenitz; sentenced to life imprisonment as war criminal.

RAMSAY, ADMIRAL SIR BERTRAM H.
Allied naval commander in chief expeditionary force in Normandy invasion; died 1945.

REYNAUD, PAUL
French Premier during German attack on France; succeeded by Pétain.

RIBBENTROP, JOACHIM VON
German Minister of Foreign Affairs; executed as war criminal 1946.

ROMMEL, FIELD MARSHAL ERWIN
Commanding Afrika Korps; later commanded Army Group B on Western front; implicated in plot against Hitler; was shot or forced into suicide 1944.

ROOSEVELT, FRANKLIN DELANO
President of U.S.; died 1945.

RUNDSTEDT, FIELD MARSHAL KARL VON
Commanding German armies in Poland, France, Russia; later commander in chief German army on Western front.

SHERMAN, REAR ADMIRAL FORREST P.
Deputy chief of staff to Admiral Nimitz.

SHERMAN, VICE ADMIRAL FREDERICK CARL
Commanding carrier task groups in South, Central and Western Pacific.

SHORT, LIEUT. GENERAL WALTER C.
Commanding U.S. Army forces in Hawaii at time of Pearl Harbor; demoted to major general and held responsible for "errors of judgment" in not preparing for Japanese attack; died in retirement 1949.

SIMPSON, LIEUT. GENERAL WILLIAM H.
Commanding U.S. Ninth Army in Europe.

SMITH, LIEUT. GENERAL HOLLAND M.
Commanding V Amphibious Corps in Gilbert, Marshall and Mariana Islands; later commanded Fleet Marine Force, Pacific.

SMITH, MAJOR GENERAL JULIAN
Commanding 2nd Marine Division at Tarawa.

SMITH, LIEUT. GENERAL WALTER BEDELL
U.S. chief of staff Allied Force Headquarters, North Africa; later SHAEF.

SOMERVELL, GENERAL BREHON BURKE
U.S. assistant chief of staff War Department; later commanding Army Service Forces War Department (formerly Service of Supply).

SOONG, T. V.
Chinese Premier and Foreign Minister.

SPAATZ, GENERAL CARL
Commander of U.S. Strategic Air Forces in Europe, later in Pacific.

SPRUANCE, ADMIRAL RAYMOND AMES
Commanding carrier task force at Battle of Midway, later Fifth Fleet.

STALIN, JOSEPH
Generalissimo and dictator of Soviet Russia.

STETTINIUS, EDWARD R. JR.
U.S. Lend-Lease Administrator; Secretary of State 1944–45; chairman U.S. delegation to U.N. Conference in San Francisco; died 1949.

STILWELL, GENERAL JOSEPH WARREN
Chief of Staff to Chiang Kai-shek; commanding general U.S. Army Forces in C.B.I. until October 1944; died 1946.

STIMSON, HENRY LEWIS
U.S. Secretary of War 1940–45.

SUZUKI, ADMIRAL BARON KANTARO
Japanese Premier succeeding Koiso; prepared for termination of war.

TEDDER, AIR CHIEF MARSHAL SIR ARTHUR
Air commander in chief Mediterranean; deputy supreme commander of Allied expeditionary forces European theater.

TIMOSHENKO, MARSHAL SEMION
Commanding central group of armies defending Moscow; later southern front.

TITO (JOSIP BROZ), MARSHAL
Yugoslav partisan leader; later Prime Minister.

TOGO, SHIGENORI
Japanese Foreign Minister at time of Pearl Harbor; sentenced to 20 years as war criminal; died 1950.

TOJO, GENERAL HIDEKI
Japanese Premier at time of Pearl Harbor; chief of army general staff; executed as war criminal Dec. 23, 1948.

TOYODA, ADMIRAL SOEMU
Commander in chief Japanese combined Fleet in Battle for Leyte Gulf; acquitted as war criminal 1949.

TRUMAN, HARRY S.
Vice President of U.S. January 1945; became President at death of Roosevelt April 12, 1945.

TURNER, ADMIRAL RICHMOND KELLY
Commanding amphibious forces, U.S. Pacific fleet from Guadalcanal through Okinawa.

VANDEGRIFT, GENERAL ALEXANDER A.
Commanding 1st Marine Division on Guadalcanal and Tulagi, later commandant U.S. Marine Corps.

VANDENBERG, LIEUT. GENERAL HOYT S.
Deputy commander in chief Allied Expeditionary Air Force and commanding general U.S. Ninth Air Force in France.

WAINWRIGHT, LIEUT. GENERAL JONATHAN M.
Commanding U.S. forces in Philippines at fall of Corregidor; prisoner of Japanese, liberated from Manchurian prison camp 1945.

WALLACE, HENRY AGARD
Vice President of U.S. 1941–45.

WAVELL, FIELD MARSHAL LORD ARCHIBALD
Commander in chief British armies in Middle East and India; later Viceroy and Governor General of India; died 1950.

WEYGAND, GENERAL MAXIME
Allied commander in chief at Fall of France, replacing General Gamelin.

WINANT, JOHN G.
U.S. Ambassador to Britain; died 1947.

YAMAMOTO, ADMIRAL ISOROKU
Japanese navy commander in chief; killed when shot down by AAF pilot over Solomons 1943.

YAMASHITA, GENERAL TOMOYUKI
Conqueror of Malaya and Singapore; later surrendered Japanese forces in Philippines; executed as war criminal 1946.

ZHUKOV, MARSHAL GEORGI
Red Army chief of staff, later Stalin's deputy commander in chief and commanding, with Konev, at fall of Berlin.

Picture Credits

1—RICHARD EDES HARRISON
2—EUROPEAN PICTURE SERVICE
4—PARAMOUNT NEWS
5—UPPER, WIDE WORLD—LOWER, PARAMOUNT NEWS
6—UPPER, INTERNATIONAL—LOWER, OFFICIAL U.S. ARMY
7—Courtesy THE LIBRARY OF CONGRESS
8—UPPER, WIDE WORLD—LOWER, OFFICIAL U.S. ARMY
9—DEVER from BLACK STAR
11—WIDE WORLD
12—UPPER LEFT, HEINRICH HOFFMAN—UPPER RIGHT, COMBINE—LOWER, KRAMER HOFMEESTER, ROTTERDAM
13—UPPER, WIDE WORLD—LOWER, DEVER from BLACK STAR
14—LEFT, DEVER from BLACK STAR—LOWER RIGHT, EUROPEAN PICTURE SERVICE
15—LOWER, HEINRICH HOFFMAN
16—UPPER, HEINRICH HOFFMAN—LOWER LEFT, DEVER from BLACK STAR—LOWER RIGHT, HEINRICH HOFFMAN
17—UPPER, HEINRICH HOFFMAN—LOWER, DEVER from BLACK STAR
18—UPPER, SIDNEY JAFFE—LOWER LEFT, INTERNATIONAL
19—UPPER, PIX INC. (both)—LOWER, MAURITIUS from BLACK STAR
20—INTERNATIONAL
21—Painting by RICHARD EURICH photographed by FERNAND BOURGES courtesy NATIONAL GALLERY OF CANADA, MASSEY COLLECTION
22–23—Painting by CHARLES CUNDALL photographed by WALTER CURTIN courtesy IMPERIAL WAR MUSEUM, LONDON
24—UPPER, painting by ERIC KENNINGTON photographed by LARRY BURROWS courtesy THE LAING ART GALLERY, NEWCASTLE UPON TYNE—LOWER, painting by NORMAN WILKINSON photographed by WALTER CURTIN courtesy MR. & MRS. E. R. HALL
25—RICHARD EDES HARRISON
26—LONDON NEWS "CHRONICLE"
28–29—UPPER LEFT, LOWER LEFT, BRITISH OFFICIAL—LOWER CENTER, COMBINE—RIGHT, BRITISH OFFICIAL
30—UPPER, PHOTO NAVARRO-MOT—LOWER, CAMERA CLIX
31—UPPER, MARGARET BOURKE-WHITE—LOWER, WILLIAM VANDIVERT
32–33—UPPER, WILLIAM VANDIVERT—LOWER AND RIGHT, BRITISH OFFICIAL
34—UPPER— BRITISH OFFICIAL—LOWER, ACME
35—UPPER, WILLIAM VANDIVERT—LOWER, ACME
36—BRITISH OFFICIAL
37–40—WILLIAM VANDIVERT
41—UPPER, DAVID E. SCHERMAN—CENTER, HANS WILD (both)—LOWER, DAVID E. SCHERMAN
42—UPPER LEFT, UPPER RIGHT, WILLIAM VANDIVERT—LOWER LEFT, WILLIAM VANDIVERT—LOWER RIGHT, GEORGE RODGER
43—LONDON "ILLUSTRATED"
44—BRITISH OFFICIAL
45—RICHARD EDES HARRISON
46—HEINRICH HOFFMAN
48—UPPER, ACME—LOWER, BRITISH OFFICIAL
49—ALL, W. BOSSHARD from BLACK STAR except UPPER RIGHT, ACME
50—UPPER, DEVER from BLACK STAR—LOWER, EUROPEAN PICTURE SERVICE
51—BRITISH OFFICIAL
52—UPPER, BRITISH OFFICIAL—LOWER LEFT, DEVER from BLACK STAR—CENTER, BRITISH OFFICIAL
53—UPPER, BRITISH OFFICIAL (both)—RIGHT CENTER, ACME—LOWER, DEVER from BLACK STAR
54—UPPER, BRITISH OFFICIAL—map by FRANK STOCKMAN & ANTHONY SODARO
55—BRITISH OFFICIAL
56—BRITISH OFFICIAL
57—Paintings by ROMAN J. FELDMEYER courtesy DEPARTMENT OF THE ARMY
58—UPPER, painting by WALTER PREIS courtesy DEPARTMENT OF THE ARMY—LOWER,

painting by WILLFRIED NAGEL courtesy DEPARTMENT OF THE ARMY
59—UPPER, painting by WALTER PREIS courtesy DEPARTMENT OF THE ARMY—LOWER, painting by ROMAN J. FELDMEYER courtesy DEPARTMENT OF THE ARMY
60—Paintings by FRANZ EICHHORST courtesy DEPARTMENT OF THE ARMY
61—MARGARET BOURKE-WHITE
62—LEFT, WIDE WORLD—LOWER RIGHT, ACME
63—UPPER, WIDE WORLD—LOWER LEFT, INTERNATIONAL—LOWER RIGHT, WIDE WORLD
64—UPPER, BRITISH OFFICIAL—LOWER, PIX INC.
65—SOVFOTO
66—HEINRICH HOFFMAN
67—SOVFOTO
68—UPPER, WIDE WORLD—LOWER, EUROPEAN PICTURE SERVICE
69—RICHARD EDES HARRISON
70—SOL LIBSOHN
72—UPPER, WIDE WORLD—LOWER, WILLIAM L. WHITE
73—FRED MASTERS
74–75—INTERNATIONAL
76—RALPH MORSE
77—UPPER, CHARLES STEINHEIMER from BLACK STAR (both)—LOWER, ACME
78—UPPER LEFT, HARRIS & EWING—UPPER RIGHT, WIDE WORLD—LOWER, MARGARET BOURKE-WHITE (both)
79—UPPER LEFT, GEORGE RODGER—UPPER RIGHT, METCALF from BLACK STAR—CENTER AND LOWER LEFT, MARGARET BOURKE-WHITE—LOWER RIGHT, N.Y. "DAILY NEWS" PHOTO BY JOE COSTA
80—INTERNATIONAL
81—STUDIO SUN
82—OFFICIAL U.S. NAVY
83—UPPER RIGHT, WIDE WORLD—RIGHT CENTER, CHICAGO "SUN-TIMES"—LOWER, OFFICIAL U.S. NAVY
84–85—OFFICIAL U.S. NAVY
86—LEFT, OFFICIAL U.S. NAVY—RIGHT, INTERNATIONAL
87—RICHARD EDES HARRISON
88—OFFICIAL U.S. ARMY
90—WALDO RUESS
91—UPPER RIGHT, CARL MYDANS—LOWER, WIDE WORLD
92—UPPER, RUDO S. GLOBUS—LOWER, WIDE WORLD (both)
93—UPPER LEFT, T. H. WHITE—UPPER RIGHT, CARL MYDANS—LOWER, T. H. WHITE
94—OFFICIAL U.S. MARINE CORPS
95—OFFICIAL U.S. MARINE CORPS
96—UPPER, courtesy THE LIBRARY OF CONGRESS—LOWER, WIDE WORLD
97—UPPER, WIDE WORLD—LOWER, WENDELL J. FURNAS
98—UPPER, courtesy THE LIBRARY OF CONGRESS—LOWER, OFFICIAL U.S. NAVY
99—Map by FRANK STOCKMAN & ANTHONY SODARO—LOWER, OFFICIAL U.S. ARMY
100—UPPER LEFT, INTERNATIONAL—UPPER RIGHT, WIDE WORLD—LOWER, OFFICIAL U.S. MARINE CORPS
102—OFFICIAL U.S. NAVY
103—UPPER, WIDE WORLD—LOWER, OFFICIAL U.S. ARMY AIR FORCE
104—UPPER, PAN AMERICAN AIRWAYS—LOWER, FRANK SCHERSCHEL
105—RICHARD EDES HARRISON
106—OFFICIAL U.S. NAVY
108–109—OFFICIAL U.S. NAVY
110–111—OFFICIAL U.S. NAVY
112—UPPER LEFT, BRITISH OFFICIAL—map by FRANK STOCKMAN & ANTHONY SODARO—LOWER, BRITISH OFFICIAL (both)
113—ALL, BRITISH OFFICIAL
114—UPPER, BRITISH OFFICIAL—CENTER LEFT, INTERNATIONAL—CENTER RIGHT, BRITISH OFFICIAL—LOWER LEFT, GEORGE RODGER—LOWER RIGHT, COMBINE
115—UPPER LEFT, EUROPEAN PICTURE SERVICE—UPPER RIGHT, ROBERT LANDRY—LOWER, GEORGE RODGER

116—UPPER, ROBERT LANDRY—CENTER, BRITISH OFFICIAL—LOWER, WIDE WORLD
117—UPPER LEFT, ROBERT LANDRY—CENTER, GEORGE RODGER—RIGHT, WIDE WORLD
118—MOVIETONE NEWS
119—OFFICIAL U.S. COAST GUARD
120—WIDE WORLD
121—UPPER, FRED MATTER—LOWER, DONALD SCHABLEIN
122—OFFICIAL U.S. COAST GUARD
123—"SIGNAL"
124—UPPER LEFT, INTERNATIONAL—UPPER RIGHT, WIDE WORLD—CENTER LEFT, SOVFOTO—CENTER RIGHT, WIDE WORLD—LOWER LEFT, INTERNATIONAL—LOWER RIGHT, RUSSIAN NEWSREEL
125—ALL, RUSSIAN NEWSREEL except LOWER LEFT, INTERNATIONAL
126–127—OFFICIAL U.S. NAVY
128—OFFICIAL U.S. NAVY
129—Painting by KENICHI NAKAMURA in custody of SCAP photographed by HORACE BRISTOL
130—UPPER, painting by TOM LEA—LOWER, painting by DWIGHT D. SHEPLER courtesy U.S. NAVY
131—Painting by DWIGHT D. SHEPLER courtesy U.S. NAVY
132—UPPER, painting by TOM LEA—LOWER, painting by ROBERT BENNEY, courtesy ABBOTT COLLECTION
133—RICHARD EDES HARRISON
134—ELIOT ELISOFON
136–137—OFFICIAL U.S. NAVY
138—Map by FRANK STOCKMAN & ANTHONY SODARO—CENTER, FRENCH EMBASSY INF. DIV.—LOWER, OFFICIAL U.S. ARMY
139—UPPER AND CENTER, OFFICIAL U.S. NAVY—LOWER, BRITISH OFFICIAL
140—WIDE WORLD
141—UPPER, BRITISH OFFICIAL—CENTER LEFT, NEWSREEL POOL—CENTER RIGHT, OFFICIAL U.S. ARMY—LOWER, OFFICIAL U.S. SIGNAL CORPS
142—BRITISH OFFICIAL
143—OFFICIAL U.S. ARMY
144—UPPER, FREE FRENCH PRESS SERVICE—LOWER, INTERNATIONAL
145—BRITISH OFFICIAL
146–147—OFFICIAL U.S. ARMY
148—UPPER, OFFICIAL U.S. ARMY—LOWER, BRITISH OFFICIAL
149—ELIOT ELISOFON
150–151—UPPER LEFT, ELIOT ELISOFON—CENTER, MARGARET BOURKE-WHITE—LOWER LEFT AND RIGHT, ELIOT ELISOFON
152—ELIOT ELISOFON
153—MARGARET BOURKE-WHITE—map by ANTHONY SODARO
154—BRITISH OFFICIAL
155—UPPER LEFT, WIDE WORLD—UPPER RIGHT, INTERNATIONAL—LOWER, OFFICIAL U.S. ARMY
156—ELIOT ELISOFON
157—ELIOT ELISOFON
158—UPPER, BRITISH OFFICIAL—LOWER, U.S. ARMY AIR FORCE from PATHE
159—UPPER, PATHE NEWS (both)—CENTER LEFT, PATHE NEWS—CENTER RIGHT, WIDE WORLD—LOWER LEFT, FRENCH EMBASSY INF. DIV.—LOWER RIGHT, ACME
160–161—ELIOT ELISOFON—OFFICIAL U.S. ARMY
162–163—OFFICIAL U.S. ARMY—ROBERT LANDRY
164—UPPER, SOVFOTO—map by ANTHONY SODARO
165—UPPER, SOVFOTO—CENTER, WIDE WORLD—LOWER, SOVFOTO
166—UPPER LEFT, WIDE WORLD—CENTER, INTERNATIONAL—UPPER RIGHT, INTERNATIONAL—LOWER, "RECOGNITION JOURNAL"
167—UPPER LEFT, PIX INC.—UPPER RIGHT, MARCH OF TIME from ACME—CENTER, PIX INC.—LOWER, SOVFOTO
168—UPPER LEFT, WIDE WORLD—UPPER RIGHT, SOVFOTO—LOWER, ACME
169—UPPER LEFT, OFFICIAL U.S. ARMY—UPPER RIGHT, MARGARET BOURKE-WHITE—CENTER, OFFICIAL U.S. ARMY—LOWER, MARGARET BOURKE-WHITE

Index

PRINTED BY R. R. DONNELLEY & SONS COMPANY, CHICAGO, ILL.

PAPER BY THE MEAD SALES COMPANY, DAYTON, OHIO